"A marvelously daring book, [...] rational arguments and powerful narratives that challenge the dominant materialist worldview of our day and age. Dale Allison brings transcendence back into religion eloquently and in the process offers readers abundant hope and ample reason for believing in the central promises of the Christian faith."

author [...]

— **Carlos Eire**

[...]g to Die in Miami

"Steeped in tr[...] world-class scholarship, Dale [...] to be written, and that few others could have. He has gifted us all with a spiritually personal and pastoral exploration of the power of extraordinary religious experiences in shaping and defining the nature of faith. In my estimation, *Encountering Mystery* will join other such works in putting to rest any notion that God's creation is limited to what we normally perceive."

— **Peter Enns**
author of *How the Bible Actually Works*

"Dale Allison offers lovely, theologically informed reflections on how mystical moments, epiphanies, visions, prophetic dreams, and other surprising encounters leave us changed—those of us who experience them directly and those of us who hear about them from others we trust. What we 'make of' these experiences, how the church has handled them, the ways they challenge pastors and other people of faith are timely matters to consider. We may, as Allison says, live in a secular age, but more and more of these stories surface as we open hospitable space for them and allow ourselves to be humbled and surprised by the joy they so often bring to us who are finding our way together on this 'darkling plain.'"

— **Marilyn McEntyre**
author of *Caring for Words in a Culture of Lies* and
Speaking Peace in a Climate of Conflict

"If you need proof that the acts of God in the world or epiphanies are not relegated to the history of Israel in the Old Testament or the exploits of the apostles in the New Testament, this book is a must-read. In *Encountering*

Mystery, Allison draws on his own experiences as well as that of numerous others who can testify to what can only be accounted for in Otto's *mysterium tremendum et fascinans*. Make no mistake, these are not a bunch of uncritically engaged idle tales, for Allison has pondered all the possibilities attached to the assumed subjectivity of such events and can attest to what those who know *know*: you cannot 'unknow' what you know without damage to the psyche. Simply put: the *Real* is still at work in the everydayness of people's lives and is literally visiting with common people who will attend to the ways of the Spirit in the world. The stories of encounter in this book demonstrate at every turn, without exception, how God is revealing, empowering, calling all to faith and how all who are believing are seeing. And here is the indisputable part, we *all* have faith enough. Inspiring and humbling!"

— **Esther E. Acolatse**
author of *Powers, Principalities, and the Spirit:*
Biblical Realism in Africa and the West

"Highly respected scholar Dale Allison dares to raise important questions that academic protocol has too often excluded. Many of the case studies he offers will challenge our own presuppositions about the world—whatever they are—and for that reason are all the more important for us to consider. Allison rightly expands the repertoire of experience that studies of religion and Scripture must take into account."

— **Craig S. Keener**
author of *Miracles Today:*
The Supernatural Work of God in the Modern World

Encountering Mystery

Religious Experience in a Secular Age

Dale C. Allison Jr.

WILLIAM B. EERDMANS PUBLISHING COMPANY
GRAND RAPIDS, MICHIGAN

Wm. B. Eerdmans Publishing Co.
4035 Park East Court SE, Grand Rapids, Michigan 49546
www.eerdmans.com

Published 2022
Printed in the United States of America

28 27 26 25 24 23 22   1 2 3 4 5 6 7

ISBN 978-0-8028-8188-5

Library of Congress Cataloging-in-Publication Data

A catalog record for this book is available from the Library of Congress.

To my brother, John

Contents

Preface

This book is unlike my previous books. Earlier volumes sought either to contribute to critical scholarship or to share, for a wider public, my thoughts on this or that. In these pages, by contrast, I am at times a sort of journalist, a popularizer writing in informal prose. This book is, above all in chapters 2-3 and 6-7, largely a report on what others have discovered. The whole is also, to be sure, a catena of my arguments and opinions. Yet while my personal take on everything is manifest throughout, my chief goal is to call attention to facts that are, despite being well established, still unknown to far too many, often with unhappy consequences.

In accord with this end and the audience I envision, the main text does not hover above long, discursive footnotes, and I pass over contentious questions at every turn. I do not, for instance, discuss whether the very idea of "religious experience"—a phrase with different associations for different writers—is coherent or useful.[1] Nor do I examine the cognitive science of religion, such an important field of late.[2] And I defend only briefly my conviction—controversial at this academic moment—that cross-cultural and cross-temporal comparisons are more than important. This is not an academic treatise. My orientation is rather pastoral, and my focus is on what ordinary people, in significant numbers, have reported and continue to report, as well as on some of the implications.

Although writing requires solitude, I am in my study only part of the time. For the rest, I am surrounded by a loving family, loyal friends, supportive colleagues, and inquisitive students. I am grateful to them all and to their roles, many and varied, in producing this book. I forgo, however, the attempt to compile an inclusive list, which would inevitably sin through omission. I must, nonetheless, acknowledge David Hufford for a conversation that planted the seeds that grew into these chapters; James Ernest of Eerdmans for his initial encouragement and continuing interest; John Wilson for generously reading and commenting (as both professor and pastor) on the entire manuscript; Bruce Greyson and Ed Kelly for expert assistance with chapters 6, 7, and 8; my wife, Kristine, for correcting early drafts; Andrew Allison for help with chapter 3; and Clifton Black and Father George Parsenios for discussions on multiple matters as well as much-needed encouragement in the year that was Covid. Finally, I recall the several pastors who, in recent times, told me that a book such as this is needed. I was paying attention.

1

Stars Descending

"Nature loves to hide itself."

—*Heraclitus*

I entered college without having planned a career or thought about how I might, down the road, make a living. My mind was on other things. Moving on from high school to college was exactly like moving on from junior high to high school: it was nothing but the expected next step. I took that step without reflection.

During freshman orientation at the nearby state university, a young man asked me about my major and my minor. I had no answer. What, I asked, is a major? What is a minor? After he explained the terms, he handed me a piece of paper with a long list of academic disciplines. I scanned the options. I then checked the two that seemed most personally relevant: philosophy for the major, religion for the minor.

I was drawn to those two topics because of what had happened a little over a year before, when I was sixteen. I was sitting by myself on my parents' back porch, under the Kansas night sky. What I was thinking about I fail to remember. I have not, however, forgotten the magical incident that redirected my life. In a moment, and seemingly without preparation on my part, the stars were not far away but close to hand. Having somehow forsaken the firmament, they were all around me. If not quite animate, they were also not wholly inanimate. These engulfing lights then announced, by what mechanism I know not, the arrival of an overwhelming, powerful presence. This presence was forbidding yet benevolent, affectionate yet

1

enigmatic. It suffused me with a calm ecstasy, a sublime elation, "a genial holy fear" (Coleridge).

The experience awakened me from what I then deemed, in retrospect, to have been a lifelong slumber. It electrified awareness and bestowed meaning. Given my cultural context, a word came straightway to mind for this fantastic Other: God. When the moment, which lasted maybe twenty seconds, had passed, I believed that I had run into God, or that God had run into me.

Of course, as I write these words, nearly fifty years after the event, not everything is perfectly vivid. Not only has time dimmed lucidity, but speech betrays the transcendent. Private event and public discourse are not the same. Yet I soon enough translated my experience into words, and I have, over the years, rehearsed them to myself. So I have, I believe, retained the gist of what took place.

I also remember what followed. My Bethel-like vision left me firmly persuaded that the word "God" refers to something more than optimistic imagination, and further that this something matters in a way nothing else does. These, however, were naked convictions, bare-boned thoughts. How was I to respond? What was I supposed to do? There was no imperative in my experience.

I soon began to speak with others about what had happened. Those who were sympathetic did not hesitate to interpret my experience for me. Jesus, they eagerly and confidently avowed, had saved me from my sins. I had been born again. I had been rescued from the domain of darkness and transferred to the kingdom of God's beloved Son. From now on I was to live, out of gratitude, a Christian life.

I accepted their interpretation even though I had already been attending a church, saying my prayers, and leading a tame life—and even though my experience had no christological component (a fact that, curiously, occurred to me only later, after I came to think for myself). Sundays thereafter found me not in my parents' liberal church but in my friends' evangelical church. Those in charge taught me what I should believe about many, many things.

Not all my high-school friends appreciated my new zeal. One in particular assailed me with questions. How do you know that anything in your miracle-filled Bible is history as opposed to fable? Given what we now know about the brain, how can you believe in a soul? Is hell not an outdated myth sensible people discarded long ago? Is it reasonable to accept the tenets of one religion when other religions hold different and contradictory tenets?

These were, to my mind, excellent questions, and I had unsatisfying answers. Soon, then, my friend's questions became my questions, his doubts my doubts, his objections my course of study. And with that I began to read. I read evangelical apologists and modern theologians, hostile atheists and biblical critics. I read philosophers and psychologists, archaeologists and biologists, scholars of Hinduism and proponents of Buddhism, as well as the parapsychologists and their critics. This is why I decided, when asked, that I would major in philosophy and minor in religion. Why not use college to investigate further the epistemological puzzles and religious quandaries that already consumed me?

After that, one thing led to another, and I eventually ended up with a PhD in biblical studies.

My meeting with the *mysterium fascinosum* in 1972 is not a parenthetical moment but rather the existential center of my entire life. I have spent my days trying to understand it and all that has flowed from it. It is the experiential foundation upon which I have built everything else. It is the source of my deep-seated curiosity about all matters religious and countless affiliated topics. Without that experience, I do not know where I would be today, but my life would not, I am sure, have been the same. Ultimately, then, I am a professor at a seminary not so much because I have the requisite credentials but because the stars came down one night when I was sixteen years old.

* * *

When I was twenty-three and in graduate school, I had another profoundly moving experience. Here is what I wrote soon after it happened:

The day before yesterday I stood in my bedroom before a window that overlooks a [cemetery with a] grove of trees, evergreen, oak, maple. The sun, close to the horizon, still lit the landscape. A cool breeze moved the trees and, blowing through the open window, stirred the air in my room. The only sound was the song of seemingly happy crickets. A few moments passed—and then, suddenly, an emotion laid hold of me. I think I should . . . call it "joy," though the word falls far short. This "joy" welled up from deep within, rapidly filled me entirely, and then passed beyond my body. No longer did I contain it, it contained me. And somehow I was enabled to see *through* the world, perceiving the depths below the shallow surface. Thus I saw, for the first time, the colors of the green things of the earth—colors brighter and more distinct than can be imagined, and yet at the same time soft: their intensity did not blind but delighted the eyes. The wind revealed itself to be a sparkling *élan*, and its appearance was like a multi-colored crystal, clear and luminous. And it spoke to me, saying: The world is full of life, overflowing from God's hand. The Golden Age, Eden, has not passed from the world; rather, people are blind, they cannot see. This that you see is always here, and always will be here. Indeed, this is what the saints shall see, walking upon the lawn of heaven.

The feeling of "joy" and my vision of nature's depth endured only a few seconds and soon began to fade. Then an odd thing happened. I did not seek to retain the experience. I no longer wished to look. Instead I wished that others might look. And in a moment of time the faces of my family and friends appeared before my mind, and I clasped my hands and prayed that they might feel what I felt and see what I saw—if not in this world then in the world to come. Having offered this prayer, I turned away from the window, assured that my petition had been heard.

* * *

With the reader's indulgence, I wish to relate one more personal experience, and then I will get to the point. The following event occurred when I was in my mid-forties. I wrote it up in an email to a friend a few hours later:

I was still in bed Sunday morning when my wife turned on some classical music (unfortunately I don't know the piece). It didn't wake me but rather brought me to that fascinating state between waking and sleeping. I entered some sort of place that was—please recall all the times you have heard mystics say that what they experienced is ineffable—entirely sky blue, composed of softly pulsating diamond crystals with large bird shadows or souls flitting through it. It was like being in the sea—this stuff surrounded me, but I wasn't exactly floating. The place itself was joy unbounded, ecstasy without compare. The music was part of it, and the bird shapes were overflowing with, singing with, happiness, as was the place itself, which I can't think of as either organic or inorganic (maybe it's like First Peter—living stones). Along with the joy was profound peace, the only thing comparable in my experience being one night in the hospital when I floated around in a morphine stupor. I experienced all this for three, four, or five seconds and then was so overwhelmed that I began to cry. My crying then brought me out of that state.

Words can't begin to describe what this was like. It will stay with me for the rest of my life. It confirms me in my belief that underneath all this mess is absolute joy. I perked up when the sermon three hours later told me that creation was the overflowing of love from the members of the Trinity; this made perfect sense. It also confirms me in my eschatological solution—an experiential solution, not an intellectual solution to be sure—to the problem of evil. As I lay in bed, I thought that if all the world and its miseries were suddenly dumped into that sky blue land, the joy would be so overwhelming and complete that all evils and regret and anger and hatred and revenge would dissipate in a second. It is so immense that it would make everything else matter less than a hill of beans. I think someone in that state would really feel that the sufferings of the present time are not worthy to be compared, etc.

This incident has helped me to appreciate Paul's uncertainty when he wrote, concerning one of his ecstatic experiences: "whether in the body or out of the body I do not know" (2 Cor. 12:3).

* * *

Having recounted my three experiences, I am wholly cognizant that many would deem them to be purely subjective and so of scant interest. They would explain them away as hallucinations of some sort, as visions without external stimulus, byproducts perhaps of glitches in my neuronal machinery. In doing so they could not only appeal to all sorts of scientific facts but also quote Shakespeare:

> Such tricks hath strong imagination,
> That if it would but apprehend some joy,
> It comprehends some bringer of that joy.[1]

While I would resist going along, I do not here mount a case to the contrary. My interest in this chapter lies elsewhere, in one undeniable fact.

Whatever the causes—be it imagination, my cerebral circuit board, extra-mundane realities, or (as I think) an even mixture of all three—my experiences have mattered profoundly. While the nature of the events is open to debate, the biographical effects are not.

I have a small piece of paper in my desk drawer. On it is a list of several out-of-the-ordinary experiences. The first line reads simply: Stars 1972. On another line is this: Cemetery 1978. The final entry is: Bird souls 1999. There are (from other years) six additional entries. I take this paper out once in a while and stare at it, mulling over the unexpected events that the key words and dates represent. Such recall imbues my life with meaning and generates gratitude.

The three experiences I have herein recounted—which, added up, occupied less than a minute of my life—have not just imparted certain feelings. They have also, via reflection, led to certain thoughts—or, more precisely, to four stanch convictions. The first is that the transcendent reality that descended from the Kansas night sky is not a curiosity, something about which I could choose to be indifferent. Not only is it, as I initially intuited, connected in some mysterious way to everything else, but nothing by comparison counts for much, or at least fails to count in the same superlative way.

Second, the theological idea of grace is not uninformed theory. Perhaps indeed grace is built into the structure of things. My experiences were in no way consciously sought, planned, or manufactured, nor were they the effects of fasting or ingesting drugs. They were not rewards for this or that, nor were they linked to a personal crisis. They seem instead to have come out of nowhere, like Paul's vision on the road to Damascus. Uninvited, they just happened. So I experienced them as surprises and received them as gifts.

My third conviction is that God can speak through the natural world. I met the maker in the stars. I beheld the divine in a cemetery garden. I experienced transcendence in shadowy birds. That the psalmist thought the heavens to declare the glory of God makes perfect sense to me, and I am inordinately fond of the passage where "I Am" speaks to Moses from a bush. I believe that a mystical presence rolls through all things, and that

> The soul can split the sky in two,
> And let the face of God shine through.

These last words are from Edna Saint Vincent Millay's wonderful poem, "Renascence," which my father asked to have read as death drew near. If, on my deathbed, I likewise have my wits, I will make the same request.

Finally, it is not that appearances can be deceiving. Rather, appearances *are* deceiving. Things are not what they seem to be most of the time. We are like Pharaoh when he looked at Moses: he had no idea what was really going on. The mysterious hierophany at the heart of the world is concealed. Seeing we do not see. "Verily thou art a God that hidest thyself" (Isa. 45:15, King James Version). Behind, beneath, and beyond the mundane face of the world, and secreted within our daily lives, is some fundamental, magical, mystical, affectionate reality.

These four convictions are not, for me, abstractions acquired from books. They are instead truths I have gathered from immediate experience. I may, I freely admit, be deluded in all this. Perhaps my brain has conspired against me, landing me in baseless fantasies. Maybe my subjective experiences have no objective correlates beyond my skull's atoms and so my beliefs are without substance. The human proclivity for error and self-deception is, speaking conservatively, enormous. Still, it is hard for me to feel that the skeptical take is more than a theoretical possibility. I have never been able to disown my experiences, to stand back and attribute them, without remainder, to tricks of the mind. They were too profoundly real, too perceptually tangible, for trouble-free reductionism. The upshot is that I cannot but perceive and interpret the world through them.

2

Behind the Scenes

"I often remember this experience, but I have spoken about it to very few people. It was just too bizarre—what would people think?"

—Karen[1]

"Until now [seventy years later] I have never mentioned it to anyone; it is too important for casual chat."

—Brandon[2]

"One does not need to be a mystic to have mystical experiences."

—Susan L. DeHoff[3]

Although the stories in the previous chapter matter greatly to me, they cannot matter much to anyone else. The justification for introducing them is not that they are important but that they are illustrative. Numinous experiences may not be common, but they are not, even in our so-called secular world, uncommon.

Evidence for this claim lies in the materials collected over the past five decades by the Religious Experience Research Centre (RERC), which Sir Alister Hardy, the renowned zoologist, founded at Oxford in 1969.[4] Suspecting that marked religious experiences were widespread, he went in search of evidence. He did this by calling on the British public for their firsthand testimonies. Today Hardy would have advertised on the internet. Back then he asked his questions in print media—in the *Guardian*, for instance, and the *Daily Mail*—and received responses through the postal service.

Those responses revealed that ordinary UK citizens, in large numbers, experience mystical raptures, see apparitions, feel the presence of the dead, perceive the unity of all things, and hear guiding voices. Many also report being overwhelmed by a loving, transcendent reality while others recount being utterly terrified by a stifling, malevolent something. On and on it goes.

Hardy, who dubbed himself a "naturalist of the numinous," was engaged in something like old-fashioned natural history. He collected human testimonies and then sorted them, classifying like with like. What emerged was the fact that mystical and distinctly religious experiences, however explained, are part of the contemporary human condition. In addition, there are clear patterns in the data. They reveal the sorts of experiences that occur again and again as well as their customary triggers (which include natural beauty and music). The data also allow us to categorize certain experiences as rare or idiosyncratic.

The RERC materials, which philosopher Jules Evans has referred to as "a sort of crowdsourced Bible,"[5] disclose that my experiences are not one-in-a-million outliers. Here is one man's testimony:

> an indescribable peace, which I have since tried to describe as a "diamond moment of reality," came flowing into (or indeed, waking up within) me, and I realized that all around me everything was lit with a kind of inner shining beauty—the rocks, bracken, bramble bushes, view, sky and even blackberries—and also myself. . . . And in that moment, sweeping in on that tide of light, there came also knowledge. The knowledge that . . . in the end "All would be well . . . All manner of things would be well."[6]

If this approximates my experience and thoughts while looking at the cemetery outside my apartment window in 1978, the following sounds like what happened to me as I lay in bed one morning in 1999:

> I woke 7 a.m & heard the sparrows in the holly-bush quarrelling as usual. With this sound still in my ears I felt myself—(I was still awake)—helped up a step, & turned to—I'm not sure whether left or right now. (I don't ask anyone to believe this—I am just content to know myself, it is true.)

I was in heaven—I have details written if of interest to you—the warmth and light was from the heart of eternal life-God—I only stood at the gate, & felt the unutterable joy. Music lifted me out of my earthly body, & for a fraction I was a part of the Love of God. Music, music—this is the key—music that uplifts the soul.

The message I received was that earthly life is just a minute moment of our lives. That those who suffer most here, are the lucky ones—if they suffer bravely, their spirits [are] safely in God's keeping, uncomplaining, for they are taken straight into the warmth & music, I only barely heard & felt.

I had to leave, & what a return. I was torn & buffeted for infinity & still to the sound of the birds chatter, found myself back in bed, crying bitterly, & begging to return to heaven.[7]

* * *

Although Hardy is now dead, his collaborators and intellectual heirs have continued to gather data and work with the archives, which are now housed at the University of Wales, Trinity Saint David. The materials, consisting of over 6,000 firsthand accounts from around the world, are fascinating on numerous counts, not least of which is the great import experiencers typically attach to what they relate. Nonetheless, most theologians and scholars of religion pay this trove no heed as they go about their business.[8]

The ignorance or indifference of so many professionals regarding the RERC and subsequent, related studies that have largely confirmed Hardy's results[9] is lamentable. It is, however, understandable. Huge swaths of the modern academy have pledged allegiance to a materialistic research program. That program, which has hardened into a doctrinaire worldview, endeavors, as a matter of principle, to reduce all phenomena to the categories of ordinary science. This is one reason for the robust tradition of discounting every claim that invokes or suggests anything beyond those categories. In particular, and with regard to out-of-the-ordinary experiences, there is a tradition of marginalization through medicalization: something must be neurologically or psychologically askew with people like me. Do not schizophrenics see visions? Do not epileptic seizures generate potent religious sensations? Do not the gullible see faces in the clouds of their imaginations? James Leuba, the influential psychologist of religion, spoke for a multitude when he ascribed mystical experiences to misapprehension and psychopathology.[10]

Skepticism is not confined to the academy. It is also at home in certain religious circles. In many churches and among many seminary-educated pastors there is a far-flung prejudice against metanormal experiences, a predisposition not to take them seriously.

I once spoke with a woman who, upon discerning that I would be sympathetic, shared her Near-Death Experience (NDE). It happened while she was giving birth, when her spinal block broke. Her report was typical for these sorts of events. She saw herself from above, traveled down a tunnel of light, and decided to return for the sake of her child. What I remember above all is that, after narrating her story, she added two remarks. The first was this. Her NDE, which she took to be an encounter with God, was the most important event in her life. The second was that she had never spoken with anybody about it before, excepting her husband; and, because of my sincere interest, she told me more about the matter than she had ever told him. I have often, recollecting her remarks, pondered the social reticence this woman felt. She was a Methodist church secretary and so spent most days around professedly religious folk. She did not, however, share her life-altering meeting with God with them.

The upshot of scientistic skepticism and theological disinterest is that multitudes, in churches as well as without, regularly keep their experiences to themselves, or tell only a select few, those they are sure will not reflexively disdain their testimony.

Years ago my then teenage (and perfectly sane) daughter suffered, while awake, a truly horrifying and deeply puzzling encounter with what she called "shadow people." Although she immediately shared her experience with me, she insisted: "Dad, you can't tell anyone, because they'll think I'm crazy." My daughter's fear is, regrettably, emblematic. A disinclination to speak about certain sorts of incidents is widespread. (Incidentally, as a testimony to how soul-shaking the uncanny can be, my daughter suffered from PTSD for ten years after her experience.)

One of the more extraordinary illustrations of people's reluctance to share their extraordinary experiences comes from Sweden. In the 1990s, researchers were studying the psychological states attending bereavement.

They interviewed fifty people in their early seventies. All had lost a spouse within the previous year. When first asked whether they had ever encountered a dead husband or wife, only a single individual (a spiritualist) answered affirmatively. After, however, the interviewers informed the widows and widowers that apparent contact with the dead is a common part of the grieving process, not a symptom of mental debility, they opened up. As it turned out, fully half had felt the presence of their departed spouse, and a third reported seeing, hearing, or speaking with a loved one.[11] One out of fifty suddenly became twenty-five out of fifty. Two percent became 50 percent. With assurance, people were honest. Without assurance, they kept quiet.

Dewi Rees, who has done as much as anyone to call attention to how often the bereaved believe they encounter the dead, wrote: "during my interviews with the widowed, I found that surprisingly few people felt able to tell others of their experiences and that they kept them secret from even close friends and relatives." This is why, according to Rees, our knowledge of these episodes has been "so scanty and distorted."[12] Self-censorship has concealed the facts. Rees added that, after speaking with a Catholic priest about contact with the dead, the pastor confessed that most congregants do not share their stories with clergy: "I would be the last person they would tell."[13]

The failure to speak about remarkable or unusual events is a well-attested motif in the relevant literature. A woman who saw an apparition told an interviewer: "My husband doesn't know. He'd think I was nuts."[14] Another experiencer confided: "I have told others but they have been hand-picked— it's not something that you tell everyone." Yet another said: "You just don't go around talking about things like this, especially when it's something close to your heart. There is a good chance you'll get laughed at or told you're crazy."[15] A daughter, when narrating her mother's experience of a vision of light, observed: "It was years before Mom took the leap and talked about this experience. She tossed out a couple of hints to close friends, but their reactions were disbelieving, even disparaging. So she kept it back."[16] One researcher, when seeking to understand negative, distressing NDEs, found data exceedingly hard to come by: "It took nine years to find fifty people who could give enough detail to create a coherent sense of such experiences. . . . The 'closeting' was so intense that even when our respondents could bring themselves to write their accounts, few were willing or able to complete the questionnaire, answer questions, or agree to an interview."[17] Then there is the elderly woman who, after having an NDE as a child, kept it to herself for decades, sharing her story for the first time when she was ninety-seven years old.[18]

David Hay and Ann Morisy, while gathering firsthand accounts of religious experiences among the citizens of Nottingham in the 1980s, discovered that 40 percent of those with stories confessed that they had never before confided in anybody about what had happened to them, "not even someone as intimate as another family member or partner. Even those who had spoken admitted that they had been pretty shamefaced about it." When asked for the reason, "everyone without exception said that they feared being labelled either stupid or mad."[19] Hay and Morisy also discovered that, the more time they spent with people and the more trust they established, the more episodes and more details they uncovered.

* * *

In 1945, when she was forty-two, the psychologist Genevieve W. Foster had an experience that, in her words, "was so far from expectation, so far from anything that I had thought in the realm of the possible, that it has taken me the rest of my life to come to terms with it."[20] Here is what, she says, happened:

> I saw nothing unusual with my outward eye, but I nevertheless knew that there was someone else in the room with me. A few feet in front of me and a little to the left stood a numinous figure, and between us was an interchange, a flood, flowing both ways, of love. There were no words, no sound. There was light everywhere. . . . Indoors and out, the world was flooded with light, the supernal light that so many of the mystics describe and a few of the poets. The vision lasted five days; sometime on Saturday afternoon I had a sense of fatigue, and could sustain it no longer, and it faded.

She goes on to comment:

> There was no one around to whom I could tell it. Roger [my husband] who is embarrassed and alarmed at the mere mention of religious ex-

perience, would have thought me utterly mad, as I surely would have thought anyone mad who told me such a story. Indeed the part of me that still adhered to my rationalist upbringing fully agreed with this point of view. . . . Yet the experience was so overwhelmingly good that I couldn't mistrust it. . . . None of my various mentors [in psychology] understood it at all. I wrote at once to Dr. [Esther] Harding [a famous Jungian analyst], though without giving her a full description; she replied immediately that such an occurrence was almost certainly to be mistrusted. . . . For me it was the most important thing that has ever happened to me.[21]

Foster (who grew up as a nominal Protestant and was, in 1945, attending a Unitarian Church) sought help not only from Dr. Harding but also a scholarly minister. The latter did no better than the former. He failed to inform her that what had happened to her had happened to others who were perfectly lucid. Instead, he mused, perhaps her experience was somehow the byproduct of menopause. "He was kind of embarrassed by the whole thing. He was really troubled, I thought. But to him it was clearly a disturbance."[22]

After this unpleasant pastoral experience, Foster understandably kept the matter to herself. Her chief comfort came from reading books, such as Evelyn Underhill's *Mysticism*. She had to go to written pages to learn about the mystical society into which she had, without her consent, been initiated.

We know Foster's story only because, almost forty years later, she decided, when facing a high-risk surgery, to inform her family about "the most important thing" that had ever overtaken her. So she wrote a memoir in which the event narrated above features prominently.

* * *

When Barbara Ehrenreich, the well-known essayist and social activist, was a teenager, she had a devastating encounter with a mysterious something. After writing about the incident in her journal, she kept it to herself for fifty-five years. She was, after all, a well-known atheist. Yet she eventually overcame her reticence and went public in a *New York Times* piece as well as in an absorbing book, *Living with a Wild God: A Nonbeliever's Search for the Truth about Everything.*[23]

One morning in 1959, when she was walking the streets of Lone Pine, California, Ehrenreich "saw the world—the mountains, the sky, the low scattered buildings—suddenly flame into life."

> There were no visions, no prophetic voices . . . just this blazing everywhere. Something poured into me and I poured out into it. . . . It was a furious encounter with a living substance that was coming at me through all things at once, too vast and violent to hold on to, too heartbreakingly beautiful to let go of. It seemed to me that whether you start as a twig or a gorgeous tapestry, you will be recruited into the flame and made indistinguishable from the rest of the blaze. I felt ecstatic and somehow completed, but also shattered. Of course I said nothing about this to anyone. Since I recognized no deities, and even the notion of an "altered state of consciousness" was unavailable at the time, I was left with only one explanation: I had had a mental breakdown, ultimately explainable as a matter of chemical imbalances, overloaded circuits or identifiable psychological forces. There had been some sort of brief equipment failure, that was all. [24]

Notwithstanding the last sentence, Ehrenreich was unable to discount or disremember her experience. It instead haunted her. After years of reflection and study, which included learning what she could about mystics and mysticism, she concluded that her encounter "was part of a widespread category of human experience." She further "decided that the insanity explanation may have been a cop-out." In other words, she "could have seen something that morning in Lone Pine." Whatever the source, one cannot deny the enduring effects of her experience, and it is fascinating to see her, in her book, speculating about the nature of what sort of being or force encountered her when she was seventeen.

Ehrenreich is exceptional. Most atheists do not publicly share their extraordinary, potentially religious experiences. [25] Nor do most scientists. This is why there is a site on the internet known as "TASTE," an acronym for The Archives of Scientists' Transcendent Experiences. It is an online safe space for scientists to post, anonymously, and without fear of personal ridicule or professional reprisal, their mystical, religious, and paranormal experiences.

The founder, Charles Tart, kept running into scientists who told him, because they knew of his offbeat interests, about extraordinary experiences that had altered their lives, experiences they felt unable to recount to other scientists. He decided to create a website where they could share their stories. While the site is no longer active, the archives remain open.[26] Among them are accounts such as these:

- "I was aware of having found an original world that we once knew but have forgotten. It always stands on our side, but we do not see it. But sometimes a glimmer opens, revealing a vision of unthinkable perfection and beauty, of superhuman harmony. The unfathomable mystery of life instantly reveals itself, of life we are the beneficiaries."

- "One night, I was sitting there alone on the rock in semi-darkness. I looked up and to my left and saw a very bright blue-white light in the sky. I continued to look at this light, and it began to approach me until it became all-encompassing to my field of view. I cannot tell you how bright the light was, but it was overpowering, yet I had no trouble looking at it. I began to sense that the light was alive, and felt that it was radiating Pure Love. (A Christian would probably call this entity Jesus, but although we attended a mainline Protestant church regularly, I did not associate the light with any particular religious figure or belief system). I felt a sense of belonging and complete acceptance, and I felt great love for the light in return. I looked at the trees around me, and knew they were trees, but saw them as the expressions of the vitality of Nature. Then all objects were appreciated as rays of one underlying wholeness, rising up to become the grass, and flowers and trees. It was like many waves on a silent ocean."

- "Without 'warning,' I suddenly had a feeling of complete peace and of complete unity with the universe. Not living in the universe, but being an integral part of it. I thought to myself, 'Something must be wrong—I don't deserve to feel this peace!,' but in spite of my best efforts to find things to worry about, such as world hunger, threats of war, etc., the peace remained. I soon accepted it, and enjoyed this persistent overwhelming feeling of peace for perhaps 10 minutes. I could not even force myself into a state of worry or anxiety. I did not attribute this to 'God' or 'Christ' at the time—it was not a 'religious' experience, just an experience of BEING.

Finally, the normal neurotic anxieties returned over a period of a minute or two. The memory of my experience sustains me to this day, and it also tells me how limiting/limited our conceptions of the Divine and of each other are. What is TRUE is beyond our manmade concepts. We need not be afraid!"

The existence of TASTE testifies to the sad state of affairs in an important sector of our current culture. Scientists pride themselves on esteeming facts. If, however, successful, highly intelligent, well-educated, and otherwise healthy individuals have surprising and profound religious or mystical experiences, then that too is a fact. We may debate what their experiences mean. What we cannot do, if honest and informed, is deny that they have such experiences and find them meaningful.

The raison d'être for TASTE was that some scientists felt too inhibited to tell their stories. They felt this way largely because so many continue to opine that mystical or extraordinary religious experiences betray psychological frailty or physiological malfunction. But this hoary polemic has become passé. It is a crude prejudice, a rejection of the religious other, no more enlightened than deeming one's own ethnic group to be superior to all other ethnic groups. Of course some who have visions or hear voices have organic disorders. That hardly requires, however, that all or most who have visions or hear voices are so afflicted.

Beyond the fallacy of depreciating the many by parading the few, there are the empirical studies of Hardy, Andrew Greeley, and others. These give no cause for pathologizing all or even most visions and metanormal claims.[27] Even without such studies, many of us need do nothing more than look at our own lives and the lives of family members and friends who have had extraordinary experiences. We do as well in the world as anyone else.

People like me should have nothing to be embarrassed about. Nor should those scientists who, because of perceived social pressure, had recourse to bearing witness in TASTE. It is human to have mystical and other hard-to-classify experiences. Indeed, the evidence supports Hardy's conviction that our inherited biological makeup fosters religious experiences (as some neuroscientists have also recently urged).[28] In any case, ignoring such experiences amounts to censorship. And reflexively attributing them one and all to pathology is deplorable.[29] Intelligent people of sound mind and body should feel free to relate what has seemingly happened to them without fear of a condescending reaction. A world in which it is otherwise is a dishonest world.

* * *

As already indicated, the situation is not much better in some churches. The implicit social censorship attending the mystical or the out of the ordinary does not automatically evaporate as we enter a house of worship or converse with members of a religious community.

Incredulity within Christianity goes back literally to day one. According to Luke 24, when the women who found Jesus's tomb empty and then saw an angel gave their report to the disciples, the dismissive response was that it was an idle tale, and they did not believe. While the story moves on from there, some of Jesus's followers remain stuck, perpetually mired in know-it-all incredulity when someone tells them anything that they cannot comfortably relate to.

Even when the doubters listen politely, their faces often betray them, and experiencers perceive the supercilious impatience and lack of real interest behind the pastoral mask. Who welcomes "the kind of patronizing acceptance that a psychotherapist offers to a psychotic patient: I believe that your hallucinations are real *to you*"?[30] The result is that countless out-of-the-ordinary experiences never come to speech in a Christian setting. Again and again, when pew-sitters have shared their stories with me, they have done so in confidence. It is the same with my seminary students, who typically wait until class is over and the others have gone before they step forward to divulge their secrets.

What everyone knows is not what everyone knows. Having extraordinary experiences and talking about them are two very different things. The belief that certain experiences are not normal moves normal people not to report them, which in turn reinforces the belief that normal people do not have them. If we are taught that only the mad or naive have a certain experience, then none but the mad or naive will report that experience. The rest, wanting to be perceived as normal, will keep quiet. The upshot is that absence from a prevailing culture does not mean absence from human experience.

* * *

Experiences are valued or derided, promoted or stigmatized, and recounted or unrecounted in accord with a social context. After the Reformation, when many Protestant divines started preaching that ghosts were not visitors from purgatory but either hallucinations or demonic tricks, Christians in Protestant lands reported fewer ghosts than previously. Thomas Woolston smugly noted: "The Ghosts of the Dead in this present Age, and especially in this Protestant Country, have ceas'd to appear; and we now-a-days hardly ever hear of such an Apparition."[31] The reason is not that people stopped seeing the dead.[32] The explanation is that, without a congenial framework for reception, a framework that Catholic theology had supplied and Protestantism deleted, people stopped recounting their experiences. Even down to the present day, "evangelical Protestants are the group least likely to say they have felt in touch with a dead person."[33]

The lack of an amenable explanatory framework can lead people not only to doubt or keep quiet about an experience but even on occasion to disremember it. A sensible Presbyterian once told me that she had seen a Roman Catholic priest levitate during Mass. Regardless of what really happened—not being there I have no opinion—she related the episode with full conviction. She clearly believed her own words. Yet when I asked her about it a few years later, my question left her clueless. What was I talking about? Nonplussed, I wondered about my recall. Later, after I shared my puzzlement with one of my sons, he told me that he too remembered her telling the story. My friend, it seems, had discarded that for which she had no file. She had failed to recall what she had once recounted. If, however, she had been a Roman Catholic of a certain stripe, the sort who believe that Teresa of Avila and Joseph of Copertino literally levitated, her memory would likely have remained intact.

While my friend's amnesia may seem hard to credit, it is only an extreme illustration of a larger phenomenon. I sometimes ask people whether or not they have ever experienced anything truly out of the ordinary. When they say no, I press on. After a bit they often dredge up from the depths some half-forgotten episode that perplexed them at the time, such as a vivid dream that came to pass, or the urgent sense that something terrible was happening to a loved one far away, which they later learned to be true. They may then shrug their shoulders and add that coincidences happen. This tames the matter for them, rendering it unremarkable. So unless someone or something prods introspection, the memory of the event that fails to fit remains below the surface, out of sight.

Not only may we have a hard time remembering something that does not match our expectations: we may even fail to notice it in the first place. Some years ago, during a public lecture, Arthur Ellison, an engineering professor at the University of London, announced that, through "psychic power," he was going to make a bowl of flowers rise into the air. He asked the audience to help him by concentrating and uttering a drawn-out "Om." He also invited six members of the audience to come forward and inspect the bowl closely. In the event, the bowl rose an inch or two from its table. The cause was not "psychic power" but an electromagnetic device Ellison had hooked up beneath the table. Nonetheless, only one of the six claimed to see a levitating bowl. Five reported seeing, against the truth, nothing at all. They failed to perceive what they believed to be impossible.[34]

The old wisdom had it that the human being is "a tool-making animal" (Benjamin Franklin), by which was meant: toolmaking distinguishes us from all other animals. It took Jane Goodall's observations about chimpanzees fishing for termites with stalks of grass to exorcize the prejudice for good. Once the traditional preconception was gone, animal behaviorists began to notice that other animals use tools, too. Octopi build fences with rocks. New Caledonian crows fashion lances out of twigs to spear larvae. Egyptian vultures use their beaks to fling rocks at eggshells in order to crack them open and eat what is inside. Black-striped capuchin monkeys split nuts by placing them on a rock and then hammering them with a stone. Now that we have permission and incentive to look, we see. Happily, something similar has, in recent decades, been happening with mystical and religious experiences.

* * *

Several times over the past sixty years, pollsters have asked Americans if they have ever had "a religious or mystical experience," that being superficially defined as "a moment of religious or spiritual awakening." Here are the numbers:[35]

	Yes	No	Don't Know
1962	22%	78%	0%
1976	31%	69%	0%
1994	33%	65%	2%
2006	47%	51%	2%
2009	49%	48%	4%

I do not read much into such statistics. In order to give them substance, one would need detailed interviews with multitudes of people. The numerical escalation, however, does interest me. I regard it as an index of social change as opposed to an index of experience. The further 1962 recedes, the more people are willing to affirm that they have had "a religious or mystical experience." One more than doubts that this is due either to a surge in divine intervention or to some dramatic transformation of our physical environment. The climbing numbers instead reflect an adjustment in the broader culture. Our *Zeitgeist* is not the same. While many redoubtable voices continue to pathologize the mystical and the metanormal, they do not dominate the social landscape as they once did. The upshot is that more of us feel permission to be candid in a way we were not before. In short, the polls do not track the number of experiences but the willingness to report them.

* * *

Many years ago, when I was in my twenties, I woke up one early morning on my back to find myself paralyzed from head to foot. I could not move a finger. I could not even, it seemed, take a breath. I thought I was suffocating. I was petrified, terrified I might die. The distress was all the more severe because I somehow sensed, near my feet and off to the left, the presence of an oppressive force or spirit. This whatever-it-was, which I recall as a nebulous darkness, was filled with malevolence directed straight at me. I remember nothing further except the profound relief when, after maybe ten to fifteen seconds, the spell was broken, and the world suddenly returned to normal.

Given my interest in non-ordinary experiences, I did not forget this one. Indeed, I have related it in classrooms over the years when lecturing to divinity students on the subject of evil. After one such lecture, a young man sent me an email that included this:

> On Saturday evening I laid down in bed with my son who is eight. He was not feeling well and had a high temperature (100–101). I fell asleep with him. While sleeping I had a dream that I had walked outside and it was night but all of the stars were gone. I don't know why but I woke up and I was lying on my back and I could not breathe. I opened my eyes and my heart was racing and I could not breathe for what seemed about 15 seconds. In the left corner of the room under a wall mirror something very dark was there and it moved and then it was gone. Just seeing it made me feel bad. I was able to breathe again and looked over at my son and I fell back asleep thinking I was just seeing things.
>
> The next day my wife came to me and said that my son had told her that he woke up in the middle of the night and the room was pitch black and there was something big moving around in the room. He described it as like a demon (whatever that means to him). He said it was about 2:30 AM. I told her that is something because I had a strange experience around that same time and we were in the room together. I had not mentioned anything to him and thought it was kind of a strange coincidence that we both saw something. My wife was weirded out by me telling her this but I don't know what to think about it.
>
> I guess I did not run because I was too scared to run. This week I was alone with my son and asked him where in the room he saw this figure and he said it was by the closet door by the mirror and it was as tall as the closet door. That was the same place I saw it. I have been looking to see if maybe the mirror makes a strange reflection but I cannot see one. Oh, yeah, my son also said that it sounded like kids but it did not talk. I do not know what to make of that.

When I first suffered sleep paralysis, I was, like my student, bewildered, without understanding. It was different when, twenty years later, I suffered my second bout. By then I had read David Hufford's *The Terror That Comes in the Night*,[36] and I was reassured by the knowledge that what had happened to me was, however frightening, something that had also happened to, quite literally, millions of others.

* * *

Early in his career, before he became Professor of Neural and Behavioral Science, and Family and Community Medicine at Penn State College of Medicine, Hufford taught at the Memorial University of Newfoundland, in the Folklore Department. In those days one of his objects of study was the Newfoundland legend of the Old Hag. Although the myth takes different forms, certain elements recur. The nucleus is this. Someone waking up or falling asleep sees or hears something fearful moving toward the bed. This is accompanied by the feeling of being strangled or the sense of great pressure on the chest. The person also suffers paralysis and an inability to cry out. Those who speak about the Old Hag or getting hagged variously explain the experience as due to a wicked spirit, a supernaturally aided enemy, a witch, a bodily ailment, or some combination of these.

Hufford, through questionnaires and interviews, discovered that many of his students not only knew stories about the Old Hag but claimed themselves to have been hagged. This was consistent with the possibility that the folklore of Newfoundland had heavily shaped or even determined their experiences and retrospective accounts. Hufford soon learned, however, that people without any knowledge of the Old Hag could tell basically the same story. He suspected this result going in, before surveying students, because he himself, years before moving to Newfoundland and becoming acquainted with the lore of the Old Hag, had once awakened to the sound of footsteps, after which he could neither move nor speak, then sensed a mortifying and repulsive evil presence that pushed down the bed and climbed onto his chest. He felt as though he was being strangled and thought he would die.[37] (And he told no one for eight years.)

Hufford's research eventually led him to outline the syndrome in this fashion:

Primary features:
- Impression of wakefulness
- Immobility (paralysis, restraint, fear of moving)
- Realistic perception of actual environment
- Fear

Secondary features:
- Supine position (very common)
- Feeling of presence (common)
- Feeling of pressure, usually on chest (common)
- Numinous quality (common)
- Fear of death (somewhat common)[38]

This is, I emphasize, a descriptive analysis, not an explanation.

We now know, thanks to Hufford and later investigators, that 20 percent or more of North Americans confront the Old Hag at least once in a lifetime. So the experience is common. It has, moreover, nothing to do with mental illness or psychosis. One researcher has commented: "it's no more patholog-ical than a case of the hiccups."[39] We further know that the phenomenon is not peculiar to our time and place. It is rather attested cross-culturally and cross-temporally. The traditional folklore of China, Japan, Southeast Asia, Alaska, and Sweden all have their own versions of the Old Hag.

The facts, as Hufford uncovered them, pushed him to favor what he calls the "experiential source hypothesis" over the "cultural source hypothesis." Behind the global folklore lies a real experience, however variously mythol-ogized or understood. The Old Hag is not the product of unmoored story-telling. More than a cultural fiction, it reflects something that happens to some of us once in a while. The basic experience is "independent of cultural models" and not occasioned by prior beliefs.[40]

This generalization includes, one should note, the sense of a threatening spirit or evil incorporeal presence. This too cannot be condensed wholly to cul-ture. However explained, it belongs to the phenomenology of the experience itself. This is why, as Hufford emphasizes, the Old Hag has moved some "psy-chologically normal, mainstream modern persons" to believe in "spirits."[41]

Another point Hufford underscores is truly startling. Western medicine and psychology, under the impulse of modern rationalism, did not, when he began his work, recognize the phenomenon that the folklore of the Old Hag encodes. Centuries ago, by contrast, people knew about this thing, as evident from the old tales of being ridden by a witch or attacked at night by an evil spirit. In fact, "until the seventeenth century the primary referent of [the word] nightmare actually was what we call sleep paralysis, and it was consistently associated with supernatural assault."[42]

But as post-Enlightenment intellectuals could not abide talk of witches or invisible spirits, they paid no heed to accounts that featured them, unless it was for the purpose of diagnosing pathology. Some experts knew that sleep paralysis—which is caused by the mechanism that prevents us from enacting movement during REM sleep—was real, but they grossly underestimated its frequency and associated it with narcolepsy. Most importantly, they failed to perceive its frequent connection with the other features of the Old Hag. When the rationalists threw away the mythology, they threw away the experience. In this way, our culture came to forget something important, dramatic, and common. So when, four decades ago, I awakened to paralysis and terror, I had no category for the event, no tradition by which to understand it.

It is one thing to underestimate the incidence of something, as we have done with rape and domestic abuse. It is quite another to fail altogether to recognize the existence of something going on fairly frequently. How could doctors, psychologists, and the general public be unaware of an experience that comes to at least one in five people? This truly dumbfounding circumstance should occasion much reflection. Hufford has observed: "one of the most fascinating social issues here is that . . . these kinds of experiences were well known in Western tradition up to three or four hundred years ago. It's not simply that Western culture never had a clue about these things. It's more dramatic than that. We erased knowledge of these experiences from the cultural repertoire while the experiences were continuing to happen. . . . That's a level of social control that's very impressive."[43]

* * *

Amputees commonly feel that they still possess a lost limb. While most of us are aware of this fact, it was not always so. Neither medical nor popular literature written before the American Civil War has much to say on the subject. Although some human beings must always have sensed lost hands, arms, and feet, few it seems said anything about it: they suffered in silence. When a few did talk, their testimonies were, it appears, regularly deemed unworthy of written record. The explanation, according to neurologist George Riddoch, is that, for much of human history, sensing an absent limb seemed "beyond reason," and "the unfortunate patient" who spoke up "was regarded as an obstinate, lying fellow or even possessed of the devil."

It was, then, "a matter better left alone. The patient himself must have often distrusted the reality of his own sensations, and even to-day among the uneducated classes spontaneous description of a phantom is rarely offered unless they [sic] are painful. Dread of the unnatural, of disbelief, or even of the accusation of insanity may be behind this reticence."[44]

As it used to be with the sensation of phantom limbs, and as it was with the Old Hag before Hufford, so is it still today in some quarters regarding mystical raptures, visions, and other salient religious experiences. Too many continue to be oblivious of the fact that the out of the ordinary is not out of the ordinary. Even more regrettably, too many blithely assume that only the credulous or victims of synaptic dysfunction have extraordinary experiences that move them to believe in more than the material world. But it is not so.

3

Bliss from Somewhere, Terror from Nowhere

"In any wilderness the unsuspecting traveler may come upon the burning bush, and discover that the ground upon which he stands is holy ground."

—Howard Thurman¹

"I've been educated and trained in a radical medical materialism, which has forced me to keep my spiritual experiences secret, which cannot be told or shared with others for fear of not being accepted as a 'sane' member of society. This context significantly hindered me from exploring the deep spiritual meaning of my experiences."

—Lucy²

Just as there are a variety of spiritual gifts, so there are, to recall the title of William James's famous book, a variety of religious experiences. Our subject is in fact a menagerie, one that is large and full of curious specimens. This makes generalizing difficult. To think about religious experience in general is a bit like thinking about animals in general. Although in both cases and for some purposes the overview from afar may be profitable, appreciation and understanding come chiefly from examining particular species.

This chapter concerns itself with two types of religious experiences. Both are well attested and intrinsically interesting. They intrigue all the more because they are antithetical. One moves people to speak of love. The other moves them to speak of horror.

* * *

The following is the testimony of the late Leslie Weatherhead, the well-known Methodist pastor and author. One murky November evening, when nineteen and a theological student, he was riding a train when this happened:

> For a few seconds only, I suppose, the whole [train] compartment was filled with light. This is the only way I know in which to describe the moment, for there was nothing to *see* at all. I felt caught up into some tremendous sense of being within a loving, triumphant and shining purpose. I never felt more humble. I never felt more exalted. A most curious, but overwhelming sense possessed me and filled me with ecstasy. I felt that all was well for mankind—how poor the words seem! The word "well" is so poverty stricken. All men were shining and glorious beings who in the end would enter incredible joy. Beauty, music, joy, love immeasurable and a glory unspeakable, all this they would inherit. . . . An indescribable joy possessed me. . . . I *loved* everybody in that compartment. It sounds silly now, and indeed I blush to write it, but at that moment I think I would have died for any one of the people in that compartment.

This was one of several experiences that made Weatherhead, in his words, "certain of the reality of some supernatural Entity which, or whom, I label 'God.'"[3]

In professing to have been overwhelmed by transcendent love, Weatherhead belongs to a great cloud of witnesses. My next illustration is from another minister, Henry Alline, "the Whitefield of Nova Scotia." A leader of the Canadian New Light movement, his experience, occasioned by self-reproach and reading the Psalms, took place in 1775:

> My whole soul was filled with love, and ravished with a divine ecstasy beyond any doubts or fears, or thoughts of being then deceived, for I enjoyed a heaven on earth, and it seemed as if I were wrapped up in God, and that he had done ten thousand times more for me than ever I could expect or had ever thought of. . . . Looking up, I thought I saw that same light [that I had seen on an earlier occasion], though it appeared different, and as soon as I saw it . . . I was obliged to cry out: enough, enough, O blessed God. . . . I will not say that I saw either of those lights with my bodily eyes, though I thought then I did, but that is no odds to me, for it was as evident to me,

as any thing I ever saw with my bodily eyes; and answered the end it was sent for. O how the condescension melted me. . . . I was ravished with his love. . . . O what secret pleasure I enjoyed! Happiness and food that the world knows nothing of: substantial food and settled joy.[4]

Alline and Weatherhead were both public figures whose experiences played a role in making them such. But countless others, whose names history will neglect, have reported comparable experiences. I content myself with testimonies from eight of our contemporaries:

- "One night I was in great distress over a family situation and cried out to God to come to me if He existed. . . . Suddenly God came. Not with a clap or thunder or a flash of light, but gently and slowly and almost imperceptibly He filled the room with His presence until he was everywhere. The comfort and warmth were indescribable. The room was Love. I was very tiny and was held in the palm of his hand and phrases like 'the everlasting arms' kept coming to me, and I said over and over again 'So this is what they mean, this is what they mean.' From then on the purpose of my life became the search for God."[5]
- "I prayed with unashamed sincerity that if God existed, could He show me some sort of light in the jungle. One day, I was sweeping the stairs, down in the house in which I was working, when suddenly I was overcome, and overwhelmed, saturated . . . with a sense of most sublime and living love. It not only affected me, but seemed to bring everything around me to life. The brush in my hand, my dustpan, the stairs, seemed to come alive with love. I seemed no longer me, with my petty troubles and trials, but part of this infinite power of love, so utterly and overwhelmingly wonderful that one knew at once what the saints had grasped. It could only have been a minute or two, yet for that brief particle of time it seemed eternity. . . ."[6]
- "I can't even begin to describe what I was feeling, but only what I know because of it. I was completely and totally saturated with love. Every molecule of my being or body or whatever you want to call it was permeated. His love is so powerful it literally touches every single molecule, atom, electron. I realized in that moment here on earth in this life, we are poorly equipped for the expression of this great love. Here, we get glimpses of love, through the nice things we do, the things we say, the

tears we shed. We can only attempt to express this through our acts and words. But in Heaven (if this is where I was), love is not expressed, it simply JUST IS!!!"[7]

- "I was aware of an invisible but very real 'Person' slightly suspended in the air before me. I perceived great power, but also loving compassion and holiness in this person and the puzzling awareness that I knew this person well, had always known him, and had seemingly forgotten him until that instant. I trust him completely as he entered into my mind communicating in a manner that could not be misinterpreted because it by-passed human thought patterns or language, imparting pure awareness. . . . I was immersed, surrounded, embraced in golden, oceanic Light, full of peace and love, joy, fulfillment, of being Home. I felt so sorry for every unkind thing I'd ever said or done. I realized we are all very precious to God and should love one another. When the vision ended, my face was drenched in tears. My heart changed. . . . I began studying the Bible, attending church and praying, beginning my journey."[8]

- "A radical surrender descended on me, a surrender of body, mind, and soul. It cleared the way for a river of living light and glorious emotion to race down through me with the force of a fire hose. It knocked me down. I lay on the floor in total awe. For several minutes the brain did not think, the body did not move. I could only experience the amazing feeling and light flowing through me. It is impossible to exaggerate the intensity of this feeling. It's like being electrocuted with joy. For me, it changed entirely my understanding of what the body and mind are capable of, virtually of what the mind and body are. After several minutes of the light and outrageously glorious feeling, my being began to settle down to a state of merely extreme bliss. . . . My emotional state now was one of what I then knew to be unconditional love. It was like a force of nature just there for everyone."[9]

- "The kitchen and garden were filled with golden light. I became conscious that at the centre of the Universe, and in my garden, was a great pulsing dynamo that ceaselessly poured out love. This love poured over and through me, and I was part of it and it wholly encompassed me. . . . It was overwhelmingly real, more real than anything I had experienced. . . . To deny it would be the ultimate sin, blasphemy."[10]

- "I was suddenly overcome by a feeling of well-being. . . . The place took on a warmth and a brightness. . . . I felt as if I had no cares at all in the world. . . . It was a moment of absolute bliss. It's hard to describe really. Just a feeling of total support and comfort and well-being. I felt as if someone was with me, and that I was to be looked after. . . . I now know that there is a higher power—whatever it is, whatever you want to call it—that loves me and is interested in my welfare. . . . Was it possible that day that I felt for the first time in my life that I was loved?"[11]

· "I . . . saw what I took to be a luminous star, which gradually came nearer, and appeared as a soft, slightly blurred, white light. I was seized with violent trembling, but had no fear. I knew that what I felt was great awe. This was followed by a sense of overwhelming love coming to me, and going out from me, then of great compassion from the outer Presence. After that I had a sense of overpowering peace, and indescribable happiness. I remember saying to myself, 'This is no dream. I am awake, and experiencing it with my whole self' . . . I awoke in the morning with a feeling of having been transformed."[12]

Despite the depth of feeling in the recollections of Weatherhead and the rest, it would be tedious to add further examples. Readers may be assured, however, that it would be easy to fill page after page with little narratives such as these. They abound.[13]

Several motifs run through the accounts I have quoted and others like them. Although each report contains idiosyncratic elements, the family resemblances are clear:

· Narrators use the English word "love."
· They conceive of this love as coming from beyond the ordinary ego, regularly crediting God as the source. They sometimes accentuate its otherworldly nature by associating it with heaven or the world to come: "all men were shining and glorious beings who in the end would enter incredible joy"; "heaven on earth"; "in Heaven [if this is where I was], love is not expressed, it simply JUST IS!!!"
· Recipients depict this love as overwhelmingly intense and evoking potent emotional responses: "I was overcome"; "my face was drenched with tears"; "it knocked me down. I lay on the floor in total awe"; "extreme bliss"; "I was seized with violent trembling."

- They often remark that words fail: "indescribable joy"; "the comfort and warmth were indescribable"; "I can't even begin to describe"; "it by-passed human thought patterns or language"; "indescribable happiness."
- They characterize the experience as of great significance and often as marking a personal turning point: "From then on the purpose of my life became the search for God"; "my heart changed. . . . I began studying the Bible"; "it changed entirely my understanding of what the body and mind are capable of"; "a feeling of having been transformed."[14]
- Many accounts refer to light, as in over half the cases quoted above: "the whole [train] compartment was filled with light"; "I thought I saw that same light"; "I was immersed, surrounded, embraced in golden, oceanic Light"; "light flowing through me"; "golden light"; "a luminous star . . . a soft, slightly blurred, white light."[15]

* * *

C. S. Lewis's *The Four Loves* attempts to map, from a Christian point of view, the various kinds of love.[16] As the title indicates, he contemplates four: natural affection (as in familial love), friendship, romantic love, and divine love. He portrays the last sort as primarily a virtue. It is the unselfish charity that promulgates God's love throughout the world.

Lewis is little interested in what one might call the affective side of divine love. He does not, to be sure, bypass it altogether. He acknowledges "the wonderful foretastes of the fruition of God vouchsafed to some in their earthly life."[17] Still, this is a passing, unelaborated remark, and his interest lies elsewhere.

Mark Fox has sought to make up the lack. His book, *The Fifth Love*, explores numinous love and how it—for want of a better word—feels to people. He is nearly alone in this endeavor. Systematic theologians for the most part shy away from writing about out-of-the-ordinary experiences (at least if the reports are outside the canon). Moral theologians are all about what people should do. And the classic literature on spirituality recognizes the perils of seeking or privileging peak experiences. Fox, by contrast, attends to what ordinary people report about life-changing encounters with what they take to be a love from beyond. Playing off Lewis, Fox calls his subject "the fifth love."

Fox demonstrates that such encounters constitute a specific subtype of religious experience. He also shows that they often occur during a personal crisis and that their long-term effects are impressively positive. Fox further reviews the prospect of reductionistic explanations. Endorphins, abreaction, and temporal lobe irregularities do not, in his judgment, explain the facts as he has uncovered them.

* * *

With Fox's work as a foundation, I wish to contribute a few musings of my own. The first has to do with secularization.

The general decline of the churches in Europe and the United States is, in terms of both numbers and influence, obvious. Equally obvious is the emergence in recent times of large structures or institutions—big business, big government, big education, big media, big tech—that operate without significant religious input. In addition, the percentage of professed atheists and the religiously indifferent continues, according to the pollsters, to climb. Despite all this, however, the prophets of the nineteenth and twentieth centuries, who confidently predicted that the tides of modern science and enlightened reason would soon wash away the sandcastles of religion, have missed the mark.

Why were the prophets of overwhelming secularity unprescient? "Secularization" is an exceedingly complex matter, and its nature and progress continue to be energetically debated. Yet it is plausible, I suggest, that powerful experiences, such as those just introduced, have, in some measure, helped thwart fulfillment of the old, overly confident predictions. Maybe the undertakers of religion botched the future partly because they overlooked the prevalence and vitality of certain superordinate experiences.

Those who believe that they have run into God's love are not going to deny God's existence, even if their culture or education has done little to implant religious sentiments in them. At the same time, encounters with the fifth love do not come with a doctrinal statement attached, so folks need not join any official religious organization. Perhaps they often find themselves, without additional guidance, in the spiritual but not religious crowd, not committed to the truth of this or that faith but rather, and more generally, persuaded that reality is much larger than they had formerly imagined.[18] In any event, such individuals will deem flat-earth materialism to be the real myth, and their presence in our society will serve as a countervailing force to secularization.

Experience of the fifth love must further function for some to attenuate the most popular objection in our age to a theistic outlook. If God is perfectly good and all powerful, how can our world be so full of evil? Why does God not step up to the plate? Or, as my wife once put it, after hearing a sermon she did not like: What's the use of being God if you don't get what you want? This is the problem of evil. Despite the formidable intellects who have tackled it, it remains, for those accepting the premises of God's goodness and power, without satisfying resolution. But an experience of transcendent love can serve as a sort of personal defeater for the skeptical conclusion that God either is not good or does not exist.

Here is the testimony of a man who, at the top of a London bus, entered some "realm of glory and light" and learned that "everything that is, is a facet of love": "For years I puzzled about this—'that everything is a facet of love'—unable to understand in the face of all the sin, diseases, etc. that this could be—but I knew it was Truth."[19] This individual recognizes that much in our world pushes against his belief that "everything is a facet of love." Yet his experience of love was so powerful that he cannot deem it illusory. For this reason, the problem of evil does not, in his case, find resolution in unbelief. The man instead retreats into his inability to understand.

It is the same with me. My experiences, as recounted in chapter 1, have much fortified my conviction that "God is love" (1 John 4:8, 16). This exceedingly counterintuitive claim is not, for me, a baseless conjecture but rather accords with my subjective apprehension on more than one occasion. This does not render me insensible to the injustices, countless absurdities, and heartless calamities all around us. Not all is right—or rather much is wrong—with this world in which, on Palm Sunday, 1994, as the children's choir was singing, a tornado struck the United Methodist Church in Goshen, Alabama. It killed twenty members. It injured almost a hundred, many of them little ones decked out for the holiday. My theological education does not much help me here. I cannot reconcile our often obscene, brutal world with the proposition that divine love enfolds us all. Which means the argument from evil is a good argument. This is why atheists incessantly appeal to it. Partially because of my experiences, however, I am emboldened not to forsake theological discourse but instead to take refuge in a mystery, and to join the ranks of the so-called skeptical theists, who stress the confines of human understanding.

* * *

In addition to discouraging full-blooded secularism in some and inserting an experiential element into the problem of evil for others, encounters with otherworldly love can also function as confirmation or clarification of a specific theological belief. As evidence of this, some of the reports that Fox catalogues take up biblical language:

- "Phrases like 'the everlasting arms' [from Deut. 33:27 and the hymn, "Leaning on the Everlasting Arms"] kept coming to me, and I said over and over again 'So this is what they mean, this is what they mean.'"
- "It is literally true that 'neither death, nor life, nor things to come, nor height, nor depth, nor any other creature, shall be able to separate us from the Love of God' (Rom 8:39)."
- "I know why God's name is 'I am' [Exod. 3:14]. The eternal nature of God as perfect love filled me with an inexpressible sense of joy."
- "There came over me a WONDERFUL sense of peace and universal love. I felt somehow united with . . . the whole world of nature . . . and realised the meaning of the words of scripture about 'not one sparrow falling to [the] ground without the Father's knowledge' (Matt. 10:29; Luke 12:6)."[20]

The same phenomenon appears in accounts outside Fox's collection. Here are two examples:

- "We seemed to be surrounded with a 'wave' of 'love,' which is the only way I can describe the feeling. It lasted about half a minute and was like nothing else I have ever experienced. It has made me realize that what St John said, that 'God is Love,' was the absolute truth."[21]
- "I had the most shattering experience of my entire life. I believe it was during a sleepless night, but it seems to have been an experience entirely out of time as we accept the notion. Without any sense perception (except that I do seem to recollect an impression of light and darkness) I was made aware of a Reality beyond anything my own mind could have conceived. And that Reality was a total love of all things in heaven and earth. 'It' enclosed and accepted everything and every creature. . . . All were 'kept' by this Power, and loved by it. I understood—then at least—the phrases 'I am that I am' [Exod. 3:14], and what I later read as 'the coinci-

35

dence of opposites. . . . ' I was put in touch with that ultimate reality for which we use the shorthand, 'God.'"[22]

Even simply to use "God" and "love" in the same sentence, as do so many who encounter the fifth love, is, in a world that sometimes half-remembers the Bible, to corroborate the New Testament insofar as it teaches that "God is love." The point is that, when an experience of transcendent love lines up with what people know of a particular religious tradition, it must function as empirical support for that tradition.

Perhaps I may add that, in my case, extraordinary experiences enhance my sympathy for what the theologians call "apophatic theology." This phrase refers to the fundamental unknowability of God, who transcends all being and is suitably spoken of via negations and imperfect analogies. As the Liturgy of John Chrysostom has it, God is "ineffable, inconceivable, invisible, incomprehensible."

One root of the apophatic tradition is the manifest ceiling of the human mind: our intellects can climb only so high. But apophaticism also has an experiential root. Coherent speech cannot effectively capture certain religious experiences. As a friend of mine told me, after a shattering encounter that featured light and love: "my former linguistic patterns were made obsolete and I'm left figuring out how to communicate in the rubble." To be immersed in the fifth love is to be enveloped in a mystery, and it is wholly natural to suppose that its source must also be a mystery, or to revert to the liturgy: ineffable, inconceivable, invisible, and incomprehensible.

* * *

Before moving on to the next type of experience, I wish to subjoin a reservation about the fifth love. Fox draws upon materials in the RERC archives. This means that he is pondering testimonies mostly from modern Western Europeans. What would happen were one to enlarge the data base? Could we find experiences of the fifth love in other times, places, and cultures? Is it part of general human experience, like hunger and thirst, or is it rather specific to our particular society, where Christianity's language of love still circulates? And do some narrate experiences of the fifth love without using the word "love" (or *amor* or *Liebe* or some such)?

These turn out to be very tricky questions. Consider this report:

> Everywhere surrounding me was this white, bright, sparkling light, like sun on frosty snow, like a million diamonds, and there was no cornfield, no trees, no sky, this light was everywhere. . . . The feeling was indescribable, but I have never experienced anything in the years that followed that can compare with that glorious moment; it was blissful, uplifting, I felt open-mouthed wonder.[23]

Although these sentences lack the word, "love," they make use of "glorious," "blissful," and "wonder," words that regularly appear in accounts of the fifth love. Also shared are association with a mystical light and the observation that the encounter was "indescribable." Is this then an experience of the fifth love without the word "love"?

The problem becomes even more acute when we set aside accounts in European languages and look beyond the Christian West. Buddhist sources speak of *piti*. This is the ecstatic euphoria sometimes attending an altered state of consciousness. Is this the fifth love by another name? I do not know. But if it is, it would mean that the theistic interpretation is not the only interpretation, that one can apprehend the experience from more than one point of view. What should we make of this Zen Buddhist anecdote?

> The roshi [teacher] scrutinized me as I entered his room, walked towards him, prostrated myself, and sat before him with my mind alert and exhilarated. . . . "The universe is One" he began, each word tearing into my mind like a bullet. . . . All at once the roshi, the room, every single thing disappeared in a dazzling stream of illumination and I felt myself bathed in a delicious, unspeakable delight.[24]

My disposition is to suppose that the RERC accounts of the fifth love likely bear witness to a broad human experience, one that is, like the Old Hag (see chapter 2), a cross-cultural reality. Yet it is also, again like the Old Hag, subject to multiple explanations. In other words, while the experience is vividly real, its reception—its phenomenology and interpretation—reflects one's culture, dispositions, and personal beliefs. This means that, while an experience of the fifth love matches the Christian dogma that God is love, it does not thereby confirm the truth of Christian doctrine generally. Hare Krishnas would find the experience consistent with their brand of devotional Hinduism, just as Irina Tweedie, a Sufi, made sense of it from within her tradition:

> On the level of emotions there was a glittering, limitless Ocean of Love
> . . . no end of it, wherever I looked . . . I could see no shore . . . it stretched
> beyond the horizon, and I was drowned in it . . . but peacefully,
> gently. . . . The nearest to Nirvana on earth. The words—Nearer to
> you than breathing, closer than hands and feet—came into my mind,
> and the sentence from the Koran: "I am closer to you than your very
> neck-vein." . . . The feeling of this sweetness, of absolute belonging, will
> haunt my memory forever. It cannot be described adequately, fleeting
> as it is, so intimate, so subtle.[25]

It makes sense that what we struggle to put into words can cause varied descriptions and carry multiple interpretations.

* * *

Unfortunately, religious experiences are not all sweetness and light. The fifth love has an evil counterpart. It is the overwhelming horror, the unparalleled terror—not unease or a sense of the uncanny but true terror—that inexplicably arrives from nowhere. In this experience, terror is not an emotional response to some proximate, perceptible cause—a grizzly bear, an enemy combatant, a car on the wrong side of the highway—but reaction to a perplexing, menacing enigma.

I first thought about the experience of unprovoked, overwhelming horror a few decades ago, when I happened upon a first-person narrative with the title, "Dance of the Leaves."[26] In this, a certain Robert Harner tells of what happened to him on November 18, 1975. While driving to give a lecture, he found himself with some extra time and decided to stop at Serpent Mound, in southern Ohio. The effigy mound, the world's largest, is shaped like a winding snake and runs over 1,300 feet.

After parking his car, Harner strolled around the monument. He found himself wholly alone. After a few minutes pondering who built the mound and why—no one really knows—he began to return to his car. While walking back, this happened:

Suddenly and without warning I was struck with the coldest, most abject, hopeless terror I have ever experienced. I felt the hair rising on the nape of my neck; I could neither move nor speak. I knew that although I was completely alone I was not really alone. I saw nothing; I heard nothing; but I felt such horror as I had never experienced before. In broad open sunlight I came close to fainting for the first time in my life. I made a futile attempt to be logical. I thought of all the reasons why I should not be frightened; it did no good.

At this juncture, the narrative takes a truly fantastic turn. Harner claims that, although there was no wind, some of the leaves on the ground began to move, in little footfalls, toward him, until they surrounded him. Although this amplified his terror, he was likewise fascinated and so decided—this was before the ubiquitous smart phone—to return to his car for his camera. With that thought, the spell was broken. The spectacle ended.

* * *

Regarding the second part of Harner's story, a skeptic might suppose that, despite his adamant insistence to the contrary, his imagination got the better of him: he turned a trick of the wind into an imagined pattern. Regrettably, I do not know Mr. Harner, who may or may not yet live. I have been unable to review the matter with him.

Regarding the first part of his story, however, I take him at his word. This is because his report, prior to the affair of the leaves, contains nothing idiosyncratic. Multitudes have reported that, for no apparent reason and without warning of any kind, utter horror descended upon them from out of the blue. Among them is one of my children. Not long ago, after he shared with me a disturbing event, I asked him to write it up. This is from the email he sent me in response:

> I had just come to bed. I recall laying on my back for what seemed only a few minutes. I suddenly had a feeling of deep dread, so I sat up. Feelings of panic rushed into my body like electricity. I had been fine and then I was filled with fear. I had a sense that a presence was in the left corner of my bedroom. I felt overwhelmed, and that this presence was emanating

hate, rage, and violence towards me. At this time I had not lifted my head to look towards it because I had been too frightened to do so.

I centered myself as best I could and then was able to glance quickly in the direction of the corner but immediately had to look away. During this glance I was able to discern only a few white streaks of light, a lot like if you were to move your eyes around quickly when glancing at a street light. I centered myself for a few moments more until I was able to look up again. This time I was able to look directly at it for a second or two.

What I saw was a dark outline of an apelike being. I could make out a squatted and hunched over body covered entirely in coarse fur or quills with long, ape-like arms. It was too dark to tell if the fur/quills were black or if the color was just hidden in shadow. I couldn't make out a face except searing-white eyes that stared back at me. There were two sets of eyes, one stacked on top of the other and overlapping slightly, like a misregistered print. One set had two very small, grey, streaky irises. Maybe one-third the size of the average human iris.

During the entire time the presence was in the room it projected hate towards me. I felt strongly somehow that it was appearing to me as a warning. I remember hearing a voice that is very difficult to describe. It was both squeaky, deep and hollow all at the same time. I remember clearly that it said "I will crush you" once and then it was gone.

Some of the dread kept returning back to me in momentary waves for the next couple of succeeding days, but that's really all I remember.

When I spoke with my son about all this, I raised the possibility that the ape-like thing he saw was the projection of his imagination, that his pattern-making mind, searching for some cause of his terror, conjured an evil creature as explanation for his acute awareness of malevolence. He did not dismiss the idea. It is conceivable, he thought, that his imagination filled in a blank, that his mind, overcome with abject horror, desperately sought an explanation and, in response, manufactured a vision or succumbed to an illusion.[27]

Whether or not that is the truth, I note that the terror was upon him before he looked around. Initially he somehow sensed, without using his eyes, that an evil presence, a mysterious force off to his left, was directing hate and violence right at him.

In talking about this event, I assured my son that what had happened to him was not rare. I had in mind experiences such as these:

- "[I was] out driving a dog-cart with my father and driver. A call is made at a cottage above a wooded hollow and for a little while I am left alone with the old mare in the shafts—there comes an overwhelming sense of evil around me and when the men return, they find me weeping bitterly, but it was not that I felt lonely or deserted. It was from the dread of some unseen force which I did not attempt to explain nor never have."[28]
- "A year and a half ago I was asleep in the night and woke very suddenly and felt quite alert. I felt surrounded and threatened by the most terrifying and powerful presence of evil. It seemed almost physical and in a curious way it 'crackled', though not audibly. It was also extremely 'black' and I felt overwhelmed with terror . . . I felt it was a manifestation directed very personally at me by a Power of Darkness. I was overwhelmed by despair and a desire to go out and kill myself by jumping in the Thames nearby, but I knew that I must withstand this."[29]
- "We had all been travelling many hours and were hot, sticky and tired. On entering the room I felt a most terrible chill, a fear I had never known. I am afraid I cannot put into words what exactly I felt, only to say that some terrible presence was in this room. . . . On the bedside table beside me was a Bible: although I am of the Jewish faith and not religious, this, even so, made me feel at that time very close to God. . . . The Bible made me feel strong, made me feel that whatever was in this room I could fight and that God would fight alongside me."[30]
- "Suddenly I became aware of a sense of the uttermost evil, so much so that I became awake. I could feel this sense of evil enveloping me. I had the terrifying impression that this evil force or presence was bent upon taking possession of me. How does one describe evil? I only knew that I was enveloped by this revolting force, so vile and rotting that I could almost taste the evil. I was in terror, so much so that I could not call out or move. A part of my mind told me that I must at all costs act or I would be lost. I recall that I managed by a great effort to stretch out my right hand and with my index finger I traced the shape of the cross in the air. Immediately on my doing this the evil enveloping me fell away completely, and I felt a wonderful sense of peace and safety."[31]

41

· "I was in a pleasant relaxed frame of mind—my idle mind—my eyes shut when I was quite suddenly 'assaulted' by a sense of Evil. I opened my eyes to see if anyone had entered the compartment of the train but it was empty, but for a single middle aged man who seemed to be snoozing in the corner. . . . I was filled with an indescribable feeling of mental revulsion and horror, but my mind seemed to work like that of a threatened animal as I tried to sense from where the threat came. I felt as if my mind was being threatened by some destructive force. . . . I left the train and was aware that the evil was with me. I felt I couldn't combat it. . . . By the end of three days this horror had departed and the memory gradually became less vivid, but it was one of the moving factors in my life."[32]

How widespread are these sorts of experiences? They are exceedingly common. We know that 20 percent or more of the general population wakes up at least once in a lifetime with paralysis, and further that three-fourths of the time this is associated with the sense of a terrifying, evil presence. This implies that, at a minimum, 15 percent of us have run into a mystifying horror. The real number must be higher given that evil presences do not confine themselves to episodes of sleep paralysis: they can also, as some of the stories just quoted reveal, disturb the wide awake.

We also know that, in 2000, the Opinion Research Business, in cooperation with the BBC, reported that 25 percent of the population of Great Britain claimed to have been, on one or more occasions, aware "of an evil presence."[33] As with most surveys, detailed follow-up would be needed to get beyond the broadest impression. Still, the high number is perhaps suggestive.

* * *

Why have people in so many times and places believed in evil spirits, or in outsized demonic figures such as the Christian Satan, the Buddhist Mara, or the Zoroastrian Angra Mainyu? There is no single or simple answer. A myriad of factors must be responsible. One cause, however, has undoubtedly been the experience of transcendent evil. What is one to think after ostensibly encountering an invisible, malignant presence? Before the ubiquity of modern skepticism and the psychologizing of everything, most would reflexively have posited an external cause—goblins or demons or an evil ghost. As one modern sufferer said: "If I were a religious man, I would certainly describe my experience as a contact with a god or devil."[34] The traditional belief in evil spirits has had, apart from culture or religious tradition, a strong experiential source.

The RERC archives contain the following testimony: "I felt the presence of such evil (as I have never experienced before or since). . . . I could neither see nor hear anything, only feel the presence of such evil. . . . Looking back and knowing what I do now about the Devil being a person and not a myth as I thought in those days, I can well believe that it was a struggle on his part to regain my soul."[35] Here belief in the devil as a myth has given way to belief in the devil as "a person," and precisely because someone encountered an evil presence.[36] I regard this change of mind as evidence for the proposition that some have believed in malevolent spirits because they have ostensibly run into them.

* * *

At this point in Western history, many in the churches disbelieve in Satan as a personal being.[37] A major reason for this is that, through the centuries, Satan and demons were invoked to explain all sorts of miserable things—wars, epilepsy, earthquakes, lightning, temptation, schizophrenia, infertility, bad crops, crib death, sexual dreams, Tourette Syndrome, non-Christian religions, fatigue at midday, the beliefs of heretics—for which we now have better explanations. The devil functioned either to explain gaps in our knowledge or, as an ideological cudgel, to demonize and discredit foes (as happens to Jesus in Matt. 12:22–24). But as modern science grew, the devil withered. Today he has so little left to do that he has disappeared completely from every modern area of knowledge. I do not recall his making an appearance in any class in elementary school, junior high, high school, or college.

And yet, notwithstanding all this, multitudes continue to have the experience of overwhelming evil, and many posit, as explanation, a supramundane cause. How then should we think about the matter?

One option is the reductionist path. Maybe the sense of horrific evil is neural flotsam, the unhappy byproduct of some blunder of the brain. Or maybe it is a not-too-distant relative of the so-called panic attack. Or maybe it has an external, invisible cause, such as low frequency sound, which can induce stress and produce unpleasant feelings.

This is not, however, the sole option. Maybe God is not the only reality beyond our earthly cave. Maybe additional powers exist, not all of them friendly. I seriously entertain this view, even though I disbelieve in the composite Satan of Christian history.

The latter's biography was concocted largely through bad exegesis. Satan became a fallen angel because readers—among them Origen and Augustine—found him in Isa. 14:12–15 ("How you are fallen from heaven, O Day Star [= 'Lucifer' in Latin], son of Dawn!") as well as in Ezek. 28:11–19 ("I cast you to the ground"). He became the proximate cause of humanity's estrangement from paradise because he was identified with the snake in Eden (Genesis 2–3). And he became, among many additional things, a choirmaster because some, after reading him into Ezekiel 28, found musical instruments in the more-than-difficult Hebrew of 28:13: "the workmanship of thy tabrets [a small drum] and of thy pipes was prepared in thee in the day that thou wast created" (King James Version). Job 38:7 seemed to confirm Satan's passion for music: "When the morning stars sang together, and all the sons of God shouted for joy."

None of this convinces me.

Yet our world is rife with evil, and laying it all at the feet of Adam and Eve's wayward offspring is an anthropocentric conceit. Our species is not all that has gone wrong with the world. Were we to vanish tomorrow at dawn, the Creator would not be able to look down and see that all is good. Drought would still slay baby elephants. Rabies would still stalk and murder raccoons. Chimpanzee communities would still splinter and go to war. Parasitoid wasps would still torment and kill beautiful caterpillars, and as Darwin confessed: "I cannot persuade myself that a beneficent and omnipotent God would have designedly created parasitic wasps with the express intention of their feeding within the living bodies of Caterpillars."[38] In short, nature would still be, without us around, red in tooth and claw, and prodigious pain and unjust suffering would remain rampant.

My public education taught me to put it all down to an impersonal, amoral evolutionary process, and perhaps it would be wisdom to leave it at that. I wonder, however, whether the divine good will has competition. Maybe it is not the only disembodied reality at large. Maybe some autonomous centers of power defy their divinely appointed telos—just like those of us created in God's image—and sometimes, for whatever reason, intersect our reality, to occasional ill effect.

I scruple to dismiss all experiences of transcendent evil as mental chimeras because I cannot, in good conscience, entertain a supramundane source for experiences of the fifth love yet be dogmatically closed-minded about a supramundane origin for any of the bleak experiences narrated above. How could I justify privileging some of the good experiences over all the bad ones? That I like one set of stories and dislike the other is not an argument. The experiences of horror, moreover, do not seem on the whole to be less subjectively persuasive than the experiences of love. Maybe the two opposing sorts of experience stand or fall together.

At the end of the day, then, I hesitate to demythologize Satan and his demons without remainder. Regarding God, we recognize that thoughts fail and that genuine mystery confronts us, and we demythologize our anthropomorphisms without becoming atheists. Maybe Satan and his demons are not wholly different. If we recognize the need to be less than literal-minded when we think about God, maybe we can decouple transcendent evil from the old myths about the devil. That Satan as we know him is a defective exegetical construct, that partisans have utilized him to vilify enemies, that he has been mistakenly called upon to explain all sorts of vexing unpleasantries, and that some enthusiasts have espied him in every dim corner and feared him beneath every unfamiliar rock need not mean that he stands for nothing beyond human imagination.

* * *

From the seventeenth century on, theologians have often debated the question, Do Satan and demons exist? Those who have urged that they do have taken the relevant biblical sources largely at face value. Those arguing to the contrary have reinterpreted the texts in this-worldly terms. But while this second alternative, which is what I grew up with, rightly welcomes modern knowledge and abandons an unimaginative literalism, it has nothing to say about a widespread experience that has helped craft ideas about transcendent evil, an experience that has not gone away but persists. This failure means that liberal theology has been woefully equipped to address those who have had the misfortune of having that experience.

Metanormal experiences of evil get mythologized. Sleep paralysis with a horrifying presence can become, as we saw in the previous chapter, the Old Hag, and encounters with frightful shadow beings can become battles with one of Lucifer's unheavenly host. One problem with much modern theology is that it typically interprets the myths about Satan and demons in psychological, theological, or literary terms while overlooking the real experiences that, in part, lie behind and are associated with those myths. It ignores the experiences while interpreting their interpretations.

* * *

Those who believe that they have encountered otherworldly evil often find themselves with no one to speak to. Sometimes this is because their social world has no place for anything beyond textbook science, so speaking up might invite incredulity or ridicule. In a conservative religious environment, by contrast, silence may be shrewd because some will imagine that horrible experiences are elicited by sin, or even that a sufferer is in danger of becoming possessed. But whatever the social or religious context, we should keep two facts in mind.

First, although people may feel alone, they are not alone. The experience of an otherworldly horror is quite common, even today. There should be some relief in knowing this. Company is comfort.

Second, there appear to be no clear patterns regarding who has the experience or when they occur or where. Merete Demant Jakobsen, who has made a special study of negative spiritual encounters, is impressed by "the randomness with which people are suddenly faced by evil. Of course, there are examples of people being on the verge of mental illness or in severe depression, but they are few. Mostly it is people who suddenly, waking up from sleep or walking in a wood, visiting a house and so on, are faced with a sense of evil that they cannot connect to a previous state of mind."[39] Again, "the recipient of these negative experiences can often not connect them to any conscious choice and feels like the victim of random onslaught."[40] Like the rain, horror falls upon the just as well as the unjust. This is simply part of being human.

4

The Hidden World of Prayer

"Prayer is wide as the world and older than history."

—*C. F. D'Arcy*[1]

"The genuineness of religion is . . . indissolubly bound up with the question whether the prayerful consciousness be or be not deceitful. The conviction that something is genuinely transacted in this consciousness is the very core of living religion."

—*William James*[2]

"Attention . . . like memory . . . is strengthened by practice and weakens when it is little used."

—*Jean-Claudet Larchet*[3]

When I was small, my Presbyterian parents told me that I should pray. I obliged, and I have honored them by praying almost every day since at least 1966. (I made a mental note of my religious activities that year because my ten-year-old self somehow intuited that his adult counterpart would be interested in what he was up to way back then.)

My mother and father failed, however, to teach me *how* to pray. For some reason, they assumed that elaboration was unnecessary. So I had to improvise. This is what I came up with. I chose to pray each evening at bedtime. I closed my eyes and imagined a medium-sized, nondescript, bare room (a rather Reformed space in retrospect). Two steps up from the floor was a dais. On the low platform was an oversized, throne-like chair. It was empty. No anthropic figure, no ball of light, nothing: God was a blank (rather apophatic in retrospect). I would enter this room in my imagination, prostrate myself before the vacant chair, and pray. My inner speech consisted most often of a bare list of names: family, friends, relatives. I had little use for sentences. Sometimes I was on my knees with hands clasped. More often I was in bed on my back, hands to the side. My words were unspoken thoughts. A bystander would have heard nothing.

A few years later, when I was a teenager, I left my parents' church for one better suited, I then thought, to my needs. The teachers there informed me that prayer should be more than imploring God to take especial note of those within my narrow circle of affectivity. The Father Almighty, they taught me, prefers prayers that include confession of sins, pleas for forgiveness, and thanksgiving. I recall dutifully trying a few times to do what they wanted. But habit prevailed, and I soon reverted to reciting names.

As I became older, however, some things did change. I eventually abandoned the room with the vacant, throne-like chair. It became but a memory. The list of names, which inevitably grew longer as I grew older, became the sole object of my mind's eye. At one point, my routine shifted from evening to morning as I began to pray while walking to work. Later on I expanded my daily routine so that petitionary prayer ceased to be central and instead became peripheral. My efforts became more focused on reflection and contemplation.

To what extent the details and development of my prayer life are either typical or idiosyncratic I do not know.[4] Perhaps no one does. The problem is that few have made serious inquiry into what people are really up to when, alone with the door shut, they pray for this or that. Pollsters have, to be sure, asked the general public, How often do you pray? and What do you pray about?[5] Furthermore, neuroscientists have studied what our brains do during religious exercises; and, over the last three decades, researchers have begun to explore systematically the psychological facets of various types of prayer.[6] We also have Tanya Luhrmann's *When God Talks Back*, a sympathetic, thoroughly engaging report on the devotional lives of members of Vineyard Christian Fellowships.[7] Nonetheless, and although private prayer remains, in our time and place, the central religious act, some aspects of the subject remain little explored.

* * *

What exactly do minds see and do when they petition God on behalf of others? I have never formed images of people while praying for them. I have instead always seen names composed of English letters, as though they were written on a piece of paper. The names do not, however, appear on a list that one could read from top to bottom. They are rather arranged geographically, being superimposed on a map of North America. I start in one place—where I am living at the moment—and then move from region to region, naming people in each area. In doing so, I rarely say to myself anything other than "I pray for" plus a name or the occasional "Lord have mercy."

No one taught me how to do this, and I have no idea how or why or exactly when it came to pass. Whatever the causes, my manner of praying appears to be atypical. Or so I have inferred from conversations with others. No one I have ever spoken with about the matter superimposes names on a map. I appear to be the inventor of this geographical system (although one individual told me that she prays by "flying from place to place"). My parents, however, are as responsible for the method as am I. By instructing me to pray without telling me how to do so, they left it to my imagination.

I have decided, after decades of informally quizzing people about petitionary prayer, that my unguided experience is that of many, perhaps even most in modern American churches. That is, while pious parents and Sunday school teachers regularly enjoin children to pray, they usually leave it at that, neglecting to deliver detailed instruction.[8] Why they are so bashful about specifics, as though this were the birds and the bees, is an intriguing question. Someone should look into it. Irrespective of the explanation, the upshot is that we grow up praying in sundry ways and diverse manners.

My prayers have always, as just indicated, focused on names, and in this I am not alone. Yet a large percentage of those who pray with names do so— again to generalize from my imperfect inquiries—not with the mind alone (as do I) but with a paper prop. They may, for instance, have a prayer list between the pages of a Bible, a list—perhaps with needs as well as names—that they go over once a day (and which they may save in order to have a record of what they reckon to be answered prayers). Or they may have scattered pieces that they gather for use during their so-called "quiet time." A few have told me that they use crayons to doodle around names.

My wife, Kris, who unlike me has no fixed time for prayer, always has an 8.5 x 11-inch piece of paper with names on it. They are not arranged geographically but by common need. One area may list people in emotional crisis. Another may have the names of the seriously ill. Recently her sheet had three names off to the side, inside a box she had penciled around them. They were the names of children of good friends, young women who were struggling with drug addiction.

Whenever she is reminded to do so, Kris looks at her piece of paper. With the names before her, she conjures images of those she is thinking of. She often says nothing and just tries, she says, to feel compassion for them. At other times, however, she utters a brief wish, such as "heal her" or "help him." Or she will, as she puts it, "hold them in the light." This is an exercise in visualization. Like me, her prayers are terse. Others, of course, use more words, and some are downright loquacious, telling the Supreme Being exactly what needs to be done.

In moving from words to images, my wife appears to exemplify the practice of the majority. Most pray primarily with pictures. But what is it precisely that their imaginations visualize? A few report envisioning people from head to toe. One woman told me that she sometimes recalls favorite photographs that include entire bodies. Another reported that she sees brief, two-second film clips of people as she prays for them. One of my close relatives, when praying for people in psychological distress, envisages them flat on a bed. He imagines that they are full of dark shadows and then summons those shadows to depart. He directs them up to the ceiling and watches them pass up through the roof. He confides that it is hard to do this when he is depressed, but if he can manage it, he feels much better. Part of him hopes that the other person does, too. I told him this sounds like a sort of long-distance exorcism. He agreed.

But these are outliers. Most people see faces, or faces with shoulders. In other words, they see headshots. It is as though they regularly pray through something like a high school yearbook, although with fewer posed smiles: prayer is too often about problems.

What do people do with these faces or busts? Many simply utter petitions while they contemplate the images. But one woman told me, "I cover the faces with light." Another reported that, when her imagination views faces, her hands "gently hold them." This is because, in the church she grew up in, her pastor blessed people by holding their faces in his hands. Her prayer is an act of imitation.

The most affecting practice I have run across comes from a former student. She says that she sees shoulders as well as faces. This allows her, in her imagination, to pick up a warm shawl and place it on the shoulders of those she is praying for. This is her daily ritual.

If people typically see the faces of those they pray for, how do they envisage God? Many do not. Their undivided focus is on those for whom they are interceding. God is in the background, an onlooker. Yet as with everything else regarding prayer, here too variety rules. One of my students told me that he regularly addresses his petitions to the letters G, O, D. An elderly Presbyterian woman once confided that she had gone through the entirety of her life praying to an old man on a throne. The man was her grandfather, who had loved her so much. She knew that God did not necessarily resemble her treasured relative, but it was altogether natural for her to conflate her aged grandparent with the Ancient of Days.

Another woman, a Pentecostal, told me that, every morning, she imagines having "coffee with the Trinity." I unaccountably neglected to ask her what the Trinity looks like. Did she think of Abraham and Sarah entertaining strangers unawares and so see something like Rublev's famous icon? I also regret that I failed to follow up with the person who told me that God, in her mind, is never alone but always surrounded by her family. I was so taken with the idea of a family portrait that includes God that I forgot to ask her about the divine likeness.

Most I have spoken with, however, do not employ an anthropomorphic picture of the Deity. They rather favor the abstract. They address a "ball of light"—I have heard that exact phrase several times—or an amorphous light. (Do these images belong to the reception history of Exodus 3, where Moses meets God in a blazing bush?) Or they pray to a pitch-black darkness or to a darkness lit up with little points of light, like stars. Two men in their twenties related that they direct requests to something like an empty computer screen. I met one person who told me that his habit is to pray to abstract shapes. His words were so nonrepresentational that I could not decipher what he was saying.

Altogether aniconic are those who never envision or utilize a symbolic representation for the Deity but instead somehow "feel" the invisible divine presence. "No one has ever seen God," they may say, quoting John 1:14. One woman remarked: "You can't see Him, but you can feel Him sitting next to you."

Conversations with others over the years and reflections on my own experience have led me to realize that most of us, typically with scant guidance, have made, consciously or unconsciously, a series of decisions about how to pray:

- We choose to concentrate on words or to focus (with different degrees of clarity) on images, or we use both words and images; or we are less conceptual, so that feelings and sensations are rather to the fore.[9] (This variation may reflect to some degree the spectrum between, at one end, the ability to see vivid mental images and, at the other end, aphantasia, the inability to perceive any images.)
- We decide in what order people appear in our prayers. (My children always come first, as is the case with most parents.)[10]
- If we use words, we can be laconic or go on at length, and we can speak aloud or silently in our minds, and we can use traditional formulas (such as phrases from the Our Father) or pray ad hoc and in our own words.[11]
- If we envisage those for whom we pray, we choose whether to see faces or faces with shoulders or something more.
- We can stare at such images in silence or utter words as we gaze at them, or we can mentally perform some action (such as embracing a face or dispelling dark shadows).
- We can regularly follow a set list of requests, or we can improvise, responding extemporaneously to news or whatever images, words, or feelings bubble up from the unconscious depths.[12] Or we can do both. (A few report that their dreams inform their prayers.)
- We can use a physical prompt such as a prayer book, an icon, a list of names on a piece of paper, or the Bible (many pray with the Psalms). Or we can write our prayers down as we say them or keep a prayer journal.[13] Or we can conduct the business of prayer wholly within ourselves.
- We can pray to God the Father or to Jesus (the latter typically imagined as he appears in artwork familiar to the one praying).
- If we pray to God, we can work with a visual representation of God or decline to do so.
- If we employ such a representation, we can make it anthropomorphic or abstract.
- We set aside a fixed time for prayer or pray at random moments or do both.

- If we fasten on a time, most of us select either morning or evening. Prayer is the first thing we do on rising or the last thing we do before going to bed. In both cases, we are typically at home.[14]
- We determine whether posture matters or is a matter of indifference. (I have no qualms about praying while upside down, as a worthwhile way to pass the time when I am on an inversion table as therapy for a sometimes unreliable back.)
- We elect to pray with eyes closed or with eyes open—although some of us, especially during lengthy prayers, regularly do both.
- We decide whether or not to combine petitionary prayer with other types of prayer—thanksgiving, silent contemplation, meditation upon a text, and so on.

All this is, I freely confess, merely and wholly anecdotal, and I have no statistics for any of my claims. But numbers would add nothing given the random and restricted nature of my inquiries. More than that, further exploration would undoubtedly introduce numerous issues and distinctions that I have ignored or failed to notice. (I have, for instance, never asked people what they see when they intercede for themselves. Is it, for some, like looking in a mirror?) I am nonetheless confident that my main point would stand. Careful, systematic investigation would confirm that creative diversity is everywhere. For every 100 people who heed the simple injunction to pray, there may be, because the imagination is in charge, a hundred different ways of responding.

One further comment on how we pray. I see names because I am literate, and I see them in English because that is my native language. An illiterate individual could never pray as I do. We can, moreover, be confident that, before the invention of the printing press and the subsequent increase in literacy, only a handful saw words as they prayed, and perhaps no one ever utilized a paper prayer list.

It is plausible that many or most people in the distant past saw faces when they prayed for others, as do so many today. Our faces are our most expressive feature and naturally represent us, body and soul. Still, I am not wholly confident about this. Although the headshot is ubiquitous in today's world, it was not always so. The photographic revolution took place less than two centuries ago. What if one grew up in the old Roman Empire, in a place where, notwithstanding busts on coins and the occasional marble head, most of the art, domestic and public, was of full human figures? Or what if one were, say, a Jew of the early third century, living in Dura Europos (on the Euphrates in what is now Syria), and were familiar with the images of human beings on the walls of the local synagogue? The archaeologists have uncovered those images, and the vast majority are of whole figures. Would recurrently seeing such images in a religious setting have upped the odds that one might, in personal prayer, see more than just faces?

Although the answers regrettably belong to unrecorded history, it is obvious that culture and technology affect our habits in prayer just as much as they affect everything else. Our imaginations work with what they have been given. I could not have prayed with mental cartography unless I had seen maps of the US in my schoolbooks. An older woman confided to me that her lifelong habit is to hold her left hand up to her left ear when she prays because "talking to God is just like talking with someone on the telephone."[15] Recently, more than one young person I queried used the verb "scrolling" in connection with prayer. Growing up with computer screens and cell phones has shaped how they pray.

Another illustration of technology herding the imagination comes from a student who told me that his prayers are patterned after Tetris, the popular tile-matching video game. Names appear at the top of his field of mental vision and move downward. He intercedes for them by fitting the falling names into the appropriate slots at the bottom. No one prayed like this before 1984, when Tetris was invented.

* * *

Leaving aside what we behold on our inner screens during petitionary prayer, whom do we pray for and what do we ask for? Here we have more than my haphazard interviews. A 2014 online survey of "Americans who pray" reported that 82 percent typically pray for "family or friends." (This strikes me as a low number. Can it really be that almost a fifth do not regularly pray for family or friends? Do so many, one wonders, pray for themselves alone?) Thirty-eight percent say they pray for victims of natural disasters, 12 percent that they pray for "government leaders," and 5 percent that they pray for "celebrities or people in the public eye." It is edifying to learn that 37 percent claim to pray for their enemies. It is unedifying to learn that 13 percent admit to praying for their favorite sports team to win a game.[16]

When people pray for themselves, 74 percent say the subject matter is often their own "problems or difficulties," 42 percent their own "sin," 36 percent their future prosperity. Lamentably, 20 percent have prayed to win the lottery, 7 percent have requested divine intervention for a good parking spot, and the same percentage has asked God that they not be caught speeding.[17]

We also have statistics from the UK.[18] An online survey of 2,069 adults, published in 2018, reported that, of those who pray, 71 percent pray for family, 40 percent for friends. Customary are petitions for healing (40 percent), for guidance (37 percent), and for one's "relationship with God" or personal "needs" (28 percent). While only 10 percent ask for specifically material needs—the small number surprises me—more than half pray "in times of personal crisis or tragedy" (55 percent). Twenty-nine percent reportedly pray in order to have the immediate practical benefit of gaining "comfort" or feeling "less lonely." Political and societal issues in the UK fail to garner much attention (9 percent). This lines up with another poll, according to which a mere 10 percent spoke to God about Brexit.[19]

*　*　*

So much for how we pray and what we pray for. What about the why? Why do we implore God to do something? What do we think we thereby accomplish? The polls do an inadequate job here, so once again I revert to what people have shared with me.

I teach at a seminary, so my social world is full of academics, pastors, and students with some theological training. They can, when it comes to prayer, be fairly sophisticated, if that is the right word. For some, it makes no sense to suppose that we can persuade Providence to do this or that. They are like John Calvin, who urged that prayer "is not so much for his [God's] sake as for ours." It directs our hearts to God. It disciplines our minds. And it prepares us "to receive all his benefits with true gratitude and thanksgiving."[20] It is not our job to rule the world, nor is it our place to instruct God on what God should be doing.

Oddly, this approach to prayer—which is overly rational to me—has a peculiar modern variant. Some contemporary atheists admit to praying regularly.[21] One, having benefitted from a twelve-step program, asserts that praying to a non-existent deity works: "If you say, 'I ought to have more serenity about the things I can't change,' versus 'Grant me serenity,' there is a humility, a surrender, an openness. If you say, 'grant me,' you're saying you can't do it by yourself. Or you wouldn't be there."[22] This pragmatic unbeliever gets down on his knees every night and says his prayers. He is not seeking to influence the world at large via a divine power he does not believe in; he is rather playing psychologist with himself.

Very few in my experience, however, think that praying to God is little more than a roundabout way of talking to themselves. More popular is the view that prayer is effective because, on some mysterious, subliminal level, we are all connected, with the result that our thoughts directly affect those at a distance. Although some who believe this fall under the "spiritual but not religious" rubric, many sit in the church pews. Perhaps Frank Laubach's *Prayer: The Mightiest Force in the World* (1946, but still in print) has here made itself felt. According to this influential book, the Christian has a "mental radio" and can "broadcast" thoughts to "subconscious minds" all around the world.[23]

The same idea recurs in other works, such as Maxie Dunnam's *Workbook of Intercessory Prayer*: "All of us, in the very depths of our being, are linked, interrelated. . . . There can be communication (such as mental telepathy) among humans other than through what we think of as normal channels. Meditative prayer is such a channel . . . through which we can send love, light, and health-giving energy to others."[24] On this view, and aside from what God is up to, our thoughts and feelings may of their own accord assist others. As John Hick, another proponent of this idea, puts it: "We are all linked at a deep unconscious level in a universal network in which our thoughts, and even more our emotions, are all the time affecting others, as others are in turn affecting us. When, in prayer or meditation, we direct our thought to a particular individual, this is intensified."[25]

This assessment also, however, belongs to a minority. Most believe that "God answers prayer." Not only this, but according to the US poll cited above, a full 28 percent of self-styled Christians affirm that "all of my prayers are answered." From one point of view, this does not surprise me, because I have again and again heard seminary students say the same thing. Yet from another point of view, this seems ludicrous. Nobody in this vale of tears who has hurled up more than three or four requests has seen them all come to pass. Even Paul confessed that, after he repeatedly besought God to remove the thorn in his flesh, it stayed put (2 Cor. 12:7–9).

A hermeneutical issue lurks here, and it reveals why, in this instance, pollsters do not get the whole story. When Christians earnestly tell me that God answers every prayer, I ask, Have you ever prayed for somebody to get well who did not get well? After they return the inevitable response, I politely point out the problem. They are never caught off guard. Most of them unfurl a version of this stock argument: When we ask, we receive, just as Jesus promised (Matt. 7:7–11), but God often answers us in ways we do not expect, ways that help us to mature as Christians. It is like a doctor who knows better than the patient, so when the latter asks for help, it may not always come in the form anticipated, yet it does come.

Interpretation of a handful of biblical passages drives this popular claim. To affirm that God answers every prayer offered in authentic faith is a way of upholding the Bible's reliability when it promises, in Mark 11:24 and elsewhere, that whatever we ask for in prayer will be ours, if we have faith. Now I think that Mark 11:24 and its parallels are hyperbolic exhortation, not assertions of an inflexible rule. Certainly the verses can hardly stand as promises not needing qualification. It is obvious, for instance, that God will turn a deaf ear to any petition, however sincere or brimming with faith, that does not accord with the divine good will (cf. 1 John 5:14). It is clear, nonetheless, why so many affirm, despite the obvious, that God consistently answers their prayers. Their exegesis leaves them no choice.

In speaking with such people, I sometimes find opportunity to pose more questions. If, as Jesus taught, "your Father knows what you need before you ask him" (Matt. 6:8), why ask? Again, if the giver of every good and perfect gift truly loves us all, why does he need a nudge to act on our behalf? Here too I rarely flummox anyone. Most have thought about these questions, or at least been told what to think about them. The standard response is: God wants us to be in on everything. Prayer allows God to work through us and so enables us to work with God. It is the Deity's way of partnering with human beings. It makes sense, then, that God waits upon us and, if we ask with informed faith, heeds our bidding.[26]

* * *

If some believe that we pray not to prod God but to move ourselves, others that our thoughts go forth into the universe and have an effect, still others that God heeds faith-filled requests by intervening in the world, there is yet a fourth group.

Polls, with their preformulated questions and yes or no answers, do not reveal its existence. I know of it only from self-reflection and candid conversations.

Many of us who pray are confused.

As I belong to this group, perhaps I can clarify by sharing some personal musings. Calvin is manifestly correct in what he affirms, if not in what he denies. Sober prayer clearly does affect us for the good. It turns thoughts inward and promotes self-reflection. It stirs us to think of others and their needs. And it fosters a sense of dependence upon God. That, however, can hardly be the end of the matter.

The notion that our prayers travel abroad and aid others is likewise sensible as far as it goes, at least for those of us who allow that we are sometimes inexplicably linked to others, as when a mother senses from afar, in the event rightly, that her daughter has just been hurt in a car wreck. I do not sneer when friends who might feel uncomfortable saying, "I'll be praying for you," instead say: "You'll be in my thoughts" or "I will remember you."

But what of God directly heeding our prayers? That the Creator wishes to work in and through us is an attractive thought, and we may at times even believe that we detect signs of this. Perplexing problems, however, beset this prevalent notion.

Long ago I wanted to believe that God answers our prayers. Real life, however, taught me otherwise. In 1987, a drunk driver slammed into a car driven by one of my dearest friends. Barbara, sixteen weeks pregnant, suffered a traumatic head injury and was comatose at the scene. Although to admit it today embarrasses me acutely, I remember feeling confident, despite the severity of her injuries, about her recovery. My grounds were theological, not medical.

Her parents were Baptist, so Baptist prayer chains were active on her behalf. She was Eastern Orthodox, so she was named in liturgical prayers across the country. And she was a lovely person with many friends, almost all of whom must have been praying for her. In short, supplications aplenty were regularly ascending for my friend and her unborn son. I cringe to recall that, one afternoon, as I contemplated how many were praying for her, I thought: We've got this covered. God cannot ignore all these heartfelt pleas, all the more as she has two little children at home. God will not let her and her baby go away. What good would come of that? But, after several weeks in the hospital, Barbara and her baby went away.

So too did my confidence in prayer. It has never returned. My prayers and those of so many others were, despite their great number and sincerity, unmercifully unanswered. Anyone who piously hazards the contrary—God answered our prayers, just not as we envisaged—is playing with words in order to deny the self-evident.

My miserable experience is, moreover, scarcely anomalous. It is rather predictable routine. Dispiriting and brutal facts repeatedly demonstrate, if we can admit the obvious, that God is not in the business of invariably or even regularly giving us what we ask for. Notwithstanding countless prayers that it be not so, hearts in every place are breaking all the time. Were God at our beck and call, the world would be utterly different: the faithful would long ago have prayed away the ills and evils that everywhere assail us.

Today, when reciting names in prayer, I am stoical. I rarely muster more than a few words. My prayers are vague and imprecise, requests whose fulfillment or nonfulfillment could never be assessed. I remain confident, because I truly believe in God, that I am heard, but I have no assurance of anything beyond that. This week, in churches around the world, millions upon millions will pray, "Thy will be done, on earth as it is in heaven," and yet, when the services let out, things will be, as ever, otherwise. Congregants will pray the same words the next week, with the same apparent lack of result, and so too the week after that.

The relationship between the Supreme Being and our prayers is a mystery to me. To pretend otherwise, to pretend that I have clear and distinct ideas about the matter, would be dishonest. Still, how could I ever cease to pray in hope for those I love, or for the broken world around me?[27]

* * *

According to a 2020 Gallup USA poll, 58 percent of us report that we pray often, 17 percent sometimes, 6 percent hardly ever, and 3 percent only in times of crisis. A scant 14 percent assert that they never pray.[28]

One reason multitudes, including individuals unaffiliated with any religious tradition, continue to pray is, quite simply, that it is hard for them not to. Praying seems almost instinctive. It feels like something we might learn to do even if never guided in the matter. Some form of prayer, it scarcely surprises, appears in all times and places.

The old saying has it that there are no atheists in fox holes. But as life is a battle, all of us are in fox holes more than once in a while. Whatever our ideology, then, most of us invoke a higher power from time to time. Surveys show that even in heavily secularized countries most people still, at least on occasion, pray.[29] One participant in a UK survey describes himself as being "at the skeptical end of agnosticism," yet he still asks God to take care of his family. He wonders "why I don't stop doing it. Sometimes I feel it's a kind of hypocrisy."[30]

If crying out in need and on behalf of our loved ones is close to inevitable, it is also true that we pray because of the immediate psychological benefits, whether or not we are aware of how this works. According to the 2018 survey of religious belief and practices in the UK, prayer leaves people feeling reassured or hopeful (40 percent), peaceful or content (33 percent), strengthened (25 percent), unburdened or released (20 percent), close to God (19 percent), guided (13 percent), loved (12 percent), humbled (11 percent), and happy or joyful (11 percent). Only a distinct minority (18 percent) report feeling the same after prayer as before.

These numbers, which have parallels in other polls, are remarkable.[31] Prayer is clearly therapeutic. One well-known study found daily prayer to be more effective than psychotherapy for dealing with emotional distress.[32] And according to a 2008 survey conducted by the American Psychological Association, 77 percent of those who pray judged this act to surpass massage, exercise, meditation, and yoga as the most effective "stress management activity."[33] The consensus of those who have studied the psychological and behavioral concomitants of serious prayer is that they are largely positive.[34]

Why does prayer—here I highlight petitionary prayer—have such positive side effects?[35] The following generalizations appear relevant:[36]

- Prayer enables us to feel useful when we otherwise cannot assist, as when we pray for victims of a tsunami in another part of the world. It gives us a sense of helping others when we cannot be with them in person, and helping others makes us feel better about ourselves.
- Imagining or feeling God to be attentively present is to conceive of oneself as being in another's company, as not being alone. Some psychologists believe that this can function as "a significant form of social support"[37] and that for this reason prayer contributes to mental and emotional well-being.[38]

- Similarly, as praying for others is a way of maintaining social connectivity with them, a means of linking ourselves to others, it is likely a partial counter for loneliness, the latter being a source of assorted troubles, including increased morbidity.[39] Elevated social connectivity also enhances immunological functioning.[40]
- Insofar as prayer nurtures optimism, hope, meaning, and gratitude, it is an effective coping strategy.[41]
- When intercessory prayer is coupled with contemplation and silent reflection, the complex activity must produce some of the well-documented benefits of meditative practices.[42]
- Praying for others is an act of self-transcendence, and reduction of self-focus appears to be associated with what one researcher dubs "authentic-durable happiness" as opposed to "fluctuating happiness," the latter stemming from self-centered behavior.[43]
- Repeating prayers that contain set formulas, such as "Lord have mercy" or "Lord Jesus Christ Son of God have mercy upon me a sinner," likely nurtures a sense of well-being, because the repetition of calmative phrases tends to decrease metabolism, lower the heart rate, and "quiet down the brain."[44]
- Prayer "can represent a kind of 'offloading' [of] troublesome matters in the form of 'turning them over to God.' This is psychologically relevant because it reduces one's overall cognitive load. . . . One is . . . able to isolate the disturbing component and hopefully remove it from consideration, at least temporarily, allowing for psychological rejuvenation."[45]

Beyond all this, meaningful and, on occasion, even dramatic experiences accompany prayer. Some report that, when praying, they have sensed God's presence in a dramatic way,[46] or felt a spiritual connection or energy,[47] or improved their visual and imaginative capacities,[48] or heard a disembodied voice.[49] There are also the idiosyncratic experiences. Here are two germane testimonies:

When I prayed, I [repeatedly] had the impression that the sun was shining brightly and sometimes was surprised on opening my eyes to find the day dull and cloudy. . . . And I think this happened only once, when praying for individuals, I saw in my mind's eye shafts of light directed downwards in various directions, as if they were illuminating those for whom I was praying. It was like wartime searchlight display in reverse, coming from above instead of ground-level.[50]

While I was kneeling, praying as I had been taught to, praying but not feeling any special reality in prayer, I was touched and for a moment picked up—not that my body left the ground, but I had the clearest sensation of the part of me that is not the body being lifted up, and I remember thinking "What is happening to me?" The sensation was as clear as if it was physical. After a moment it passed and I was left wondering. I have since from time to time felt bent down with worship when praying, or in other ways deeply moved by worship, but these are emotional experiences and quite distinct from this first physical experience which has never recurred.[51]

Experiences such as these, however one accounts for them, must fortify the belief that prayer is worthwhile, which must in turn up the odds that those who have them will continue to pray.[52]

* * *

Despite the psychological benefits, many who pray, when asked to explain why, refer above all to the correlations they perceive between prayer—for them the cause—and what happens later—for them the effect.[53] Here is the common claim: "Well, you know how y'pray, well I prayed and he [a sick loved one] was all right. I was here on my own, he was on the operating table. . . . I prayed for him to get better, I'd got nothing else. . . . It has given faith, really. I know God is good after that. I pray, and God acts."[54]

Winston Churchill articulated the same conviction a bit more eloquently:

I found [during battle] that whatever I might think or argue, I did not hesitate to ask for special protection when about to come under the fire of the enemy: nor to feel sincerely grateful when I got home safe for tea. I even asked for lesser things than not to be killed too soon, and nearly always in those years, and indeed throughout my life, I got what I wanted. This practice seemed perfectly natural, and just as strong and real as the reasoning process which contradicted it so sharply. Moreover the practice was comforting and the reasoning led nowhere. I therefore acted in accord with my feelings without troubling to square such conduct with the conclusions of thought.[55]

Churchill went on to quote Pascal: "The heart has its reasons which reason does not know."

Churchill realized that he was here not in the land of logic, and I have found that, when Christians begin to talk about prayer, many forsake all sense. I once heard a young woman eagerly relate that, after running out of gasoline on the highway, she recalled that Jesus had turned water into wine. So why, it occurred, could he not turn water into gasoline? She prayed over her canteen, emptied it into the gas tank, and drove down the road to the filling station. (I doubt she was lying. The water likely pushed forward what little gas was left, which was just enough to get her to the pump. My guess is that her engine ran rough for a bit.)

Even more remarkably, a teenager informed me that once, while driving, he was "convicted to pray." Believing that prayer requires shut eyes, and trusting that God was in control, he closed his eyes and started speaking to Jesus. Pious task completed—his prayer cannot have lasted long—he opened his eyes to find himself in the middle of a wheat field. (Maybe I should concede that this was a sort of minor miracle. Neither driver nor car was worse off for the folly.)

Several years ago I read about the Pray at the Pump Movement. This was 2008, and gas prices were elevated, hurting especially the lowest on the economic ladder. In response, religious activist Rocky Twyman advocated prayer. He and like-minded others huddled around gas pumps in various American cities and beseeched the Almighty to reduce the cost. Twyman declared: "Prayer is the answer to every problem in life. If the whole country keeps on praying, we can bring down prices even more, to even less than $2."[56] When rates dropped that summer, Twyman credited God.

Gas prices, however, go up and down all the time, and common sense requires that we give coincidence its due. Sometimes the unemployed pray for a job and get one. Sometimes farmers pray for rain and it rains. Sometimes children pray for a sick mother and she gets well. Yet if no one ever prayed, the unemployed would sometimes be hired, and it would sometimes rain, and sick mothers would sometimes get well.

Maybe Churchill was just lucky. A veteran of D-Day once told me that, as people fell all around him on a Normandy beach, he prayed, and he was certain his prayers saved his life. This is Christian solipsism. Did bullets puncture only those who failed to pray or had nobody at home praying for them? Likewise with Churchill. Although he survived battles, we can be sure that many who fought beside him took bullets and perished despite fervently imploring to be spared. Churchill's narrative reflects, in my view, his sense of his own importance in the grand scheme of things. Whether it discloses anything about Providence's special solicitude for the future Prime Minister is another matter.

Correlation does not demand causation. When I walk into the kitchen in the morning to feed our two cats, Luna and Westley, they run out of the room and into the dining room, then race back in through a second door. This daily routine is highly counterintuitive. One would expect them to move straightway to me, or to the cabinet holding their food, or to the spot where their food will soon be. Yet every morning they scurry out of the kitchen only to come directly back in. The explanation, I believe, is this. One day Luna happened to be exiting or entering the kitchen right before being fed. She inferred that maybe her action caused her food to appear, so the next day she did the same thing. As the same result obtained, she did it again the day after that. Soon enough her habit was fixed. At some point, Westley also figured things out and joined her. And now, every morning, they run out and back when I show up to feed them.

* * *

Discriminating between divine agency and other causes is just one of the issues attending our vexed subject. Paul remarked that we "do not know how to pray as we ought" (Rom. 8:26), and I cannot abide a claim to fulfilled prayer that opens with, "When I was a freshman in college, I lost my fountain pen."[57] God is not a handy tool with which to overcome inevitable inconveniences. We can, in our freedom, ask for anything we desire, but our desire is no good guide as to what truly matters; and if something does not truly matter, it is not a fit subject for prayer. Origen was right: "If we be given the spiritual gifts and receive illumination from God in the full possession of the things that are truly good, we shall not waste words over such an insignificant thing as a shadow."[58] Some prayers have more merit than others.

Even when we rise above praying for trivialities, we remain woefully underinformed. Looking back upon decades of life, I know that I have learned more from the worst of times than from the best of times. This means my most valuable lessons have come from what I prayed would go away and leave me alone. I have grasped what was good for me only retrospectively. Would it then not be foolish for me now to want God to act at my behest?

Even more pressing is the problem of disparate outcomes. A few years before a drunk driver ran over my friend Barbara, the same thing happened to me, one street over and less than a mile away: an inebriated man sped through a red light and crushed my car. I came very near to dying on the spot, and it was a week before I was assured of any future at all. Now I could, were I so disposed, imagine that, since I recovered, God answered my prayers and those of my family and friends. My father thought this, thought that God graciously responded to the desperate prayers cast up on my behalf. I cannot go along. For this would entail that, for no discernible reason, God failed to respond as generously to the prayers uttered on Barbara's behalf. What sense would that make, especially as many who prayed for me also prayed for her? Whatever the explanation for our dissimilar fates, it cannot lie in prayer.

While I am firm on this last point, for the rest I remain largely confused. Although I affirm that God acts in the world and that our prayers count for something, I do not know how to connect the two things—in part because I have no lucid idea as to how I might identify an act of God.

Perhaps divine benevolence works or even incessantly works through what we dub coincidence, so that to distinguish the latter from Providence, as I implicitly did earlier, misses the mark.[59] After all, how can anything be outside of God if "in him we live and move and have our being" (Acts 17:28)? Matters are even more perplexing if one wishes, as I do, to think of God as an agent within the regular course of nature. When I return thanks for bread, I do so sincerely, as though God had something to do with what is on my plate. Yet I do not imagine that, between farm and table, anything happened that would astound an atheist. My narrative as to how wheat is planted, harvested, trucked off to grain elevators, and so on would not differ appreciably from that of someone who never utters a blessing before meals. What exactly then am I doing when I thank God for food, especially when I recall that many, through no fault of their own, have no food for which to give thanks? Am I simply converting an emotion into words, behind which lies no coherent thought?

* * *

But then there are the stories that, if they happened as told, inevitably astound us. In these the correlation between petition and ensuing circumstance so staggers that the claim of answered prayer appears not unreasonable. Here are two such stories.

(1) Pentecostal preacher and author Judson Cornwall (1924–2005) once climbed onto the roof of his church for an inspection before the shingles were to be fixed. It was a cold, wintery Saturday, and he lost his footing on some ice. He found himself on his chest, sliding headfirst for the edge, without anything to grab. Had he continued, he would have taken a long fall onto a pile of bricks below. But just as his head passed the roof's end, he unaccountably came to a stop—"as though I had hit something." "It was not a gradual slowing down—it was sudden." He then gingerly turned himself around and slowly scooted back up to the steeple, finally making his way safely into the church, aware of having survived "a close call."

It is the sequel that seemingly makes this a story about answered prayer. The next day, at church, a woman in Cornwall's congregation shared with him that, as she was doing the dishes the day before, she felt an overwhelming compulsion to pray. Immediately, without even drying her hands, she hurried to her bedroom, got on her knees, and began to pray—for what she did not know. But "when the spirit of intercession lifted, she asked the Lord what she had been praying for." She then had a vision of her pastor sliding toward the edge of the roof of their church, after which she saw "the hand of God" stop him.[60]

(2) Ken Gaub (1935–) is an itinerant pastor and evangelist. Years ago he was travelling in Ohio with his musical family and other musicians.[61] They were going from church to church and concert to concert in two large motor coaches. One day they drove into the parking lot of a pizza parlor just south of Dayton. Everyone went in for dinner, except for Gaub, who stayed behind. He wished to be alone. In an emotionally difficult place, he was uncertain whether he should continue in ministry. "I seemed to have used up all my faith in ministering to others. Even my sense of humor was hollow."

As Gaub wrestled with his thoughts, he decided to get some fresh air. Looking around, he spotted a Dairy Queen and walked over for a Coke. As he made his way back to the bus, he heard a phone ringing. Looking around, he realized that the sound was coming from a phone booth in front of the filling station on the corner. (This was long before cell phones became omnipresent.) It rang and rang. Supposing that it might be someone in an emergency, he eventually picked up the receiver and said, "Hello." He heard an operator say, "Long distance call for Ken Gaub." He reflexively laughed: "You're crazy!" Then, not wanting to seem rude, he added: "This can't be! I was just walking down the street, not bothering anyone, and the phone was ringing." The operator asked: "Is Ken Gaub there? I have a long distance call for him."

Gaub then thought, "I know what this is! I'm on 'Candid Camera.'" He glanced around, smoothing his hair to make sure he looked OK. Seeing no camera, he asked the operator how the call could be for him. She again asked, "Is Mr. Gaub there or isn't he?" After he said, "As far as I know at this point, I am," he heard another voice say, "Yes, that's him, operator. I believe that's him." Gaub then began speaking with the caller. She informed him: "I'm Millie from Harrisburg, Pennsylvania. You don't know me, but I'm desperate. Please help." Gaub responded: "What can I do for you?"

The woman had been writing a suicide note. At the same time, she was pleading with God for a way out. In the midst of her turmoil, she remembered seeing Gaub on television, and it occurred to her that, if only she could speak with him, maybe he could help. Soon thereafter, a series of numbers entered her mind. She wrote them down, hoping against hope that maybe God had revealed to her his office number. She then dialed the number, which rang the phone booth in Ohio, near which Gaub happened right then to be passing.

Gaub and his caller were of course convinced that God had arranged it so that they could speak with one another. She hung up reassured that God cared about her enough to work a miracle. He came away exhilarated that God obviously wished to continue working through his ministry. As he returned to the bus he announced to his wife, "Barb, you won't believe this! God knows where we are!"

In retelling these two stories, I do not insist on their veracity. I have met neither Judson Cornwall nor Ken Gaub (whose versions of Christianity put them outside the ecclesiastical circles in which I usually find myself). Nor have I attempted to contact anyone involved in their narratives. I admit the possibility that their firsthand accounts are no closer to the truth than the

Egyptian tale in which Simon the Shoemaker, in order to defeat Muslim opponents, prays for a mountain to move, after which it moves.[62] I observe only three things.

First, while some disdain all such stories as beyond credence, others embrace them because they believe whatever tallies with what they want to believe. Still others, such as myself, find ourselves between these two extremes. I am persuaded that baffling events occur, that God is active in the world, and that sometimes those two circumstances overlap. Yet I also know that the world is full of edifying tales that are not true or only partly true, and further that being an eyewitness ensures neither one's integrity nor inability to embellish. Without further investigation, then, the best I can do, when running across stories such as those told by Cornwall and Gaub, is: That would be wonderful, but who knows? Maybe. Maybe not.

Second, to affirm that some stunning account of answered prayer merits belief and that God was the agent creates a pastoral difficulty. If a desperate woman reached Ken Gaub because she prayed and miraculously saw a phone number, why is it that nothing at all seems to happen when so many others, in equally desperate straits, cry out to God day and night? No edifying answer commends itself to me. I affirm, with Plato, that, "regarding the good things, God and no other is the cause, but of the evil things we must look for many different causes, only not God" (*Republic* 379C). But why are "the good things" so unevenly distributed, and why are they so often withheld without regard seemingly to degree of need, faith, or prayer?

There is, moreover, the practical point that most congregations have a Job or two in them, so when someone unfurls a remarkable account of apparently answered prayer, some will inevitably compare what has happened to others with what has not happened to them. They may ask, What's wrong with me? It is a sad fact that "often we blame ourselves when our prayers seem to effect nothing, and deplore our lack of faith, or love, or persistence."[63]

Others of us will become disillusioned not with ourselves but with God.[64] Iris Dement's haunting ballad, "The Night I Learned How Not To Pray," relates how, notwithstanding her fervent prayers, her baby brother died after falling down the stairs. Why pray, she sings, when "God does what He wants to do anyway"? Anyone unprepared to respond to that question with more than Christian platitudes has no business passing on reports of answered prayer.

Finally, and irrespective of what one makes of stories such as those of Gaub and Cornwall, they continue to circulate. Preachers recount them from pulpits, authors share them in books, and the internet is filled with more of the same. As long as this is the case, multitudes will continue to believe that God, at least on occasion, answers prayer. This circumstance will, in turn, encourage people to continue saying their prayers.

* * *

Prayer is not, however, a constant, insulated from cultural forces. As observed above, technology can reshape it. This is why some pray as though talking on the telephone, others as though scrolling on a computer screen. Of most interest to me, however, is how prayer relates to the matter of attention.

YouTube, Facebook, Instagram, Twitter, Snapchat, LinkedIn, texting, television, video games, movies, email, vlogs, and virtual reality are re-wiring our plastic brains and (even if it is unclear how to measure this objectively) compressing our attention spans. This is important because, with the exception of the spontaneous cry for help, prayer is a form of dedicated attention, even a type of self-induced trance. It is an act by which one withdraws from the outer world and moves to the inner world of darkness and imagination. This requires, for all but the most short-lived, casual, or perfunctory prayers, the ability to focus on an internal state of affairs for at least several minutes.

The exponential explosion of screens—there are now more screens than people—must make this harder. Let me make my case by drawing a comparison.

The omnipresence of screens has unquestionably disturbed another activity that requires focused attention. I refer to reading words on plain, unadorned paper. This irreplaceable task has become more difficult for most of us in the last two decades.

We do not need scientific studies in order to prove this, although such research exists.[65] All we need to do is examine ourselves—at least those of us who are not digital natives, who are old enough to remember life before personal computers and smart phones. We know firsthand that we are more easily distracted now than we once were. Four decades ago, before a computer displaced a typewriter at the center of my desk, I was far less restless, better able to sit for hours and lose myself in an old-fashioned book, fiction or nonfiction. No part of my brain incessantly wondered whether I had a new email, or felt the lack of color and movement when staring at plain black letters on a white page.

Philip Yancey, who in the following must speak for a multitude, recently confessed:

> I am going through a personal crisis. I used to love reading. I used to read three books a week. But I am reading many fewer books these days, and even fewer of the kinds of books that require hard work. The Internet and social media have trained my brain to read a paragraph or two, and then [to] start looking around. When I read an online article . . . after a few paragraphs I glance over at the side bar to judge the article's length. My mind strays, and I find myself clicking on the sidebars and the underlined links. . . . Worse, I fall prey to the little boxes that tell me, "If you like this article, you'll also like . . ."

Yancey went on, in partial explanation of his plight, to refer to the work of neuroscientists, who have found that "when we learn something quick and new, we get a dopamine rush; functional-MRI brain scans show the brain's pleasure centers lighting up." He ended by mourning the loss of deep reading, the sort that "requires intense concentration . . . and a slower pace," a reading that nurtures "both spirituality and creativity."[66]

As with reading, so must it be with prayer. If the latter, like the former, involves (in the words of Howard Thurman) "the total process of quieting down" and cannot "be separated from meditation,"[67] if prayer, that is, requires a form of prolonged, focused attention, and if ever-proliferating screens hamper our ability to muster and maintain such attention, then they must likewise hamper our ability to pray.

The much-publicized claim that, in the age of the internet, the average human attention span has shrunk to less than that of a goldfish appears to be fake news.[68] Yet when we first read that bulletin, it did not sound implausible. We know what is happening to us.

A few years ago, psychologists at Harvard and the University of Virginia wanted to learn how people would react when placed in a bare room with nothing to do but think for fifteen minutes. (The study included, in addition to college students, people recruited from a church and a farmer's market.) The researchers gave participants this choice: either you can sit alone with your thoughts, or you can push a button that will give you a nasty electrical shock. The vast majority found sitting and thinking both difficult and unpleasant—so unpleasant and difficult that they preferred to push the button and inflict pain. On average they pushed the button seven times. They preferred pain over being alone with their thoughts for a mere quarter of an hour.[69]

How likely is it that people who cannot bear to be alone without distraction, who are instantly restless without external stimulus, will carve out lengthy periods for private prayer of any sort? Had I been one of the psychologists, I would have asked participants how often they meditate or pray in solitude. I would have anticipated that the more time they spent alone, the less often they would have pushed the button. In any case, as all of us continue to give increasing time to the electronic devices sponsored by the merchants of attention, as we habituate ourselves to hyperimmediacy, rapid task switching, and continuous partial attention, one wonders about the long-term effects upon the hidden world of prayer.

My intuition on this matter—the more screens, the less prayer—seems to line up with results from Baylor's 2017 survey of American values.[70] When asked whether technology has improved their relationship with God, 38 percent disagreed and 31 percent strongly disagreed, for a total of 69 percent. On the other side, 4 percent strongly agreed and 14 percent agreed, a combined sum of only 18 percent. Even more interesting is this: the more people said they prayed, the less they confessed to feelings of "technological addiction." At one end of the spectrum, 33 percent of those who never pray had such feelings. It was 29 percent for those who reported praying only occasionally. At the other end, only 17 percent of those who purported praying several times a day confided to feeling addicted. In other words, the more prayer, the less addiction to technology.

If we tend to have our most compelling religious experiences while alone—"very few reports of religious experience are connected with church services"[71]—one wonders what happens when, with screens at our constant beck and call, or rather with us at their constant beck and call, we find it increasingly hard to put them away and spend time by ourselves, without any company, real or virtual. One also wonders how common it is to have profound religious experiences while watching a screen. I know of no data on this, but my guess is that it is less than for walking in a forest, or staring at stars, or praying alone in one's room with the door shut.

5

The Lore of Angels

"I find it fascinating that even though angels are symbolized or somehow represented almost everywhere we look (for example, their images can be seen in church paintings, our home décor, and even as guardian-angel charms or trinkets in our cars), when someone talks about a vision involving an angel . . . it's somehow considered fringe."

—David Kessler[1]

"Statements of the prevalence, distribution and clinical significance of visionary experiences have been dramatically incorrect throughout the past century."

—David Hufford[2]

"Those who see and hear things that 'are not there' are the majority of people. This is the elephant in the room of psychology and psychiatry."

—Allan Kellehear[3]

One morning in the 1960s, Mickey Rooney, the late Hollywood actor, sat in the booth of a Lake Tahoe casino coffee shop.[4] He was despondent. A series of personal tragedies—his wife's murder, his mother's passing, a friend's death by the bottle—had occasioned unbearable dismay. He had little heart for the future.

In the midst of his gloom, a busboy, dressed in white, appeared at his table. Looking kindly at Mr. Rooney, he whispered, without preface or explanation: "Mr. Rooney, Jesus Christ loves you very much." The boy then turned around and walked off into the kitchen.

Mr. Rooney did not return a word. He sat and ruminated upon the lad's unelaborated sentence. After a time, he determined to speak with the youngster, whose uninvited but timely utterance had set him to thinking new thoughts. Not seeing the youth anywhere in the dining room, he made inquiry of the hostess: "Say, I'd like to talk to that busboy who was working our table."

"Which busboy?" she asked.

"The one with the light-blond curls," Mr. Rooney said. "Sort of surrounded his head like a helmet."

"Hmmm," the hostess replied, "we don't have a busboy like that. No boy here with blond hair."

"Naw," the actor said. "He was just talking to me."

"Well you can certainly go back in the kitchen and look."

Mr. Rooney did just that, without result. He could find no blond busboy in white.

The failure to locate the busboy, far from marring the experience, turned it into a better anecdote, one tinged with mystery. For in his autobiography *Life Is Too Short*, Rooney expresses his conviction, formed on the spot in Lake Tahoe, that his much-needed encouragement came from an angel, from a supernatural being who temporarily adopted a terrestrial costume to impart wisdom and then, mission accomplished, miraculously disappeared: "All of a sudden my flesh crawled, and the hair stood up on my arms. I knew I'd been visited by an angel. 'God,' I said, 'who am I that you should send an angel to me? I, who have been paying so little attention.'"

Without either naively commending this story as evidence for divine intervention or disdainfully dismissing Rooney's interpretation—in fairness, I was not there—what interests me is the nature of the narrative. It belongs to a well-established literary type. Many stories about people entertaining angels unawares feature this outline:

- Individual in physical or mental distress.
- Unexpected appearance of a stranger dressed in white.
- Distress relieved through stranger's word or deed.
- Inexplicable disappearance of the stranger or subsequent failure to identify or establish the stranger's existence.
- Conviction that the stranger must have been an angel.

This sort of short story—the mysterious angel in white (AIW) story—is well represented in the many, sometimes best-selling books that purport to recount true stories of modern people encountering angels. Joan Wester Anderson's *Where Angels Walk*, for example, tells the story of Sandy Smith.[5] After a nasty car wreck, she awoke to find herself in a secluded alcove of the Delaware Memorial Hospital (Ohio). Looking at the dried blood on her clothes and arms, and uncertain about the condition of her travelling companion, she began to weep. She then lost consciousness.

Upon awaking, Sandy discovered that someone, sitting beside her, was gently stroking her hand: "I'm not positive it was a woman, and it hurt too much to turn my head, but I could tell that she had long, almost-white hair and pale skin. Her clothing was white too, but I couldn't see if she was wearing pants or a skirt."

The tranquil touch brought reassurance. Even more consoling was the strange sound emanating from the stranger, who spoke not a word. The sound was "like a song, not in a conventional sense, but almost like millions of voices blending together in the most extraordinary tones." Because of this, Sandy concluded that she was in the presence of "a supernatural being," whose comforting tones helped her to sleep. She insists she was not hallucinating.

When Sandy awoke again, the mysterious stranger was gone. An ordinary nurse was instead caring for her, a nurse who told her that she must have dreamt about the woman in white: "I've been right outside this alcove ever since they brought you in, and no one's been near you." The nurse added that no one on the floor that day was fair-haired, and that every extra hand was in the emergency room, working on her injured girlfriend.

* * *

One does not explain away AIW stories and their strong structural and thematic resemblances by classifying them as friend-of-a-friend tales. Not all of them are devoid of factual content. Many accounts—including the two I have cited—are undoubtedly firsthand. What one rather suspects is that certain experiences lend themselves to being interpreted by the same cluster of traditional, well-known motifs.

Here Scripture plays a role. It contains passages in which angels suddenly appear and disappear, others in which angels assist people in need, still others in which angels are clad in white.[6] Such passages, moreover, belong to both individual and collective memory. So when a stranger in light clothing aids someone in distress, and anything out of the ordinary seems to occur, the elements are in place for interpreting, remembering, and recounting events as a brush with an AIW.

All this seems obvious enough. Indeed, most AIW stories can, with scant effort, be reasonably explained as the overinterpretation of mundane events. When a stranger pushes a car out of a ditch or crafts encouraging words and then disappears while remaining unidentified, that stranger (especially if sporting white) may become an angel.

I recall in this connection a news story from 2013. It had to do with a car crash near Center, Missouri. A young woman, hit head-on by a drunk driver, was stuck in her Mercedes. Pinned between her front seat and the steering wheel, she could not work herself free. Nor, after an hour of trying, could emergency workers get her out. Frustrated and increasingly anxious for the girl's welfare—she obviously had broken many bones—the responders held hands and prayed with her. Thereupon a man in priest's garb appeared, even though by that time the road had been blocked off a quarter mile in both directions. The priest offered a prayer. He then assured everybody that the woman would be OK. Immediately thereafter, the heavy equipment to cut the girl out arrived. She was soon free. With that task completed, the workers looked around to thank the priest, who had much encouraged them. He was gone. Nor did they see any other bystanders. Nor did they see any vehicles that did not belong to the police or emergency workers.

Soon some began to wonder if the priest had been an angel. Their speculation quickly became news, and this was the headline in one British tabloid: "The Riddle of the Angel Priest: Holy Man Appeared from Nowhere to Pray with Trapped Girl and Rescuers in Traffic Accident; Told Them She Would Be OK and Then Vanished."[7] The language is deliberately charged (no doubt for the purpose of upping sales): "riddle," "angel," "holy," "appeared from nowhere," "vanished." We have here a story of angelic intervention in the making, even though in this case the helper wore not white but the apparel of a Catholic priest.

Unfortunately for overeager purveyors of the supernatural, after the news began to spread, a flesh-and-blood priest recognized himself in the story. He conscientiously let the world know that it was he who had happened upon the accident and uttered a prayer. He had not "appeared from nowhere" but rather wandered onto the scene. He had not "vanished" but simply walked away. He was not an "angel" (in the first sense in the dictionary) but a Roman Catholic pastor. There was no "riddle."

* * *

Almost as popular as AIW stories are those that feature the miraculous defeat of gravity.

According to Katherine C. Calore of Olathe, Kansas, when she and her sister, Carol, were about eight and six respectively, the two learned to climb a large tree in their front yard.[8] One day, with Katherine above her, Carol slipped off a branch. Yet she did not, her sister claims, fall and hit the ground as expected. She rather "floated, like a piece of paper, back and forth, until she landed on the ground far below, on her feet." She was unhurt. The explanation for this fortunate outcome? An angel, Katherine inferred, must have intervened.

Another illustration of an alleged slow fall concerns a woman named Janie and her five-year-old daughter.[9] Soon after moving into their new house, the little girl, wearing a Superman costume, climbed up the fourteen-foot scaffold inside the still-unfinished circular staircase in the middle of the entrance hall. In her imagination she was being brave. But when she looked down, she discovered how high up she was. Becoming frightened, she lost her balance. She then slipped, screamed, "Mommy help," and fell from the scaffold. Janie was too far away to do anything but watch. Yet as she looked on, it was as if an invisible arm stretched out beneath her daughter and gently laid her down on the floor. When the medics arrived, they found, to their amazement, neither bruise nor broken bone. The girl was no worse for her fall.

If some narratives recount a slow fall from above, others feature invisible hands that help here below. One cold spring morning, when Mrs. Jean Blitz of Wichita, Kansas, was several months pregnant with her fifth child, she stepped onto her front porch to see whether or not the milkman had yet made the day's delivery.[10] Too late she realized that ice had glazed the concrete, that the footing was hazardous. Her feet did not hold.

As her hand had no handrail to latch onto, it seemed certain she would hit the concrete hard—no little matter given her gravid condition. As her posterior approached the pavement, however, time seemed to slow down, and two strong arms not only caught Jean but stood her up against the door. Thinking that her husband had fortuitously happened by at a life-saving moment, she turned to speak her relief and gratitude to him. Instead of her husband, who later confirmed his lack of participation, she saw only an empty doorway. There was no one there at all. Her inference was immediate. Some formless and invisible force had first slowed Jean's fall, then straightened her up, then set her safely off the ice. An angel.

* * *

If we refuse to adopt the popular expedient of explaining things by denying their occurrence, how should we evaluate stories of angels beating gravity? It is natural to have reservations.

The stories I have related—stories whose details I am in no position to affirm or deny—are told as angelic rescues. Yet no out-of-the-ordinary beings were seen. Nor did a divine voice provide clear exegesis. In each case, belief in angelic agency was an inference, an act of interpretation. The Bible has undoubtedly made itself felt here. Psalm 91:11-12—which the popular books about angels incessantly cite—has this: "For he will command his angels concerning you to guard you in all your ways. On their hands they will bear you up, so that you will not dash your foot against a stone." These words are well-known. They appear not only in a psalm but also in Matthew and Luke. The gospels quote them when reporting how the devil once tempted Jesus to throw himself off the pinnacle of the temple in Jerusalem (Matt. 4:6; Luke 4:10-11). It seems likely, then, that a familiar biblical motif—angels can rescue saints from a perilous fall—has been drawn upon to explain falls unattended by harm. In other words, angels do not, in the stories just told, appear visibly in the dramatic moment. They rather show up via reflection.

Do the events require this? The stories I have introduced contain three main motifs: someone falling or slipping, perception of something peculiar, and unexpected non-injury. That these point us beyond the mundane is not self-evident.

Whatever time may or may not be, our experience of it varies. As all who have had unpleasant jobs know well, time sometimes seems to slow down. The fact is dramatically manifest in the proverbial experience of people in dire distress seeing their lives pass before their eyes. Athletes also sometimes perceive the deceleration of time.[11] A longtime NFL quarterback, John Brodie, once observed that, during many plays,

> time seems to slow way down, in an uncanny way, as if everyone were moving in slow motion. It seems as if I had all the time in the world to watch the receivers run their patterns, and yet I know the defensive line is coming at me just as fast as ever. I know perfectly well how hard and fast those guys are coming and yet the whole thing seems like a movie or a dance in slow motion.[12]

Since we can, whatever the mechanism, experience time's passage at different speeds, when someone says, "I felt as though I fell in slow motion," that need not inform us about the objective, measurable rate of descent. What would a video recorder have detected?

Neither does the failure of a fall to issue in injury stump us. People who plummet more than the height of a one-story house usually do at least sprain an ankle. Sometimes, however, luck is with us. Twenty years ago I fell about ten feet from a tree limb and walked away unscathed. I did not think about angels.

People have slipped off the sides of cliffs and plunged down mining shafts without meeting their Maker, and much more often than one might suspect, they have fallen out of buildings five or more stories high and, because they landed just right on just the right surface—such as an evergreen tree or a canvas car top—walked away relatively unscathed. Cats of course regularly fall off high apartment ledges without apparent ill effect—there is indeed a small scientific literature on this—and, incredibly, there are a handful of reports of skydivers surviving when a parachute failed to unfurl, although assuredly not without injury. Then we have the story of the teenager who, still strapped to her seat, fell about two miles after her plane, while flying over Peru, disintegrated in the midst of a violent thunderstorm. She suffered only minor physical harm—a gash in her leg and a broken collar bone—seemingly because the treetops of a forest cushioned her landing.[13]

With such facts in mind, the proposition that occasionally a boy might fall out of a tree or a little girl from atop a fourteen-foot scaffold and not suffer harm does not beggar belief. It must happen on occasion, maybe more than on occasion.

In order, then, to feel truly perplexed, we require more than the feeling of sluggish descent and the circumstance of non-injury. We need another element, an onlooker who avows, I saw so and so fall, and he or she seemed to float, to come down like a leaf instead of an acorn.

The first story recounted above, that told by Katherine Calore, does contain this element. Yet the excessively succinct narrative is from a fifteen-year-old memory of an eight-year-old's perception, and the line of sight on her sister's fall was not from the side but from above. Did this foster an optical illusion? One cannot do much with this story.

The second report, that about a five year-old and her fall from a scaffold, also fails to meet my criterion for genuine puzzlement. The mother called an ambulance. This makes one doubt whether she really, as she had convinced herself, saw her daughter alight gently upon the ground.

Although it does not involve a fall from a great height, I have run across a report that, if true to the facts, would make one think twice. It concerns a three year old, Danny Agnese of Bethpage, New York.[14] One morning the little boy was recklessly running full tilt across his living room rug when he tripped and fell headfirst toward the sharp corner of a table. But, as his horrified mother looked on, the child's forward fall was suddenly and inexplicably halted. Somehow he was stood up and moved over, to continue on his happy, oblivious way.

It is the sequel that gives this story its punch and sets it in the long-term memory. The next day, we are told, Danny, while at play, suddenly looked up and addressed his mother: "Mommy? I saw a beautiful lady. With wings." The mother, supposing her son to be recounting fantasy, replied, "Really, Danny? What is the lady like?" There followed this: "She's nice. She caught me yesterday, so I did not hit my head against the table. . . . She said she was going to watch over me and keep me from getting hurt."

The story of Danny's deliverance has two witnesses—one to an inexplicably interrupted fall, one to an extraordinary being. If everything happened as told—obviously a large if—one might be hard-pressed for a humdrum explanation.

The same suggestiveness attends an analogous story in Hope MacDonald's *When Angels Appear*.[15] When MacDonald's sister, Marilyn, was eight years old, she made the near fatal mistake of running in front of a car. As her parents and others watched helplessly, she was hit and thrown very high into the air. Upon falling hard to the pavement, the little girl rapidly rolled toward a large open sewer. But, to the amazement and relief of the onlookers, her progress was instantly and inexplicably halted right at the edge of the sewer. Later on, in the presence of her family and doctor, Marilyn, surprised at everyone else's bafflement, offered the explanation: "But didn't you see that huge, beautiful angel standing in the sewer, holding up her hands to keep me from rolling in?"

This episode from MacDonald's book resembles the story in Anderson's volume. One might wonder whether we have here a new urban legend in the making. The difficulty, however, is that the accounts are not fictitious friend-of-a-friend tales. Indeed, in one instance the alleged events concern the author's sister. Whatever explanation we adopt, then, it will not be rooted in the evolution of folklore.

* * *

The old form critics classified biblical materials according to type. Rudolf Bultmann, for instance, observed that the miracles of Jesus, as recounted in the canonical Gospels, fall basically into four categories: healings, exorcisms, raisings of the dead, and nature miracles. In the same way, most—not all—of the stories in the modern books on angels belong to standard types. One book organizes its materials under three headings: visions, rescues, healings.[16] I prefer a more capacious analysis, one that itemizes the two types of stories illustrated above:

- Visions of beings of light (while one is awake, asleep, or near death).[17]
- Helpers/protectors from nowhere (the AIW belongs here).[18]
- A hand on a shoulder that warns, prompts, or pushes one away from danger.[19]
- Anti-gravity rescues.[20]
- Disembodied voices that warn or prompt.[21]
- Mysterious light(s) or "light forms" or "balls of light" that seems conscious.[22]
- Spontaneous or unexplained remission of disease/miraculous cures.[23]
- Beautiful or ethereal music of unknown origin.[24]

That so many modern accounts of angels belong to one of these eight types implies that, when individuals talk about themselves, they do so under the influence of stories they have heard or read. People implicitly know how to craft their reports—what themes to stress, what motifs to highlight—so that that they are not wholly anomalous but rather akin to the reports of others. In this way, like is assimilated to like, and matching patterns are created. At the same time, the resemblance of stories also tells us that some people are likely having comparable experiences. The reports are in part similar because many experiences, however explained, are similar.

* * *

So far in this chapter I have retold and remarked upon several stories featuring angels as though there might be something of interest or value in them. Is there?

Theologians and biblical scholars generally ignore the popular books that showcase intervening angels.[25] Their indifference has multiple sources. Professionals spend most of their time reading other professionals. Why waste time engaging amateurs? (I am a biblical scholar and have not seriously perused a popular book about the Bible in perhaps decades.) Furthermore, miracles pervade the books about angels, and many people are incredulous regarding most or even all miracle claims. These doubting Thomases are sure that pious anthologies of anecdotal stories are uncritical, their authors untutored in the ways of deception and self-deception. The uncredentialed authors must be, it is assumed, unaware of how readily human beings import meaning into nothing but coincidence or dupe themselves by fabricating fictions via misperception, inaccurate recall, and conscious and unconscious embellishment.

Then there are those whose theology is exclusively Christocentric, so that their interest in angels—which have traditionally been at the periphery of most Protestant dogmatics—is on a par with their nonexistent interest in the old pagan gods.

One further suspects that many are disinclined to pay heed to works that are presumed to be, because of their sensationalistic subject matter, blithely insensitive to the problem of evil. Is it really helpful, in this post-Holocaust age, to parade stories of miraculous deliverance when they are so few and far between, when most people in need of rescue never get rescued? "Why would God work a miracle to open a garage door, while allowing millions to perish through injustice and hunger?"[26]

I, however, am of another mind. Despite their popular and generally trusting, even naive nature, the books by Anderson, MacDonald, and others warrant, I believe, our attention. They are not, for the most part, collections of recycled stories. They rather report what someone known to the author has claimed, or what someone who sent a letter or email to the author has claimed. These books in fact often tell their stories in the experiencers' own words.[27] One volume even includes photographs and brief biographies of all the storytellers.[28]

This does not, I should stress, mean that the narratives are true to the facts. One would be gullible to move without further ado from a firsthand account, however sincere, to what really happened. Nevertheless, many stories that feature angels effectively dispel the notion, bankrupt yet annoyingly still widespread, that miracle stories may be dismissed because they are always third- or fourth- or fifthhand, always and everywhere the product of an unconstrained chain of rumor. Sometimes, and far more often than one might anticipate, they are firsthand.[29]

A related reason for attending to these popular tomes is that they are repositories of human experience. Although the editorial commentary is sometimes heavy, the religious interpretation in the accounts themselves is often light, and separating the stories from the editors' narrative frames and the experiencers' explicit interpretations is frequently possible. Despite, then, the recurrent imposition of the elastic, almost all-purpose concept of "angel" upon an array of truly disparate phenomena—visions, unexpected healings, disembodied voices, and so on—many reports give us access to what people sincerely think they witnessed—and not always, by the way, without some critical awareness. The literature contains remarks such as these:

- "I . . . questioned myself, since my child did not see it."[30]
- "Was this all my imagination? Was this really happening to me?"[31]
- "I am still puzzled about this incident."[32]
- "I always wondered about this."[33]
- "Was it simply a coincidence?"[34]

The work of Emma Heathcote-James bolsters my conviction that we have here a legitimate area of study, at least when patterns in the reports recur. Her work *Seeing Angels: True Contemporary Accounts of Hundreds of Angelic*

Experiences (2002) is a popularization of her doctoral dissertation at the University of Birmingham.[35] It confirms that, on the whole, the popular books accurately reflect what many of our contemporaries have to say. Heathcote-James reports on and analyzes the first 350 responses she received to requests for firsthand encounters with angels. Her narratives line up seamlessly with those in the less academically oriented works. That is, *Seeing Angels* also features anti-gravity stories, heavenly music, help from strangers, and the rest, all attributed to angels.

We have one more reason for not snidely ignoring the popular books on angels. They remind us of the crucial fact, emphasized throughout these pages, that we cannot equate what people divulge publicly with what goes on privately. The truth is that multitudes keep some meaningful experiences, including experiences they ascribe to angels, tucked away safely in their memory banks, or share them with but a handful. The following three testimonies are from Heathcote-James's book:

- "At the time [after the experience] I was too shocked to share the experience with even my family, and ever since have only told it to a few."
- "The experience I relate is a one-off thing for me, and is something I only ever shared with my husband. This is because it is very personal and special, not because I doubt its authenticity."
- "I have told very few people of this experience as it's so very precious to me, but wanted you to maybe include it in your research."[36]

In line with these statements, Hope MacDonald reports that, when she started speaking publicly about angels, people began to share their stories with her, and most of them had "three things in common: they had never shared their story with anyone before; they felt the experience had made a great difference in their lives; and they all thanked me for giving them the opportunity to share their angel story." She writes further: "I didn't find anyone who had an angel story who went around broadcasting it, who got up on a soapbox and proclaimed the experience, or who even tried to convince another person it was true. In fact, most were very reluctant to share the experience at all."[37] Many or perhaps even most angel stories are well-kept secrets.

* * *

Angels are not always disguised or entertained unawares. They may also appear as numinous beings of light. Indeed, our contemporaries see angels often enough, or at least beings they call by that name. The numerous books on angels as well as other sources document sighting after sighting.[38] Here are four illustrations:

- "A very tall, glowing figure was next to his bed [the writer's dying father] all the afternoon and evening. . . . As I held his hand, I became aware of a ten-foot presence kneeling on the opposite side of the bed, looking intently into my dad's face. The figure was tall, dressed in brilliant white, flowing robes, and glowing with a sparkling force which was eminently powerful."[39]

- "I just kept on crying. And then this voice said, 'What's the matter? Why are you crying? What is it? Tell me.' And I just said, 'I'm sorry. I'm really, really sorry.' And she said, 'What are you sorry for?' . . . I opened my eyes to look at her. And standing there was this huge being in a brilliant white light. It was the most beautiful thing I've ever seen in my whole life. Words just can't express . . ."[40]

- "In 1959 my father died suddenly. . . . I was bereft, heartbroken. . . . Suddenly in bed one morning about the time I'd awake I looked in the corner of the bedroom & there was a being such as I had never seen. It was pure gold. I looked at the face so loving & all about the head the most beautiful golden curls & wings that were like overlapping fronds, it seemed a tall being. I could see the flowers on the bedroom wall through its being. It faded. At the time I felt awe I thought later such as the shepherds would have felt in the fields [see Luke 2]. As the being faded I felt happy, so happy & joyous."[41]

- "From behind us we heard the murmur of muted voices in the distance, and I said to [my sister] Marion, 'We have company in the woods this morning.' Marion nodded, and turned to look. We saw nothing, but the voices were coming nearer. . . . Then we perceived that the sounds were not only behind us but above us, and we looked up. How can I describe what we felt? Is it possible to tell of the surge of exaltation that ran through us? Is it possible to record this phenomenon in objective accuracy and yet be credible? For about ten feet above us and slightly to our left was a floating group of glorious creatures that glowed with spiritual beauty. . . . There were six of them, young beautiful women dressed in flowing white garments and engaged in earnest conversation. If they were aware of our existence they gave no indication of it. . . . Neither Marion nor I could understand their words. . . . It would be an understatement to say we were astounded."[42]

I could go on at length with similar accounts. They are legion. A 2005 survey of Canadians found an astonishing 5.8 percent of those polled reported seeing an angel.[43]

This is, of course, not only a modern experience. Human beings have been having visionary experiences of luminous figures for centuries. We find this in the Book of Daniel:

On the twenty-fourth day of the first month, as I was standing on the bank of the great river (that is, the Tigris), I looked up and saw a man clothed in linen, with a belt of gold from Uphaz around his waist. His body was like beryl, his face like lightning, his eyes like flaming torches, his arms and legs like the gleam of burnished bronze, and the sound of his words like the roar of a multitude. I, Daniel, alone saw the vision; the people who were with me did not see the vision, though a great trembling fell upon them, and they fled and hid themselves. So I was left alone to see this great vision. My strength left me, and my complexion grew deathly pale, and I retained no strength. Then I heard the sound of his words; and when I heard the sound of his words, I fell into a trance, face to the ground (10:4-9).

This account is in several respects reminiscent of the old Zoroastrian tradition about the enlightenment of Zoroaster:

Zoroaster went at dawn to the bank of the river Daiti, to make the hom-libation. . . . When he came up from the water . . . he saw Vahman . . . in the shape of a man, fair, bright, and radiant. . . . He wore a garment like silk . . . which was as light itself. And he was nine times taller than Zoroaster. And he questioned Zoroaster: "Who are you? Whose are you? What is your chief desire? In what are you diligent?" And he answered: "I am Spitaman Zoroaster. My chief desire . . . is righteousness. . . ." And Vahman bade Zoroaster: "Go forward to the assembly of the divine beings."[44]

Nearer our own time is this entry from Cotton Mather's diary:

A strange and memorable thing. After outpourings of prayer, with the utmost fervor and fasting, there appeared an Angel, whose face shone like the noonday sun. His features were those of a man, and beardless; his head was encircled by a splendid tiara; on his shoulders were wings; his garments were white and shining; his robe reached to his ankles; and about his loins was a belt not unlike the girdles of the peoples of the East. And this Angel said that he was sent by the Lord Jesus to bear a clear answer to the prayers of a certain youth, and to bear back his words in reply. Many things this angel said. . . . Among other things not to be forgotten he declared that the fate of this youth should be to find full expression for what in him was best. [45]

Rather than cite additional reports, which might weary readers, I wish to observe that we can make some generalizations about visions of angels, old and new. More often than not they occur during times of stress or confusion. The experiences themselves are usually short-lived: a figure appears out of nowhere, is seen or heard, and just as suddenly disappears. In addition, as they typically bring comfort, encouragement, warning, or important information, angels work for the good, as with Jesus in Gethsemane: "an angel from heaven appeared to him and gave him strength" (Luke 22:43).

Beyond these large generalizations—to which there are always exceptions—diversity reigns. Angels appear to children and adults, to those near death and those in good health, to those who are wide awake and (as with Jacob in Genesis 28) those who are sleeping. Angels may be large or small, with wings or without, young (as always on traditional icons) or (much less often) old, male or (at least in the modern world) female; and they may be seen in whole or in part. (A few visionaries glimpse feet or wings alone. Others, strangely enough, report not seeing a face because the head was too far above, out of sight.) Sometimes angels become visible and say not a word. Other times they appear precisely in order to speak (as habitually in Scripture). They are usually white, silver, or golden but once in a while red or blue (never, so far as I recall, green). Although most often a single angel is noticed, there are reports of people perceiving two or more angels at once.[46] Finally, angels normally appear for the purpose of assisting someone, but occasionally an angel glimpsed takes no notice of the percipient, as if its business is elsewhere.

* * *

We have always known that unaided brains can delude themselves and behold what is not there. When Macbeth saw his deceased father, he wondered whether the ghost before him was but "a dagger of the mind, a false creation" produced by a "heat oppressed brain." Today the scientific study of idiosyncratic perception is a large, academic field. It proceeds on the assumption that visions are, as a rule, hallucinations, perceptions of what is not there, and that the causes must lie solely within skulls.[47] Should we not, then, assume that each and every vision, including each and every vision of an alleged angel, is, in the words of an old cataloguer of superstitions, "grounded on no other Bottom, than the Fears and Fancies, and weak Brains of Men"?[48]

Despite so much learned opinion against me, I doubt that we should. I side rather with Wolfhart Pannenberg: "the thesis that we must regard all visionary experiences as psychological projections with no basis in reality cannot be regarded . . . as an adequately grounded philosophical postulate."[49] All-too-briefly, here are a few reasons why I have an open mind on this matter:

(1) Although the sense that an experience is real does not, in and of itself, require a stimulus external to the percipient,[50] we should nonetheless keep in mind that many who report seeing angels are firmly convinced that they were not hallucinating. Perhaps their confident conviction counts for more than nothing.

(2) There are stories in which more than one person sees an angel. I have already quoted two illustrations of this. Here are two more:

- "Suddenly I saw two bright lights, about the size of a ten-year-old children [sic], standing in the corner of the room, between the wall and a sideboard. I didn't want to interrupt Bo [my boyfriend], and did not say anything about this apparition. I knew for certain that they had come through the wall. By chance I had looked at my watch; it was about 7.40 pm. When Bo wanted to leave, he asked me: 'Did you see anything unusual earlier?' I asked: 'Where?' 'Over there in the left corner of the room!' This was exactly where I had seen them. I pretended not to know anything, and asked, 'What was there?' 'It looked like two little angels.' But the angels had no wings—neither of us had seen wings. I asked Bo: 'When was this?' He said: 'At about quarter to eight.'"[51]

- "Suddenly there was a man in white standing in front of the [baptismal] font about eighteen inches away. He was a man but he was totally, utterly different from the rest of us. He was wearing something long, like a robe, but it was so white it was almost transparent. . . . He was just looking at us. It was the most wonderful feeling. Not a word was spoken; various people began to touch their arms because it felt like having warm oil poured over you. The children came forward with their mouths wide open. Then all of a sudden—I suppose it was a few seconds, but time seemed to stop—the angel was gone. Everyone who was there was quite convinced that the angel came to encourage us."[52]

If these recollections and others like them are not wholly misleading, they make unswerving skepticism more difficult. To recall the common sense of Deuteronomy, the evidence of two or of three witnesses is stronger than the evidence of a single witness (19:15).

(3) To hold that, since many visions are purely endogenous—a fact no one denies—all must be purely endogenous, is a logical fallacy. It is equally fallacious to contend that all objects are physical because many objects are physical.

(4) If all angelic visions are illusory, one might expect them to accord with the beliefs of a percipient or a percipient's culture. While they most often do, there are striking exceptions. These are the words of a woman who saw what she did not expect to see: "In the bright white light, I could see the outlines of angels. . . . As I didn't believe in angels, I was confused at to why I was seeing this. I was seeing things I didn't believe to be true. Why was this happening?"[53] Equally intriguing are these words, which are a mother's recollections of the deathbed visions of her ten-year-old daughter, Daisy:

During this time she dwelt in both worlds, as she expressed it. . . . Mrs. W., one of our kind neighbours, was reading to her these words from the [New] Testament: "Let not your heart be troubled. In my Father's house are many mansions. I go to prepare a place for you" (John xiv, 1, 2). Daisy remarked, "Mansions, that means houses. I don't see real houses there. . . ." I [the mother] said, "Daisy, don't you know the Bible speaks of heaven being a beautiful city?" She said: "I do not see a city," and a puzzled look came over her face. . . . Daisy exclaimed . . . "Is it not strange? We always thought the angels had wings! But it is a mistake; they don't have any." Lulu [a friend] replied, "But they must have wings, else how do they fly down from heaven?" "Oh, but they don't fly," she answered, "they just come."[54]

Whatever else was going on with Daisy, she was not dutifully following the religious script of her family and friends.[55]

(5) One wonders why, if there are no divine emissaries to be seen, natural selection has programmed so many of us to see them. One wonders especially about the angels who so often, as we will see in later chapters, show up to comfort the dying. What is their evolutionary utility? Or is this phenomenon a by-product of some adaptive trait? But then what trait? Equipping survival machines with the ability to hallucinate reassuring light forms near death seems a roundabout way of achieving whatever evolutionary purpose it is supposed to achieve. One might rather expect evolution to terrorize expiring carriers of genetic material. A dying woman who was seeing angels, after being reassured that other terminal patients reported the same, said: "If there's no God and everyone is seeing this, how incredible our body is to make us experience this, that it could have been engineered at random to give us peace at our death."[56]

(6) To hold that some visions of angels may not be wholly illusory is not to eliminate the subjective component in perception or interpretation. Experts inform us that all perception is projection, active construction as opposed to passive reception and so, to some extent, imaginal. Regarding the objective and the subjective as antithetical is a crude disjunction. In response to incoming electrical and chemical signals, our inner theatre—for lack of a better metaphor—shows us a film. As one expert puts it, "perhaps we are hallucinating all the time and what we call perception is arrived at by simply determining which hallucination best conforms to the current sensory input."[57] We can also, however, show ourselves films without the

usual input, as when dreaming or on drugs or under hypnosis. To entertain the possibility that some visions are more than all-in-the-mind illusions is not to hold that some special experience is independent of thoroughly psychological and neurochemical mechanisms. It is instead to posit that our virtual reality machines can respond to mind-independent input from sources beyond the reach of current science. I recall what a professor of psychiatry said of his vision of Jesus: I "was fully aware that what I saw was a product of my own brain. I felt that God was, as it were, using my mind as a projectionist uses a projector."[58]

(7) Whatever one thinks about angels, visions of them do not reliably indicate pathology. Recent authorities do not regard having a vision as either a symptom of schizophrenia or the product of delirium, drugs, alcohol, or brain lesions.[59] "A substantial minority of the population"—anywhere from 10-25 percent, depending on the study—"experiences frank hallucinations at some point in their lives," and "for every person who receives a diagnosis of schizophrenia . . . it would appear that there are approximately 10 who experience hallucinations without receiving the diagnosis."[60] While visions are associated with certain pathological states as well as with stress and trauma, they are far from being exclusively coupled with such states. Many see visions without being in any way mentally or physically compromised.[61]

I introduce the preceding points not because I foolishly aspire, in a couple of pages, to convert anyone to my point of view. The subject is far too complex and controverted for that. I urge only that, while skepticism is certainly understandable, it is not obviously inevitable.

* * *

Even if one agrees with me, the vexing problem of agency remains. Many move from seeing a reassuring figure of light to the Christian idea of an angel. Others make the same move when a disembodied voice instructs them to do this or that, or when they hear exquisite music with no apparent source, or when they benefit from an amazing coincidence, or when a stranger lends a much-needed hand and then vanishes.

Yet such events do not befall Christians alone, which means that the Christian interpretation is not the only one on offer. Anyone familiar with the popular lore of other religions knows this; so too those acquainted with the stories that parapsychologists—who do not subsume all the relevant phenomena under the single category, "angel"—have been amassing since the nineteenth century.[62]

The same fact is on display in Heathcote-James's *Seeing Angels*. This book advocates neither an exclusivist theology nor a specifically Christian view of things, and a chart at the back has these statistics on the religious affiliations of the (UK) respondents: Protestant (including Anglican) 39.1 percent, unknown (none given) 28.9 percent, Catholic 6.3 percent, agnostic 5.7 percent, new age 4.6 percent, lapsed Christian 4.3 percent, atheist 4 percent, Christian convert 3.4 percent, Jewish 1.7 percent, Muslim 1.4 percent, Buddhist 0.6 percent.[63] Heathcote-James's conclusion? Not only do "people from all cultures, backgrounds and faiths relate fundamentally the same types of experience," but "agnostics and atheists have the same kinds of experiences as believers in orthodox religions."[64]

I can illustrate the problem of interpretation with two stories. The first concerns a small boy, Eric, and his mother.[65] Eric reported that, while he was asleep, his ceiling fixture descended and hovered above his bed, all the time shimmering brilliantly. While his mother did not believe him, she knew he was not in the habit of telling tall tales; and the following night "an insistent voice" roused her from sleep to announce that Eric's light was in her room. This reportedly happened next:

A brilliant, radiant, scintillating [object], shaped like a gigantic snowflake, lingered at my doorway. I felt a presence, an aliveness. It was warm, peaceful, good. As I watched, it began slowly to recede, then fade, then was gone. I noted the time, determined to prove I was not asleep, and ever so slowly came to the realization that I, no more than my ten-year-old, could . . . put a name on this wondrous thing. Was it an angel in its natural state, not artificially clothed in human disguise?

The mother remembers something like a gigantic radiant snowflake that mediated a "presence" and gave her warm feelings. She very cleverly construes this as an angel "in its natural state." No one, however, knows what an angel undisguised looks like. It could also have occurred to her, were she so moved, to identify the strange light with the spirit of a dead person, or with a friendly entity from a neighboring dimension, or with some form of ball lightning that, because of its peculiar electrical charge, evoked pleasant feelings; or she could have confessed bafflement in face of the unknown. The experience itself did not dictate the interpretation. That had to be read in.

My second story took place on August 26, 1989. On that evening, Joyce Robinson-Brim, while standing at an open kitchen window, saw "the purest, brightest light" she had ever seen. "It was as white as snow with a sparkle of what appeared to be mercury riding in the center."[66] The light appeared "out of nowhere without sound or warning," as if "a piece of the moon" had come down just beyond her window screen. She immediately wondered whether this was God or "an angel of the Lord, but why on earth would God appear to me?" Soon, however, she had a second thought: Unidentified Flying Object. Unnerved, she backed away in a daze.

Later Joyce's mother recounted seeing, while sitting outside, a light that illumined the whole back porch, and her nephew relayed that lightning had lit up the dining room, kitchen, and backyard. There had been, however, no storm that evening. Joyce called the Air Force and NASA to ask whether anyone else had reported a peculiar light. They were of no help. Still without an answer, her thoughts turned again to her religious faith. In the end she decided that the light must have been Jesus, who "wanted me to know that He is just as real today as He was back then."

In narrating this episode, Joyce raises five distinct possibilities. The light was God. Or it was an angel. Or it was a UFO. Or it was lightning. Or it was Jesus. What it truly was, I have no clue. All that matters here, however, is that, once again, the experience did not interpret itself.

* * *

The equivocal nature of many of the stories about angels is obvious. Not only do visionaries and others read their religious ideas into their experiences but, as observed earlier, it is not difficult to account for many AIW and slow fall stories by positing that people often lay biblical templates over events that may be mundane. Given, in addition, that "extremely improbable events are commonplace,"[67] many coincidences that get attributed to angels are surely just that, coincidences.

Yet after we have given critical reflection its due, we must concede that some stories, if they do not stray into fiction, would move almost all of us to use the word "angel." Not every experience is a Rorschach inkblot. Consider these words:

As she [a young mother] looked out the [kitchen] window into the back yard, she noticed that the garden gate had been left open. Her little three-year-old daughter, Lisa, had toddled through the gate and was sitting casually on the railroad tracks playing with the gravel. The mother's heart stopped when she saw a train coming around the bend and heard its whistle blaring persistently. As she raced from the house screaming her daughter's name, she suddenly saw a striking figure, clothed in pure white, lifting Lisa off the tracks. While the train roared past, this glorious being stood by the track with an arm around the child. Together, they watched the train go by. When the mother reached her daughter's side, Lisa was standing alone.[68]

As with most of the stories in this book, I offer no judgment as to what really happened. Were it true, that would be lovely. Alas, I see no way, given my distance from the event and its principals, to adjudicate the matter. What I can say is this. If I were to see a "glorious being" rescue my daughter from an oncoming train, I would not posit that I had projected an angelic mirage and, in addition, somehow managed psychokinetically to lift my child to safety. I would rather infer, using my Christian language, that an angel had saved her. Would this not be the sensible thing to do?

* * *

I have, in the previous pages, taken a stab at what might lie behind some of the modern stories featuring angelic intervention. At this point I lay that endeavor aside and ask how the stories function for their readers.

Most obviously, they entertain. The books that showcase angels are strings of pleasant short stories with five basic elements:

- Introduction of protagonist.
- Portrayal of distress or difficulty.
- Unexpected, supernatural intervention.
- Resolution of problem.
- Interpretation.

The stories typically run from one to four pages. Convoluted plots are absent, as are extended arguments. Lengthy attention is not required. Everything is short and sweet, and the endings are happy. These are the marks of entertainment in the post-*Reader's Digest* age.

It is entertainment with a purpose, however. The various compendia of angel stories are designed to inspire, to encourage people not to lose heart. The first-person accounts do this chiefly by persuading readers that they are not alone. The books are, insofar as they supply evidence of God in a largely secular world, implicit attacks on atheism.[69] More than that, the angels in these stories communicate divine attention and compassion. Their sympathetic intervention makes God, through intermediaries, a social being who cares. Note this statement, which is interchangeable with a hundred others: "As I got to the stairway to come up, standing there was a lovely, tall, white shining being. Nothing was said, but there came over me a warm sense of peace and quietness. Then I knew I was not alone, and that experience sustained me through a trying time in the days ahead."[70] Perhaps this individual already believed in God, or even that God is love. There can be, however, a chasm between perfunctory doctrinal assent and first-person experience. Furthermore, even when one does not have such experience, reading about others who seemingly have can bring reassurance: we are not alone.

The potential downside to this, of course, is that some will inevitably wonder why God has never sent an angel to make things better for them. Here is the testimony of one such individual:

> I do believe that there is a Higher Power . . . but I don't think that He has any say in our lives. . . . I guess it's kind of sad for my kids, but there's no religion in my house. Before this [time of desperate need] I believed in God. I said prayers every night. I believed that He would take care of me. It sounds so weird to say this right now. Catholics have this thing called a guardian angel. When I was a kid, my guardian angel took care of me, but at the lowest, worst time in my life, when I needed my guardian angel and God, they were nowhere to be found.[71]

Many of our authors, however, are aware of the problem of disparate fates and address it head-on. Near the beginning of her book, MacDonald asks, "Where was the angel when my friend's three teenage children were suddenly killed by a train at an unmarked railroad crossing?" Here is her response:

No one has the answer. . . . Most of the time there isn't any answer. We know that during the days when Jesus lived on earth, He didn't heal every blind, sick, and crippled person in the entire city of Jerusalem. He didn't stand at the entrance of each tomb and call every person back to life as He did Lazarus. When you read through your Bible, you find that God did intervene in certain circumstances; but those circumstances were the exception, not the rule. God does send some angels to rescue His people from time to time, but those instances are rare.[72]

This is not a sophisticated philosophical or theological statement. It serves well enough, however, for practical purposes. Seemingly remarkable interventions occur only now and then, and no one can say why some are rescued or favored with a vision and others are not.[73]

Yet another function of the popular books on angels is, almost inevitably, promotion of a particular theology. This theology can be overt, as when authors read their doctrines into and out of accounts by framing and editing them so that they promote some version of evangelical or conservative Protestantism. When this happens, there may be references to the Trinity or the blood of Jesus, or even calls for readers to convert.[74]

Other books, by contrast, remain self-consciously ecumenical. Their celestial beings are non-denominational and do not insist on a confessional response to their therapeutic ministrations. In these works, angels are vaguely Judeo-Christian, and the religious affiliation of experiencers does not matter. An angel can appear to Protestant, Catholic, Jew, or to one without any religious affiliation. As one author has it, "angels are not restricted by race, religion or creed of any kind."[75] The message is clear: doctrine is not the most important thing in the world.

My last observation about function is that the popular books on angels are ethical tractates, literary exercises in moral formation. They illustrate and reinforce multiple imperatives. Anderson's *Where Angels Walk* draws to a close with the refrain that, what angels do, "we can do for each other."[76] If angels "lift our hearts and give us wings," if they "sit silently with us as we mourn," if they offer us "opportunities to turn our suffering into bridges of healing and hope," if they "furnish information, provide food," and "buffer the storms of life," then "we can do that for each other." "Full-time angels," being beyond our beck and call, are "completely unpredictable." This is why part-time angels are so important. Angels like you and me. Few of us may identify a celestial being during our lifetime. . . . But we can all be angels to one another. We can choose to obey the still small stirring within, the little whisper that says, "Go. Ask. Reach out. Be the answer to someone's plea. You have a part to play. Have faith." We can decide to risk that He [God] is indeed there, watching, caring, cherishing us as we love and accept love.

This call to assist others retrospectively turns Anderson's book into ethical exhortation. She is calling for the *imitatio angelorum*, the moral imitation of the angels.[77]

In like manner, the final chapter of *In the Presence of Angels*, by Lonnie Melashenko and Timothy Crosby, is entitled, "You Can Be an Angel."[78] It includes a long list of ways in which Christians can act like angels. These include: "Invite someone to dinner who never gets invited to a dinner"; "Pray for an enemy, and ask God to show you something good you can do for him"; and "Imagine yourself a contestant in a one-day contest for 'kindest person on earth.'"[79] In short: You have seen what angels do. Go and do likewise.

One may be disappointed that the angels do not seem concerned about the larger world. They are mum about economic disparity and class divisions, about racism and sexism, about commodity fetishism and environmental folly. Yet this is to expect too much from our genre. I am fairly sure that the conversations on suicide hotlines rarely touch upon the great social and political issues of our day. It is the same in our books, and for a similar reason. The focus, given the percipients' circumstances, is not on the current state of our culture and its collective sins. It is rather on aid coming to individuals in the moment, individuals in immediate personal crisis. This scarcely entails, if I may so put it, that angels care about nothing else.

* * *

Some of my colleagues are perplexed that I read and ponder popular books on angels. Is it not a waste of time for an educated mind to bother with tales told by the gullible? But I pay attention to these books for the same reason my colleagues pay attention to the daily news: they want to know what is going on in our world.

A survey a few years back found 54 percent of Americans reporting that they had been "protected from harm by a guardian angel."[80] The number is astonishing. I suspect it reflects the far-flung influence of writers such as Joan Wester Anderson and Hope MacDonald, writers who have subsumed a miscellany of experiences under the rubric "angel."[81] If so, they have had a remarkable impact upon our culture. That is reason enough to think about their books. Perhaps I have not thought about them rightly, but at least I have tried.

6

Approaching Death

"This happens all the time, but no one wants to talk about it. . . . It's like this: I want other doctors to refer their patients to me; and I want to be seen as competent, technically astute, and on top of cutting-edge treatments. If I went around telling people that my patients were having deathbed visions, do you think I'd be taken seriously?"

—A doctor[1]

"Almost without exception, everyone starts his or her story with something like: 'I've never told anybody this, and if I did, they'd put me in the nuthouse—but this is what I experienced.'"

—A hospice worker[2]

"Studies suggest that as many as 60 percent of conscious dying patients experience end-of-life dreams and visions, but the actual number likely is higher because the phenomenon is considered underreported by patients and family members for fear of embarrassment."

—Henry L. Davis[3]

Some deaths are wretched and best forgotten. A week before she passed, my maternal grandmother was moved out of her nursing home into a critical-care facility. Although she was able, until almost the end, to play the piano as always, her mind had been, for months, evaporating. She would stare at her TV without awareness of the content. At some point she began to utter sentences that we assumed—perhaps wrongly in retrospect—were devoid of meaning. In her final days, she began repeating, like a stuck, old-fashioned record player, "Help me, help me." The memory haunts. No one in my family knew how to respond to her unsettling plea. I confess that all I could think of was the ending to a 1958 sci-fi horror movie, *The Fly*. At the film's end, a man who has been turned into a fly through an experiment gone dreadfully wrong cries out, as a spider devours him, "Help me, help me."

All deaths are not, thank God, so miserable. Many gather meaning to themselves in one way or another. In this chapter and the next, I briefly survey some of those ways. In doing so, I look first at experiences that sometimes precede death. After that, in the following chapter, I look at so-called near-death experiences. Those involved in both sorts of experiences often give them religious meaning. When taken at face value, moreover, they suggest a world beyond this one. Of course, whether we should take them at face value is a matter of passionate dispute.

* * *

Once upon a time, most died where they had lived, in their homes. Today, half of us instead expire in hospitals or nursing homes. The circumstance permits some to avoid ever standing at the bedside of one who is dying.

It is otherwise with hospice nurses and critical-care workers. It is their business to attend the dying. In doing so, they have become our society's most qualified observers of death. They are intimately familiar with what regularly happens one to three months before the end, one to two weeks before the end, and in the final days and hours before the end. They know all about the depression, restlessness, anxiety, confusion, delirium, somnolence, temperature fluctuations, difficulty swallowing, stertorous breathing, and other woes that often presage the human exit.

Yet not all is grim. Those who recurrently behold death and its approach often tell strange and edifying stories, and if one ponders enough of them, patterns begin to emerge. It is now established beyond doubt, for instance, that a surprisingly high percentage of the dying have visions of some other realm, or report seeing deceased loved ones or angelic beings. It has also become quite clear that many can sense in advance that death is drawing near.[4] The hospice folk have a name for this: Nearing Death Awareness.[5]

Occasionally in fact a patient appears able to predict the day of death. One man—who had lived as a skeptic and rationalist—blurted out: "Enough . . . enough . . . the angels say enough . . . only three days left."[6] Another declared: "Three days left. Three days left. I know I have three days left. But my family won't let me [go?]. They won't."[7] Both were right: they died in three days.

Even when it is not obvious to the attending professionals that death is near, some patients appear to discern, for reasons unknown, its proximity. Here are the reflections of a paramedic, who has found some deaths to be "very unnerving":

> They know, for whatever reason. They have a prescience. It's a definite feeling that they have that they are gonna die and I would say ninety-five percent of the time they end up dying in front of me. And it's very disturbing to me. There were many cases where, really, I did not think that they were ill enough, and then, for whatever reason, they would suddenly have a cardiac arrest, and I would say, "Oh my God, he told me this."[8]

Less dramatic and more usual is the general sense that the end is in the offing—not immediately near but not far off. In conveying this idea, the dying typically use symbolic language. Why they should do this is a fascinating question. Perhaps some instinctively forsake the literal because they are facing the unknown. Perhaps others reach for a metaphor because they have seen or sensed something they cannot describe prosaically. Whatever the cause, the nonliteral dominates. People speak of getting ready for a big dance, or of attending a big dinner, or of waiting for a big storm. The common, underlying notion is, obviously, preparation for a major event.

Travel metaphors are most frequent. One study reports that 40 percent of the terminally ill speak in one way or another of taking a trip. The dying will, for example, indicate that they need to pack a suitcase, or that they have to find their ticket or passport, or that they must get ready for a bus or plane. One woman exclaimed, "Yellow bus! There's the bus!" Her granddaughter asked, "Who is driving that bus, Grandma?" The answer was: "Not sure. Not sure . . . but lots of angels."[9] One man cryptically said, "I'll be getting into the car then, but I haven't done anything wrong."[10] Another confidently announced that he was ready to catch "the next available bus."[11]

My wife's aged cousin died not long ago. She was afflicted with uterine and ovarian cancer. She also had malignant spots in her lungs and brain. On top of that, she suffered from atrial fibrillation. Surgery was not an option, and death was indubitably near. She nonetheless refused to resign herself to the obvious. She told my wife, a cancer survivor, that she was her inspiration, because she had survived a serious bout with cancer and resumed a normal life. In other words, this eighty-five-year-old, riddled with multiple inoperable tumors and suffering from a serious heart condition, was absurdly hoping to get well. Despite this denial, however, some part of her clearly knew the truth. One day she enigmatically proclaimed to my daughter, who was attending her: "I am reluctant to travel." She could have said, "I do not want to die." She instead chose a metaphor.

Whether my wife's cousin ever reconciled herself to the inevitable we do not know. She said nothing over her last ten days. But whatever her ultimate mindset, many do recognize the inevitable and can even welcome it. Most sentences about metaphorical travel do not signal reluctance or recalcitrance. They rather indicate acquiescence to the unescapable.

Such sentences, it seems to me, obliquely make a metaphysical claim. To take a journey is to move from here to there, to travel from where one is now to where one will be later. No one gets on a train or bus in order to arrive at oblivion. Those who summon a travel metaphor are, then, implicitly affirming some sort of continuation beyond this life. Their metaphors reflect the hope or conviction that their physical end will not be their utter end. This is why they do not speak about the chalk being erased, or the house burning down, or the cardboard being recycled.

This is not all. Lisa Smart, who has made a study of last words, has observed that the dying do not talk about jogging or taking a stroll: "While a couple of people have said, 'Get my coat; I have to go,' no one yet has been recorded as saying, 'Get my tennies. I am preparing for a long walk.' The transportation metaphors involve outside agency—someone or something beyond our own physical body transports us."[12]

Those who sense that they are leaving this world for another know that they are not in charge of the move. They are getting on the bus, not driving it; they are getting on the train, not conducting it. I am reminded of the old idea that angels come for the saints at death.[13] To be carried away by angels is perhaps the ancient equivalent of getting on a bus.

* * *

In the middle of the nineteenth century, a French doctor wrote: "In certain diseases, the senses acquire an extraordinary delicacy on the approach of death, when the sick person astonishes those about him by the elevation of his thoughts, and the sudden lucidity of a mind which has been obscured during many long years."[14] Similar are these words from a British physician, of the same century: "We have all observed the mind clear up in an extraordinary manner in the last hours of life, when terminated even in the ordinary course of nature; but certainly still more remarkably when it has been cut short by disease, which had affected, for a time, the intellectual faculties."[15]

These remarks represent once common knowledge. Hippocrates, Cicero, Plutarch, and Galen, as well as doctors in the eighteenth and nineteenth centuries, reported cases of the confused or cognitively inert becoming, shortly before death, perfectly lucid.[16] William Munk, in a book published in 1887, remarked that lucidity before death "has impressed and surprised mankind from the earliest ages."[17]

The phenomenon, however, barely shows up in the medical literature of the twentieth century.[18] It seems to have been largely forgotten until 2009, when a German biologist, Michael Nahm, published a survey of relevant cases and coined the phrase *terminale Geistesklarheit*, which comes into English as "terminal lucidity." He offered this description: "the (re-)emergence of normal or unusually enhanced mental abilities in dull, unconscious, or mentally ill patients shortly before death, including considerable elevation of mood and spiritual affectation, or the ability to speak in a previously unusual spiritualized and elated manner."[19]

To illustrate: Scott Haig, the well-known medical columnist and clinical professor of orthopedic surgery at Columbia University College of Physicians and Surgeons, had a patient, David, whose lung cancer, as so often happens, had metastasized to his brain. David's speech, as a result, was slurred. Then he became incoherent. Then he could no longer move. He eventually became wholly unresponsive. According to Haig, he showed "no expression, no response to anything we did to him. As far as I could tell, he was just not there." A scan revealed that cancer had eaten most of his brain. And yet, an hour before his death, and after he had already begun to breathe irregularly, he awakened. He smiled, spoke clearly to his gathered family, and held their hands. Only then did he slip away. The attending nurse opined that it was "like a miracle." This was Haig's verdict: "It wasn't David's brain that woke him up to say good-bye that Friday. His brain had already been destroyed. Tumor metastases don't simply occupy space and press on things, leaving a whole brain. The metastases actually replace tissue. Where that gray stuff grows, the brain is just not there."[20]

Even Alzheimer's patients can exhibit terminal lucidity. One ninety-one-year-old woman had been wholly unresponsive for five years. Nothing hinted that she recognized anyone, including her daughter, who was her caretaker. Nevertheless, a few minutes before she died, she began to engage in a coherent conversation. She spoke about death, her church, her family. Her daughter was, naturally enough, utterly baffled at her mother's momentary return to her earlier, articulate self.[21]

In a similar case, a woman with Alzheimer's had not spoken with or recognized anyone for years. Yet a week before she died, she abruptly stirred from insentience and began conversing with her granddaughter, asking questions about the family and offering advice. Her granddaughter was taken aback by this flabbergasting flash of vitality and later remarked: "It was like talking to Rip Van Winkle."

These last two accounts not only illustrate terminal lucidity but give a sense of what is usually communicated. As Smart has noted: "of all those I interviewed . . . no one had a story in which angry or spiteful words were spoken during the window of lucidity. Most of the stories included final requests for favorite foods or final reconciliations or pronouncements of love."[22] Another expert has related that the most common themes are memories, preparation for death, final wishes, bodily issues (such as hunger), and awareness of imminent departure.[23]

During what part of the dying process does terminal lucidity occur? One study of forty-nine cases, not all with dementia, reported that 43 percent of the episodes took place on the last day of life, 41 percent happened during the final two to seven days, and 10 percent occurred eight to thirty days before death.[24] These numbers explain why some medical practitioners use the term "sunset day": terminal lucidity often occurs on the final day. There are, however, cases of individuals with debilitating disorders gradually becoming lucid during the weeks leading up to death.[25]

How often do these sorts of enigmatic events occur? No one knows, although it seems that while they are not rare, to claim they are commonplace would be too much. One small survey of ten caregivers in a nursing home showed that seven were familiar with terminal lucidity.[26] A larger study of forty-five Canadian hospice or palliative care volunteers found that 33 percent professed witnessing the phenomenon.[27] A review of 338 deaths at a Korean teaching hospital uncovered only six instances;[28] but a study of a hospice in New Zealand found six cases of lucidity in 100 deaths;[29] and Alexander Batthyány, a cognitive scientist associated with the Viktor Frankl Institute in Vienna, maintains that about 10 percent of patients with dementia display terminal lucidity.[30] Whatever the numbers turn out to be after further inquiry, they will likely be low enough so that informed families and friends of the unlucid should not get their hopes up, yet high enough that they should be prepared just in case.

Terminal lucidity has been documented not only in those with brain tumors and dementia (including those scoring high on the Global Deterioration Scale) but also in schizophrenics, victims of stroke, and patients with meningitis. The evidence is now sufficiently robust that mainstream medicine acknowledges the reality of terminal lucidity (and distinguishes it from lucid interludes that can occur long before death). The National Institute on Aging in fact recently funded research into the phenomenon. Its hope is that study of the transient recovery of long-lost clarity might lead to improved understanding of cognitive decline, and so to improved treatment of Alzheimer's and dementia.[31]

Why did the medical literature overlook this phenomenon until quite recently? While one can only speculate, one factor may have been wariness to bring up a subject that does not, on its face, prop up a materialistic model of the mind.[32] How do wrecked brains of various sorts heal themselves, if only for a bit? Some earlier writers, including Christian apologists, appealed to the puzzling circumstance as evidence for the existence of a soul.[33] More recently, Batthyány has asserted that "terminal lucidity seem[s] to stare at you in the face, and shout, 'No, you're more than your brain,' because obviously you've got a very non-supportive brain that wouldn't generate clear, consistent, coherent and reactive communication."[34] It is notable that Nahm, who gave terminal lucidity its name, suspects that the phenomenon is not the brain's last hurrah but the self's awakening to something new. He doubts that this life is all there is, that death is a never-ending nothing.[35]

* * *

Those who experience terminal lucidity speak not only with family and caregivers. They sometimes converse with figures no one else sees. Lyon White of Sussex reports that his mother, Peggy, after her long bout with Alzheimer's, was admitted to a hospital. No longer able to talk intelligibly, her words amounted to nothing save "gobbledygook." One day, however, as Lyon entered his mom's room, he heard her talking. She was chatting with her father, a policeman who had been murdered while on duty. The subjects of conversation included Peggy's deceased husband and his love for her. Lyon could not believe what he was hearing. His mother's condition had left her unable to compose a coherent sentence or even to enunciate clearly a single word. Yet here she was doing both—until becoming aware of Lyon's presence. After that, she slipped back to her uncommunicative state.[36]

Speaking with or to the unseen is hardly confined to cases of terminal lucidity. The phenomenon is instead quite common across all sorts of deaths. Here are five brief accounts:

- "It was as if my dad were speaking to my mom—who had died ten years earlier—by phone, and I heard only his end of the telephone call. He was so excited and happy. It was hard to believe that it was just imagination. Something very real seemed to be going on."[37]

- "She [a dying aunt] said, 'I can't wait.' I [the niece] said, 'What do you mean?' And she said, 'I am sitting here and I am having conversations with my twin and her sisters who had died before her.' She was in that other place and communicating, this was real for her, with her friends, her sisters."[38]

- "All of a sudden she [a dying cancer patient] opened her eyes. She called her [deceased] husband by name and said she was coming to him. She had the most peaceful, nicest smile just as if she were going to the arms of someone she thought a great deal of. She said, 'Guy, I am coming.' She didn't seem to realize I was there. It was almost as if she were in another world. It was as if something beautiful had opened up to her; she was experiencing something so wonderful and beautiful."[39]

- "I recall the death of a woman who was the victim of . . . malignant cancer. Her sufferings were excruciating and she prayed earnestly that death might speedily come to her and end her agony. Suddenly her sufferings appeared to cease; the expression of her face, which a moment before had been distorted by pain, changed to one of radiant joy. Gazing upwards, with a glad light in her eyes, she raised her hands and exclaimed, 'Oh, mother dear, you have come to take me home. I am so glad!' And in another moment her physical life had ceased."[40]

· "Much to my surprise she [the speaker's mother] not only sat up in bed but leaped over the bottom rail of the bed, saying 'Jim [her deceased brother], wait for me, don't go . . .' She was looking at the wall behind where I sat and obviously saw something I did not."[41]

In addition to speaking with those not physically present, the dying may also, as the last two accounts suggest, see them. Legions of stories have patients staring into space and seemingly beholding something others do not behold. Upon being asked, they may report that they see mom or dad or some other beloved relative or friend.

This is not something new under the sun. The Zohar, a Jewish work from thirteenth-century Spain, says at one point: "For we have learned: When a person is about to depart the world, his father and relatives are present with him, and he sees and recognizes them. And all those with whom he shared the same run in that world, they all gather around him and accompany his soul to the place where she will abide."[42] This is a large generalization, and the authority for it is not the Bible or one of the great rabbis but simply, "We have learned." Evidently this is the voice of experience.

Here is Frances Power Cobbe, the prominent Victorian suffragette and antivivisectionist, writing at a time when most deaths still took place at home:

In almost every family or circle, a question will elicit recollections of death-bed scenes, wherein, with singular recurrence, appears one very significant incident—namely, that the dying person, precisely at the moment of death, and when the power of speech was lost, or nearly lost, seemed to see something; or rather, to speak more exactly, to become conscious of something present (for actual sight is out of the question)— of a very striking kind, which remained invisible to and unperceived by the assistants. Again and again this incident is repeated. It is described almost in the same words by persons who have never heard of similar occurrences, and who suppose their own experience to be unique, and have raised no theory upon it, but merely consider it to be "strange," "curious," "affecting," and nothing more. It is invariably explained, that the dying person is lying quietly, when suddenly, in the very act of expiring, he looks up—sometimes starts up in bed—and gazes on (what appears to be) vacancy, with an expression of astonishment, sometimes developing instantly into joy, and sometimes cut short in the first emotion of solemn wonder and awe. If the dying man were to see some utterly-unexpected but instantly-recognized vision, causing him a great surprise, or rapturous joy, his face could not better reveal the fact.[43]

Cobbe illustrated her generalizations with several stories. This is one, "given in the words of a friend on whose accuracy every reliance may be placed":

I was watching one night beside a poor man dying of consumption; his case was hopeless, but there was no appearance of the end being very near; he was in full possession of his senses, able to talk with a strong voice and not in the least drowsy. He had slept through the day and was so wakeful that I had been conversing with him on ordinary subjects to while away the long hours. Suddenly, while we were talking together, he became silent, and fixed his eyes on one particular spot in the room, which was entirely vacant, even of furniture; at the same time a look of the greatest delight changed the whole expression of his face, and after a moment of what seemed to be intense scrutiny of some object invisible to me, he said to me in a joyous tone, "There is Jim" [the man's dead son]. . . . "Don't you see him? There he is," said the man, pointing to the vacant space on which his eyes were fixed; and when I did not answer, he repeated almost fretfully, "Don't you see him standing there?"
I answered that I could not see him, though I felt perfectly convinced that something was visible to the sick man, which I could not perceive. When I gave him this answer, he looked quite amazed, and turned round to look at me with a glance almost of indignation. As his eyes met mine, I saw that a film seemed to pass over them, the light of intelligence died away, he gave a gentle sigh and expired.[44]

Stories like this continue to come from deathbeds. They are common enough that the experience has an acronym—DBV, for "deathbed vision." Here are three modern illustrations, cut to their essence:

- Patient: "Have you seen them?" Hospice nurse: "No, I haven't. But I believe that you do. Are they here now?" Patient: "They left a little while ago. They don't stay all the time; they come and go." Hospice nurse: "What is it like when they're here?" Patient: "Well, sometimes we talk, but usually I just know that they're here. I know that they love me, and that they'll be here with me when it's time." Hospice nurse: "When it's time?" Patient: "When I die."[45]

- Patient: "I saw an angel." Hospice nurse: "Tell me what happened." Patient: "When I woke up there was an angel sitting in the light from the window." Mother of patient: "Angela, it's a sign from God!" Patient: "Mother, I don't believe in God." Mother: "That doesn't matter. You've seen God, or at least a messenger from God." Patient: "Does it matter who it is? Isn't it enough to know that there's someone so loving and caring waiting for me?"[46]

- "George appeared to be conversing with someone in the corner of the room, where hundreds of other patients had described seeing angels and deceased loved ones. He was saying, 'Mom, I'm not worthy to go with you. You go on.' I [a hospice doctor] listened. George was having a conversation with his [dead] mother. She was trying to help him but he was refusing her help."[47]

The literature on the subject of DBVs—as distinguished from hallucinations during delirium, which are typically annoying and rarely involve deceased relatives—is now very large. One takeaway is their surprising prevalence. In the 1960s and 70s, Karlis Osis and Erlendur Haraldsson asked doctors and nurses in the northeastern US as well as in Uttar Pradesh in northern India about their experiences with the dying. They received 1,708 usable questionnaires, approximately half of which they followed up with detailed interviews. "After-life related apparitions" turned out to be frequent, being reported by approximately half of respondents. Additionally, patients without medication had more apparitional experiences than those with medication; visions were not associated with specific medical conditions but occurred across the spectrum of afflictions; half of the visions lasted five minutes or less; incidence was independent of age, sex, and education; and "religious beliefs failed to affect the nature of the visions of another world."[48]

In 2005, a study of over 500 hospice patients and their caregivers in the US reported the following:[49]

- Eighty-five percent of patients had "survival-related" visions.
- Ninety percent of these reported seeing parents and siblings; 90 percent saw angels; 30 percent reported seeing God or Jesus; 5 percent saw "evil beings."
- The onset of visions was unrelated to medication and fevers.
- Incidence had nothing to do with age, gender, education, or religious affiliation.
- Visions typically lasted from one second to five minutes.
- Beginning three days before death, purported spiritual presences were often continuous.
- The interval between onset and death averaged four weeks.

Another study from the early 2000s, this an online survey, found 218 out of 525 caregivers and doctors reporting DBVs (41.5 percent).[50] Since then, a nationwide survey of the bereaved families of cancer patients in Japan found 21 percent (of 2,221 respondents) confirming a loved one's DBV. (The Japanese word for this is *Omukae*, which denotes an otherworldly escort for death's journey). Eighty-seven percent of the experiences involved deceased persons—most commonly parents—while 54 percent were of "afterlife scenes."[51] Another Japanese study, this of 575 bereaved families, found a full 39 percent reporting DBVs.[52] A survey in Moldova of 102 Christian families who had lost a loved one six to twenty-four months earlier found thirty-seven reporting an even mix of near death "visions" and "unusual dreams."[53] Interviews of 104 families in India produced similar results (with the additional outcome that Muslims were less likely to report DBVs than Hindus).[54]

More recently, fifty-nine patients in a hospice unit in a suburb of Buffalo, New York, were interviewed on multiple occasions about their experiences.[55] Eighty-eight percent reported having an end-of-life dream or vision (ELDV), and 99 percent of those said that their experiences were "real." The researchers also related that ELDVs, over against delirium, "typically occur in patients who have clear consciousness, heightened acuity, and awareness of their surroundings. ELDVs are also memorable and recalled with clarity. ELDVs differ most from hallucinations or delirium by the responses they evoke, including inner peace, acceptance, and the sense of impending death."[56] In short, they typically function in positive ways.[57]

The most common experience—half the time a dream, half the time a waking vision—involved encountering deceased relatives and friends. Incidents of this sort climbed dramatically in the weeks before death. A chief conclusion of the study was that it is a mistake "to medicalize these [ELDVs] and suggest that they hold very little value," for that "would be detrimental to the dying individual's ability to communicate, find closure, and experience meaning at the end of life."[58]

It is not possible to put all these studies together, run a meta-analysis, and come up with stable statistics about incidence. Different definitions of the subject were used, different methods were employed (questionnaires and interviews), and different people were consulted (patients, families, clinicians). This does not, however, disallow some confident generalizations. Concerning, for example, the content of these experiences, much more often than not the dying see and speak with deceased relatives whose perceived purpose is to bring comfort or serve as escorts to a new world.[59] Osis and Haraldsson found 91 percent of identified apparitions were of this type. Reports of religious figures, such as Jesus or angels, are much less frequent, at least in reports from the Western world. Occasionally, a figure will go unidentified. One little girl's final words were, "Who are all those people standing there, mommy?"[60]

The dying report seeing not only people but also catching glimpses of otherworldly locales:

- "It is very beautiful over there."[61]
- "Where have I been? Oh; I will tell you. . . . I've been billions and billions of miles away to a Happy Land. Oh! how glorious! I can't describe it and I'm going back there. . . . I was never so happy in my life."[62]
- Hospice nurse: "Clare, what are you seeing?" Patient: "It's that place, you know, you were there." (The nurse had earlier shared her NDE with the patient.)[63]
- "I can see and hear the most beautiful things and you must not worry."[64]
- "Oh, it's so beautiful, so blinding. So beautiful. Blinding."[65]
- "It's beautiful. It's so beautiful! Is this what heaven looks like? There are mountains and bright green grass; the colors are so brilliant."[66]
- "Please . . . don't ever be afraid of dying. I have seen a beautiful light and I was going towards it. . . . It was so peaceful I really had to fight to come back."[67]

One wonders whether the last words of Steve Jobs—"Oh wow! Oh wow! Oh wow!"—were occasioned by sight of an otherworldly landscape. His family reports that he spoke these words as he appeared to be looking past them.

* * *

What are we to make of all this? The pastoral response is obvious. Deathbed visions and auditions are a regular part of the dying process and no cause for concern. Indeed, they typically bring comfort and so have therapeutic value, both to the dying and those alongside them.[68] If, then, a loved one who is not in delirium sees or hears what others cannot see or hear, the informed response is not to call for more medication but for sympathetic listening and, if appropriate, open-ended queries.[69]

As to the inevitable question, What is really going on? one possibility is that brains, as they stumble toward extermination, see what is not there. Many will reflexively opine that this is the only credible assessment. They can appeal to dying patients who see spiders crawling out of TV screens or doctors sprouting turkey heads. Given, however, that caregivers often remark that interaction with unseen relatives appears to be quite different from run-of-the-mill hallucinations, this is not the only option. We have cause to wonder whether, at least sometimes, something truly extraordinary may be taking place.

One reason for contemplating this possibility is that the dying themselves believe this. In the Buffalo study, 99 percent of those who had ostensibly encountered the dead took their experience to be real, not hallucinatory. That is a truly remarkable statistic, and it is the more impressive when one adds that a visionary experience can liquidate unbelief. In one case, for instance, a dying woman who had earlier said, "I don't have any religion" and "I've never believed in God or anything like that, I'm just not interested," a woman who held that death ends everything, had a dream that, in her words, "wasn't really a dream," a dream about "a lovely place." Her daughter commented: "She knows she's dying, but now she seems to know that she will somehow continue to exist afterward. Mother's always maintained that people simply cease to exist after death, but now she's seen somewhere else." The daughter, also a skeptic, found her own disbelief challenged by her mother's change of mind: "I still don't believe any of those religious stories, but I no longer believe that when I die I'll just come to an end."[70]

Maybe such conversions should count for something. So too the fact that the dying sometimes report seeing people not known to them to be dead. Here are four illustrations:

- "My brother, John Alkin Ogel, died in Leeds. . . . About an hour before he expired, he saw his brother, who had died about 16 years before, and John, looking up with fixed interest, said, 'Joe, Joe,' and immediately after exclaimed with ardent surprise, 'George Hanley!' My mother, who had come from Melbourne, a distance of about forty miles, where George Hanley resided, was astonished at this, and said, 'How strange he should see George Hanley; he died only ten days ago.' Then, turning to my sister in law she asked if anybody had told John of George Hanley's death; she said 'No one.' My mother was the only person present who was aware of the fact. I was present and witnessed this."[71]
- In 1968, Janet T. gave birth to a baby who died after only two days. Her grandmother was, at the same time, dying in another city. The news was kept from her. At one point the grandmother began to tell Janet's father that she was having visitors. Although he saw nothing, she became calm and happy. Yet she was puzzled, because her late husband carried a baby. But then she announced: "It's one of our family. It's Janet's baby. Poor Janet. Never mind, she'll get over it."[72]
- "One day Su [a terminal patient] seemed very puzzled. 'Why is my sister with my husband?' she asked. 'They are both calling to me.' 'Is your sister dead?' I [a hospice nurse] asked. 'No, she still lives in China,' she said. 'I have not seen her for many years.' When I related this conversation to the daughter, she was astonished and tearful. 'My aunt died two days ago in China,' Lily said. 'We decided not to tell mother.'"[73]
- "The day he [Mr. Sykes, an Alzheimer's patient] died was different in a very eerie way. He sat up in bed and spoke as clear as a bell, talking just like anyone would, but not addressing us. He was looking upward with bright eyes and carrying on a conversation with 'Hugh.' He spoke loud and clear to Hugh, sometimes laughing but usually just conversing as though the two were sitting in a coffee shop having a chat. Mr. Sykes's wife told us that Hugh was alive and in good health, but . . . we learned shortly afterward that Hugh had keeled over with a fatal heart attack right about the time that Mr. Sykes miraculously came back to life."[74]

Accounts such as these refer to what have been dubbed "Peak in Darien experiences." The term comes from Keats's "On First Looking into Chapman's Homer." The poem ends with Cortez—a mistake for Balboa—staring at the Pacific for the first time:

> Then felt I like some watcher of the skies
> When a new planet swims into his ken;
> Or like stout Cortez when with eagle eyes
> He star'd at the Pacific—and all his men
> Look'd at each other with a wild surmise—
> Silent, upon a peak in Darien.

Frances Cobbe entitled her essay on experiences that presage death "The Peak in Darien: The Riddle of Death." She thought that the dying, by their looks and actions, sometimes reveal that they have beheld, "from their peak in Darien . . . an Ocean yet hidden from our view."[75]

We now have enough of these experiences for one collector to observe that there are at least three main types. The first involves seeing someone who died recently. The second involves seeing someone who died some time ago. The third involves seeing someone the visionary had never known.[76]

* * *

We have yet another reason for entertaining the possibility that deathbed visions are not always purely endogenous. In the middle of the listless, academic prose reporting on one of the Japanese studies referred to above, one trips over this remarkable sentence: "In some cases, not only patients themselves but also health care professionals or family caregivers see the visions."[77] The same unelaborated claim appears in a summary of a study conducted in the UK: "the apparitions were seen rarely by others in the room, usually by children, very rarely by hospice or hospital staff."[78] "Very rarely" is not the same as "never."

Neither article, regrettably, bothers to elaborate. Other sources, however, offer support for and help to fill out the laconic assertions. Here are the words of a nurse who believes that she felt what her dying patient reported seeing:

This gentleman was in a very weakened debilitated condition where he needed two people to care for him when he just started talking, and he sat bolt upright in his bed and this was something very unusual because he was preterminal . . . and he sat bolt upright and started this conversation just straight off the cuff and he was looking over towards the doorway . . . and he was talking to the doorway and I myself felt another presence in the room. . . . and I said to him "who are you talking to?" And he said, "Oh, that's my brother." So he went on talking for a little bit longer and I asked him another question you know, "Are you finished talking with your brother yet?" And . . . I felt the presence gone. And with that he lay back down again, like he didn't have any strength to hold himself up any longer.[79]

One can shelve this account as being about nothing more than someone's feelings ("I myself felt"). More intriguing, then, are occasions when it is not the patient who has a vision but a bystander, or when both do. One pastoral care worker stated:

This angel was sitting on her [a dying patient's] bed and I asked her if she was all right and she said, "Well I don't know." I asked her what was the problem and she said, "I think I'm going mad," so I said: "What makes you think you're going, you know [mad]?" [She said:] "Well, there's someone sitting on the bed beside me," and I said, "Well, I can see it too." "Thank goodness for that," she said.[80]

After a woman in her 70s died in the north of England in 2004, Penny Sartori interviewed the husband and daughter separately. The former claimed that, as he held his wife's hand, he had seen, "as through my wife's eyes," a bright light, out of which stepped "a tall person" with outstretched arms, and "he was waiting there as if to give her a welcoming hug; there was a sense of peace and love." The daughter had this to say:

Whether I saw this or it was a picture of it in my head I don't know. . . . All of a sudden, I could see her [mother] walking into the distance on a path. . . . I looked around and saw this tall person—I don't know who he was. She walked toward him on the path. When she reached him he took her into his arms as if in a warm welcoming embrace that was full of love. Mum's breaths got shallower. And then there were no further breaths and the image or scene disappeared.

A third person present at the death, a son, saw nothing remarkable at all.[81]

A similar account comes from an American woman who recalled the death of her grandfather in 1965:

I heard granddaddy calling out to his wife, Hazel. Grandmom had died nine years prior, so I thought he must be losing his mind. I ran down the hall to make another attempt to help him. I was amazed to find him sitting up, smiling with his arms reaching out. The room was filled with a warm, bright light. He spoke to grandmom, who was standing at the foot of the bed. Neither of them acknowledged my presence. She was there but a brief moment, and when granddaddy laid back down, his soul escaped with her. He died with a smile on his face.[82]

Raymond Moody, the chief figure in the modern study of NDEs, has his own story of this type. As his mother was dying of lymphoma, he, his wife, his two sisters, and their husbands were gathered round the bed. While they were holding hands,

the room seemed to change shape and four of the six of us felt as though we were being lifted off the ground. . . . I felt a strong pull, like a riptide that was pulling me out to sea, only the pull was upward. "Look," said my sister, pointing to a spot at the end of the bed. "Dad's here! He's come back to get her!" Everyone there reported later that the light in the room changed to a soft and fuzzy texture. It was like looking at light in a swimming pool at night. . . . It was as though the fabric of the universe had torn and for just a moment we felt the energy of that place called heaven. . . . My brother-in-law, the Reverend Rick Lanford, a Methodist minister, summed it up best when he said, "I felt I left my physical body and went into another plane with her. It was like nothing that had ever happened to me."[83]

The literature holds a surprising number of such stories.[84] Taken together, they will give the broadminded occasion for thought.

* * *

One cannot be broadminded about everything, however, and the next phenomenon may transgress the reader's boggle threshold. Nonetheless, as with everything else in this chapter, the witnesses are there.

Toward the end of Martin Scorsese's 2011 documentary *George Harrison: Living in the Material World*, the ex-Beatle's wife, Olivia, speaks about her husband's death. Her words are these: "There was a profound experience that happened when he left his body. It was visible. Let's just say, you wouldn't need to light the room, if you were trying to film it. He just . . . lit the room." She is clearly reticent to share this experience, maybe even a tad embarrassed. She is also just as clearly not deploying a metaphor. She is talking about some sort of literal, extraordinary light.

Whatever really happened at George's deathbed, his wife's words mirror a motif in the Christian tradition. An old monastic source, the *Apophthegmata Patrum*, or the *Sayings of the Fathers*, has this to say about the death of Sisoes, one of the so-called desert fathers:

> It was said of Abba Sisoes that when he was at the point of death, while the fathers were sitting beside him, his face shone like the sun. He said to them, "Look, Abba Anthony is coming." A little later he said, "Look, the choir of prophets is coming." Again his countenance shone with the brightness and he said, "Look, the choir of apostles is coming." His countenance increased in brightness and lo, he spoke with someone. Then the old man asked him, "With whom are you speaking, father?" He said: "Look, the angels are coming to fetch me . . ." Once more his countenance suddenly became like the sun.[85]

This is a hagiographical account, and how much actual memory it preserves is anyone's guess. Given, however, the countless modern reports of DBVs, at least the part about seeing the dead sounds true to life, or rather true to death.

The narrative about Sisoes is not an isolated anomaly. A supernal light at death is also part of the biographies of—to pick a few names at random—

Saint Benedict the Moor (d. 1589), Saint John of the Cross (d. 1591), Saint Joseph of Copertino (d. 1663), and the Venerable Mother Mary Maddalena Bentivoglio (d. 1905).[86] Although Protestants may reflexively dismiss such claims about people outside their tradition, we are not here dealing with unanchored folklore or tales from the age of legends. Because of the Roman Catholic canonization process, we have depositions from eyewitnesses regarding each of these individuals. Whatever the explanation, it is a fact that witnesses testified under oath before God that they had seen something remarkable at the bedsides of the aforementioned worthies.

The phenomenon, or at least firsthand testimony to it, is not confined to the past. Nor is it associated exclusively with the profoundly pious. Catherine Crowe, in the middle of the nineteenth century, offered the generalization that "luminous emanations" are occasionally seen around dying persons.[87] She could, were she alive, make the same claim today. In order to persuade the reader that I am right about this, here are ten testimonies, all firsthand, all from recent times:[88]

- "The room became uncomfortably bright, so bright that when I shut my eyes I couldn't shut out the light. But still it was comforting. In the light I could feel her [the speaker's wife]. She had gone physically but was still with me in spirit. . . . [The light was] vivid and bright, but not in the way that we see with our eyes."[89]
- "When Mom died, everyone present saw the room fill with light from 'an angelic presence.'"
- "About one week prior to my sister's actual passing, a bright white light engulfed the room. It was a light that we all saw and a light that has stayed with us ever since. I felt an intense love and connection with everyone in the room, including other 'souls' that were not visible but that we felt the presence of."
- "Suddenly there was the most brilliant light shining from my husband's chest and as this light lifted upwards there was the most beautiful music and singing voices, my own chest seemed filled with infinite joy and my heart felt as if it was lifting to join this light and music. Suddenly there was a hand on my shoulder and a nurse said 'I'm sorry love. He has just gone.'"[90]
- "Suddenly I was aware that her father [my grandfather] was stood [sic] at the foot of her bed. My mother was staring at him too and her face was lit

up with joy. It was then that I saw her face appeared to be glowing with a gold light. The light began to leave through the top of her head and go towards the ceiling. Looking back to my mother's face I saw that she was no longer breathing."[91]

- "Dad passed away in the early 1980s. At the moment of his last breath, I was at his side, holding his hand. I believe my eyes were closed. At this point I can only say that everything disappeared and was replaced by a bright white consuming light. Within this was total peace. No pain, no thought, no time. It could have lasted seconds or minutes. I have no awareness of its duration."

- "Odd tiny sparks of bright light . . . [emanated] from around my brother's body. Not many, just 2 or 3 very brief instances. I did not mention this to anyone else present. However, my brother's wife noticed the same thing and mentioned it, so I told her that I too had seen this."

- "I've always felt it was a miracle. . . . [We] sat there, and his face [that of the speaker's father] was really drawn with pain, when all of a sudden I saw a light go from his chest, over his head and up through the window. . . . When we got back home that night I said to my mom, 'That was a strange thing with Dad today,' and before I could go any further she said, 'I know what you're going to tell me, because I saw it too.'"[92]

- "It wasn't that it [my father's head] was just hot. It actually glowed! My brother and I both saw it. Our father's head glowed!"[93]

- "There was what I can only describe as a white light or form around the top of her [the witness's great aunt] head and face area. Her face looked so radiant in all that very bright light. . . . This light or form gradually disappeared from around her head and face area and what remained was what I can only describe as a 'total stillness' in the room."[94]

These statements—which are, I reiterate, from eyewitnesses—could, in theory, derive from erroneous misperceptions of natural lights. Or, one might speculate, emotional stress somehow led to seeing what was not there.

Then again, not just relatives but caregivers also report seeing luminous phenomena around the dying. Indeed, a questionnaire given to end-of-life caregivers in England and the Netherlands in the early 2000s found a third of the English caregivers and half of the Dutch caregivers reporting seeing, sometime in the preceding five years, a light "surrounding or emanating from the [dying] body."[95] More of the same comes from a recent study involving six nursing homes, a cancer hospital, and a palliative care unit in Brazil. Of the 133 healthcare professionals asked, forty-three (32 percent) reported perceiving at least once, in the last five years, "a radiant light" enveloping a dying person.[96]

These are flabbergasting statistics. Behind them apparently lie experiences such as this one, reported by a hospice nurse:

> When I was a student nurse . . . I saw her [a dying woman] draw her last breath. Right then a light that looked like vapor formed over her face. I never had felt such peace. The head nurse on duty was very calm and told me that Mrs. Jones was leaving her body. . . . I saw a luminous presence floating near the bed, shaped somewhat like a person. The head nurse saw the light in the room and this tremendous light coming from Mrs. Jones's eyes but not the presence. The nurse encouraged me by saying that she had witnessed similar appearances at other times.[97]

A British administrator offered this generalization: "A light often [surrounds patients]; especially my therapists often report on a light around patients and more towards when they die."[98]

The most thoroughly researched case of this sort known to me has to do with a sixty-eight-year-old man who died in Southern California in 1981. A chaplain at a large hospice told a friend, Elizabeth McAdams, that multiple people had witnessed a glowing light around the dying patient's head. Her interest piqued, McAdams interviewed both family members and hospice staff. Half a dozen told her a similar story. One administrative nurse said: "Close to the patient's head I saw a very golden fine line around the head. . . . I also saw the aura when the room was darkened." Another nurse reported: "I was able to see a yellow aura visible around the patient's head. Several other members of the staff were able to clearly see it also." According to yet a third nurse, "suddenly, there was this cast of light around the man's head. I almost came unglued. I absolutely could not believe it. I kind of screamed out, 'My goodness, I see it!'" One son said: "It was a glow very close to the head, a half circle. It went out about an inch from his head. It was gold or yellowish." Here is the chaplain's testimony:

I saw a light around his head. I saw it from various positions. . . . I went out several times and saw the glow every time I returned to the room. Later that evening, I happened to go back, the evening shift was on, and there were family members in the room, at least four men at that time. Two of them said they could see it, and the other two couldn't see it. . . . I saw a layer of light around his head, about 2 to 3 inches in depth. I saw it have a bulge at times that went out to the thickness of about 8 to 12 inches. I saw another light like a half circle or arc, separate, about 2 feet from the glow on the patient's head.[99]

If this account stood alone, one might, despite the several witnesses, pay it no heed. But, as is by now obvious, this peculiar report is not one-of-a-kind. Put otherwise, the old hagiographical motif of the dying light stems not from unalloyed legend but is informed by firsthand reports.

* * *

Might there be a mundane explanation? In 1842, Sir Henry Marsh, the famous Irish physician, published a short book entitled *The Evolution of Light from the Living Human Subject*.[100] In this he related several then-contemporary, well-attested accounts of luminescence before and near death. Many persons, he recognized, attribute such light to "supernatural agency," construing it as a sign of "divine favour and acceptance." He thought, however, that "the known and established laws of nature" account for the facts, and that "revealed truth" is "founded on a basis too firm to need" any sort of "miraculous interposition." In other words, the age of miracles is over. As for the real cause, Marsh posited phosphorous "generated in organic bodies at the period of incipient decomposition." As proof, he appealed to a pitiless experiment in which he had participated. A hapless dog, injected with phosphorated oil, produced, with the lights extinguished, expirations "beautifully luminous"—until it died in agony, five minutes later.[101]

To my knowledge, no one today hews to Marsh's hypothesis. More up-to-date sounding is the possibility that death releases a surge of photons and that these, once in a while, through means unknown, become visible.[102] Strangely enough, cameras that can detect a single photon reveal that our faces give off more light than the rest of us.[103] Still, science is nowhere near establishing such a hypothesis. I note it only as a curiosity. I am left wondering whether, once one subtracts the rare cases of luminous bacteria and such,[104] some luminosities around deathbeds present us with something truly strange and exotic.

*　*　*

End-of-life Experiences (ELEs) or Deathbed Phenomena (DBP) are the most common names for the phenomena introduced in the preceding pages. Also included in these labels, although not considered here, are startling death-bed coincidences, unearthly music without a source, and the sense of the presence of the newly departed.[105]

Although still at the margins of modern medicine, reports of and generalizations about ELEs and DBPs are no longer outlawed subjects, confined almost exclusively to religious hagiography or the literature of parapsychology. They have rather moved into mainstream journals, such as the *American Journal of Hospice & Palliative Care*, the *Archives of Gerontology and Geriatrics*, and *Alzheimer's and Dementia*. The old borderlines have been redrawn.

The chief gain in our knowledge is that unusual experiences attending death are much like the Old Hag (as discussed in chapter 2). A hundred years ago, few knew anything about them. Even today many know little to nothing about them. And yet they are not rare. In fact, the more data we gather, the more widespread they reveal themselves to be. Just as Alister Hardy taught us that mystical experiences are common, so medical researchers and hospice workers have taught us that deathbeds can be peculiar places. Transformative experiences are as familiar to the dying as to the healthy. In life and death, the ostensibly transcendent accompanies us.

Three further observations before turning to the next chapter. First, ELEs have likely persuaded or encouraged human beings in many times and places to believe that death is not a wall but a door, not a dead-end but a thoroughfare. Indeed, the existence of ELEs likely helps explain how belief in an afterlife originated in the first place and why such belief has been so widespread. If in the past, as in the present, the dying sometimes reported speaking with and seeing the dead, and if in the past, as in the present, curious events sometimes enveloped deathbeds, it is perfectly understandable that many posited something beyond breath's cessation.[106] This does not, I grant, mean that the inference, when made, was right, only that it was not an unfounded, anxious guess. It was rather born of experience. We cannot, of course, go back in time and figure out how beliefs about the afterlife and ELEs were intertwined, but that they ran wholly separate courses at any time or place makes no sense.

Second, we face the question of what we might think for ourselves. The problem is that the evidence is not all on one side. Multitudinous deaths are, to outward appearances, dull or miserable affairs without incident, events utterly devoid of transcendence. When one adds that human perception and testimony can go astray and that modern materialistic science has successfully explained so much, one may feel compelled to hold that, at death, the candle gutters and goes out.

This chapter is not the place to adjudicate this debate, which at times has extended into theological circles. But I have offered, if briefly, a few reasons why some of the phenomena reported above seem genuinely puzzling. Dismissing them one and all as anecdotal, moreover, requires that large swaths of our fellow citizens are absolutely wretched observers or wholly untethered from the truth. I prefer to think that at least some of them are halfway decent witnesses, and that all the testimony, taken together, pushes against reduction to the ordinary.

It is not without interest, in this connection, that ELEs, as already noted, sometimes convert skeptics. A terminal patient who called himself an atheist told a hospice doctor: "in the last few days, I've been seeing and experiencing things that seem beyond my control and outside my belief system. I am looking at life from a new perspective." He went on to ask about hallucinations in the dying and then confessed that he was seeing "bright white and very comforting" apparitions. Later he saw his deceased parents and went on to speak of "angels."[107]

Less dramatic yet still suggestive is this account:

> I was nursing my friend who had definite views that there was no afterlife. In her last couple of hours she became very peaceful and arose from her unconsciousness periodically saying clearly and happily such phrases as "I will know soon," "come on, get on with it then, I am ready to go now," and "it is so beautiful." . . . She was very obviously content, happy and at peace. It was a wonderful experience for her partner and me.[108]

More generally, a 2013 survey of terminal patients in Switzerland reported that, of the sixty-eight patients who explicitly associated an ELE with God, nine had previously categorized themselves as atheist or agnostic.[109] Such cases mark conversions.

To my mind, ELEs raise the odds that expiration of the body is not expiration of the self. Terminal lucidity, deathbed visions, and the rest move us to think twice, to wonder what is real and to ask what might await us in death.

* * *

Finally, as death nears and the familiar gives way to the unfamiliar, what captures most of our attention? According to hospice chaplain Kerry Egan, we do not, when death is at hand, live in our heads, "in theology and theories." Nor do we "use words of theology to talk about God." We rather speak about the families "we are born into, the families we create, the families we make through the people we choose as friends." Her theological take on this is that "people talk to the chaplain about their families because that is *how* we talk about God. That is *how* we talk about the meaning of our lives. That is *how* we talk about the big spiritual questions of human existence." Moreover, "we should learn from those who are dying that the best way to teach our children about God is by loving each other wholly and forgiving each other fully—just as each of us longs to be loved and forgiven by our mothers and fathers, sons and daughters."[110]

This may not sit well with some of us. Having spent our lives sponsoring a particular set of religious ideas, we might balk at the theological disinterest or what we may take to be the shallowness of the modern mind. Yet the dying, when they go on about their families, are usually preoccupied with love, faith, forgiveness, and reconciliation. How could any of us complain about that with integrity? Do we not love God by loving the image of God?

7

Death from Within

"It was the sheer distance of my anomalous experiences from their experience and training that silenced the rabbis whom I approached. It was not necessarily a dismissal of my plight, although it felt like that each and every time. . . . They simply lacked the tools to make sense of my experience, and so, to their discredit, they didn't even try."

—Elizabeth G. Krohn[1]

"He had tried to tell a few friends and relatives about it but they thought he was crazy. He told me I was the first person who had taken him seriously."

—Steve Taylor[2]

"The nurse told me in a cold, matter-of-fact manner that if I continued to talk that way a psychiatrist would be called in. With that pronouncement, I became very frightened. I figured that if the medical profession thought I was crazy, I had better keep silent about the whole affair."

—Edith[3]

It is astounding how much frightful trauma the human brain can sometimes endure without apparent ill effect. On June 8, 1992, Arthur Ekvall, twenty-nine, of San Diego, California, awoke suddenly from a sound slumber. An exploding pain filled his head. His first thought was: aneurysm. His second thought, informed by looking around, was more accurate. Across the room stood Jessie Solis, his one-time friend and ex-roommate, and Jessie was reloading a crossbow. Clearly comprehending, despite his injured brain, what had transpired, Arthur jumped up and wrestled the weapon away from Solis, who fled the premises.

With his enemy scattered, Arthur dialed 911. The police, upon arrival, were dumbfounded. The conscious victim had an arrow sticking through his head. This, however, was not comedy. The arrow had pierced the neck just below the left base of the skull and then passed upward, emerging above the left eye.

Surgeons unscrewed and removed the tip of the arrow and then used Vise-Grips to pull the shaft out the back. The operation was a success. Mr. Ekvall's brain, left eye, and vertebrae were unharmed, and in three days he walked out of the hospital, suffering nothing worse than a scar over his left eye—and, perhaps, designs on revenge.

When I read the news releases about Arthur Ekvall, I recalled the story of Phineas Gage and his notorious misadventure of 1848. As a consequence of an explosion, a thirteen-pound iron tamping rod, three and a half feet long and an inch and a quarter in diameter, entered his skull just below his left eye. It exited at the top of his skull. Yet he did not die. He in fact made a full physical recovery, although his personality took a turn for the worse.

Unlike Arthur Ekvall, Gage lived not just with severe damage to his brain but without a portion of it. Remarkably enough, the medical literature documents many such cases. The interested reader may consult that old and frightful treasure house, Gould and Pyle's *Anomalies and Curiosities of Medicine*.[4] It dedicates several pages to the grisly subject.

How much brain can we do without? One of my former students did just fine after the surgical removal of an entire hemisphere to stop severe seizures. She earned A's in both Fundamentals of Hebrew and Introduction to the New Testament. Indeed, she told me that, after her hemispherectomy, her IQ had, by official measurement, gone up.

How can these things be? The late John Freeman, the famed neurosurgeon at Johns Hopkins, was honest: "We don't really know."[5]

Even more perplexing are the brain scans that have revealed skulls filled mostly with water.[6] Sometimes the back pressure of fluid in the ventricles—the series of channels and reservoirs in the lower and middle brain through which the cerebrospinal fluid circulates—forces the overlying brain tissue against the cranium. The tissue is not just pushed upward: the pressure also destroys white and, to a lesser degree, gray matter. The result is that fluid-filled ventricles can occupy up to 95 percent of the cranium. In other words, a human head may be almost wholly inflated with a liquid that looks like water. Although most individuals with acute hydrocephalus suffer physical and mental disability, this is not, bizarrely, always so. Some with radically reduced brain tissue are not socially or intellectually enervated. The situation is so unexpected and puzzling that one recent researcher has seriously suggested that we entertain the possibility of information storage at the subatomic level or in some extracorporeal region.[7]

* * *

It is one thing to manage without the greater part of one's brain. It is quite another to be dead, so that there is no brain function at all. What happens then?

We can approach this question, which matters to everyone, any number of ways. We might, for example, consult the writings of philosophers for arguments for and against an afterlife. Or we might appeal to our scripture or religious tradition for the answer. Often, however, debates have included purportedly empirical observations. Some, for instance, and as observed in the previous chapter, have claimed to see the dead. Others have testified to hearing a loved one in the voice of an entranced medium. In recent times, so-called near-death experiences (NDEs) have taken center stage. Some contend that these experiences back the belief that we do not fade into oblivion. Many, of course, adamantly dispute this.

Most are by now familiar with the stereotypical NDE.[8] Commonly reported features include:

- looking down upon one's body;
- reviewing, replaying, or evaluating one's life or episodes from it;[9]
- sensing a movement from darkness to another realm;
- encountering a brilliant light or being of light;
- meeting dead loved ones;
- feeling a strong sense of peace and well-being;
- running up against a limit or barrier; and
- being sent back to earthly life or choosing to return.

As these items are very far from invariant—few reports if any include them all—and as they are recalled in no fixed order,[10] "the NDE is best regarded as a collection of typical sub-experiences: a variable combination of a number of possible elements from an established repertoire, the details of which differ on a case-by-case basis for reasons which remain largely obscure."[11]

The modern study of NDEs began with Raymond Moody's 1975 best-seller, *Life after Life*, a book that sold millions of copies and was translated into a dozen languages.[12] Five decades on, we have learned much.

(1) The NDE is a more or less coherent phenomenon. Multitudes have reported, independently of one other, variations on "a common range of patterns."[13] Those who have been in death's vicinity are, to be sure, far from telling the same story. Many have no story at all while others recount their idiosyncratic tales or relate nothing but obvious hallucinations. Nonetheless, countless narratives bear a distinct family resemblance. The stereotypical NDE is a real experience.[14]

(2) Culture alone is not the explanation. I know a man whose young son, after undergoing surgery, claimed to have met Jesus. When asked for clarification, the child related a standard NDE. This youngster had been, up to that point, kept at home due to mental issues, and his parents were certain he knew nothing about NDEs. Yet he reported one. In this he is not unique: it is the same with other youngsters.[15]

As for adults, NDEs sometimes confute their expectations, including the expectation that death is oblivion.[16] One woman remarked: "Nothing about the event was on my radar or in my conscious storehouse of concepts."[17] Another said: "I was always a professed atheist, but after my experience I know there is [a] God."[18] One man stated: "I would say—and not being religious at all—that there must be something after death, which I never believed in before."[19] One recalls A. J. Ayer's famous NDE: it quite surprised him.[20] His attending physician claimed to hear the famous atheist confide: "I saw a Divine Being. I'm afraid I'm going to have to revise all my various books and opinions."[21] Again, John Wren-Lewis, before his NDE, was a Death of God theologian who "dismissed all mysticism as neurotic escape-fantasy." After his NDE, he underwent "a radical change in attitude to life as a whole" and articulated his experience via the language of religious mystics.[22]

Also unsupportive of the cultural source hypothesis is the independence of many accounts. At this point in time, of course, after all the best-selling books and their authors' appearances on Oprah, it is not so easy to find stories altogether uninfluenced by the post-Moody materials. Yet researchers in the 1970s did not have this problem, and the main patterns were established by then. Further, they appear in accounts from earlier times.[23] The point is effectively conceded by those who have sought to account for NDEs chiefly by means of oxygen deprivation, hallucination-inducing medications, the release of endorphins, or temporal lobe dysfunction: these are not appeals to social or cultural circumstances.

(3) The NDE is cross-cultural and cross-temporal.[24] It is not the invention of our time and place. Not only do we have contemporary reports from all around the world,[25] but there are recognizable variants of the NDE in premodern sources. The best guide here is the work of Gregory Shushan.[26] He has shown, by combing through accounts from missionaries, anthropologists, and early explorers, that indigenous peoples in Africa, Oceania, and North America were familiar with the main elements of NDEs—with leaving the body, passing through darkness to light, meeting the dead, receiving information, having their lives examined, and so on. The cultural differences are there, but so too are the parallels. In Shushan's words, the NDE is a "pan-human experience," and "the fundamental interpretation of NDEs appears to be universal . . . *this is what happens when we die.*"[27]

(4) Although the NDE is not the unadulterated product of language and culture, it is hardly independent of them. We perceive, remember, interpret, and narrate all our experiences, including NDEs, in accord with our personal predilections, cultural assumptions, linguistic concepts, and tacit knowledge.[28] We never, wherever we go, leave ourselves behind. If modern Americans—who are familiar with images of trains, cars, and subways entering tunnels—sometimes speak of passing through a dark tunnel, this element is quite rare in hunter-gatherer cultures. In like fashion, while a Buddhist may see a light and call it Buddha Amida, a Christian may see a light and call it Jesus. Similarly, the accounts of NDEs from the Middle Ages, promoting as they do old Catholic ideas about heaven, hell, and purgatory, sound as though they are from the Middle Ages.[29] And NDEs told today by small children, who more often report meeting "a lady" than "an angel," typically sound as though they are from children. Just as water takes the form of the container holding it, so NDE narratives are shaped by those who experience and recount them.

(5) If, before Hufford, the Old Hag was not a recognized syndrome, so similarly with the NDE: the phenomenon was not, before Moody, well known in the modern West. There had been the occasional book as well as short accounts in popular publications such as *Guideposts* magazine, but the NDE did not become a meme until the 1970s and 1980s. It was only then that, for society at large, the trickle of stories became a flood, and those paying attention began to grasp the true scope of the phenomenon (which continues to grow as the science of resuscitation advances; by one recent estimate, twenty-five million people worldwide have had an NDE[30]).

(6) If, in the century before Moody, the vast majority of scientists, doctors, and care-givers knew nothing about NDEs, there was a time when stories of both positive and negative experiences were abroad in the West.[31] As with the Old Hag, so with the NDE: commitment to the materialist view among academic elites obscured knowledge of a real phenomenon. Those with stories to tell generally shrank from doing so, cognizant that the disparaging, all-purpose word "hallucination" would be their reward. Even today many continue to hold their stories close. What is the point of baring your soul if the smug response is, "They've decided it's just oxygen deprivation, right?" or "Must've been a dream"?

(7) The NDE does not signal pathology. The vast majority of reports come from individuals who are psychologically healthy and "do not differ from comparison groups in age, gender, race, religion, religiosity, mental health, intelligence, neuroticism, extroversion, trait and state anxiety, or relevant Rorschach measures."[32] Beyond that, the aftereffects of most NDEs are, on the whole, positive and life-affirming.[33]

* * *

Although NDEs fascinate for any number of reasons, their chief interest for most doubtless lies in the issue of whether they offer support for the possibility of a life after this one and, if so, intimate anything about its initial nature. Unfortunately, as with most subjects that truly matter, the learned do not speak with one voice. So there can be no effortless, we-need-not-think-about-this-for-ourselves appeal to the consensus. What, then, might one hazard to think?

I incline to the less skeptical side. This is partly because I am, on other grounds, not a materialist in any of its iterations, reductive or nonreductive. I regard materialistic monism as "a large-scale culturally constructed error."[34] That the mind is corporeal in origin and destiny is, in my view, neither a necessary inference from the data nor even the best inference: too many facts stand in the way.[35] So the possibility that NDEs are more than brain-based hallucinations, more than the sputtering gasp of dying neurons, does not imperil my worldview.

It is different for medical materialists, for whom the relation of mind to brain is that of flute to music: destroying the former terminates the latter. But if awareness is entirely a function of the brain, then why, when the latter is shutting down or temporarily offline—as during prolonged cardiac arrest—do so many remember experiences that are vivid, coherent, detailed, meaningful, and life-changing?[36] Almost all NDErs "report that, during the experience, their thinking was clearer, faster, and more logical than ever before."[37] Indeed, "the more severe the physiological crisis, the more likely NDErs are to report having experienced clear and complex cognitive and sensory functioning."[38] Why do they not rather experience delirium or mental agitation, dysfunction or confusion? And if survival is everything for evolution, why should gasping, expiring brains feel bliss instead of overwhelming panic? What is the evolutionary gain? Natural selection cares not for us but for our genes, which only the living can pass on. Why, then, would it ease us into death rather than terrify us unrelentingly?

The skeptical literature, to be sure, makes a go of it, giving us explanations that appeal, for example, to the effects of brain anoxia, the release of endogenous opioids, or some other physiological circumstance.[39] The truth, however, is that the neuroscientists failed even vaguely to foresee, before Moody, the NDE or anything like it. The attempted explanations—which fall short in multiple ways[40]—are, in effect, after-the-fact rationalizations in the service of the materialist paradigm. This hardly entails that they are false, but they do amount to a sort of ad hoc apologetics for the unexpected.

My disposition to dispute reductionistic proposals is also consistent with the near Cartesian certainty with which so many experiencers speak. A few years ago, I was on a panel with a philosopher, coauthor of a book that reduces NDEs to materialistic circumstances. After we were done speaking and answering questions, a man from the back of the room walked up and chatted with my fellow panelist. When this audience member later strolled over to me, I asked him about his prolonged conversation with the other speaker. He chuckled and said: "I told him that he doesn't know what he's talking about." The man went on to share with me his own NDE. He emphasized that, having himself gone down the tunnel of light and so on, it was impossible to disbelieve. He said, with perfect assurance, that he knew.

This reminded me of a former colleague who was dying of lung cancer. Between visits to the hospital, he would come into school to see friends. One afternoon, when I was in his office, this professor told me that he had always assumed that "all that stuff about near-death experiences is bunk." Recently, however, during surgery, he had found himself inside a classic NDE. He was no longer, he confessed, a skeptic. Firsthand experience had converted him.

My late friend belongs to a cloud of witnesses. Most NDErs insist that their experiences were not dream-like or confused but real, even hyperreal. A recent survey found that, of 1,122 NDErs, 95.6 percent claimed that their experience was "definitely real." Another 4 percent thought it was "probably real." That adds up to 99.6 percent.[41] That is about as unified as human testimony or opinion can get. Here are some typical sentences:

- "I once more acknowledge the reality of what I experienced and maintain emphatically that I never at any other time in my life experienced the truest reality so clearly, down to the most factual intensification of what was felt."[42]
- "It's reality. I know for myself that I didn't experience no fantasy. There was no so-called dream or nothing. These things really happened to me. It happened. I know. I went through it."[43]
- "Never, ever did I think it might have been a dream. I knew that it was true and real, more real than any other thing I've ever known."[44]
- "This was more real than anything on earth. By comparison, my life in my body had been a dream."
- "It was very real. It's as real as you and I are."[45]
- "I thought to myself for a while, it didn't happen. But then I thought to myself, Boy, you were there and it really did happen."

Such testimony coheres with the fact that, according to standard psychological measures, memories of NDEs are closer to memories of real events than to imagined ones.[46]

Now I am not naive here. I freely concede that subjective conviction can be no more than suggestive. Brains sometimes mislead minds, and we know for a fact that undoubted illusions can be hyper vivid and even seem "more real than real."[47] Beyond that, human beings can, intentionally and unintentionally, manufacture fictions. (A notorious illustration of conscious deceit is the 2011 best seller *The Boy Who Came Back from Heaven*, since pulled from the shelves.) Still, unless there are extenuating circumstances, we normally heed human testimony, especially when the numbers are large; and in the matter to hand, the chief extenuating circumstance is belief in physicalism, according to which consciousness apart from an operational, online brain is impossible. If that belief does not regulate one's thinking, then the abundance of independent, vivid testimony—which includes statements from individuals who changed their minds after going through the experience—nudges one in a certain direction.

This is all the more so as one fails to see why evolution would select for whatever mechanism generates the false sense of an NDE's veracity. What survival advantage follows from that? Failing a decent answer, maybe the statements of those who claim to have seen for themselves should count as much as the conjectures, however learned, of outsiders looking in, especially as the latter so often have heavy personal investment in explaining away the seemingly astounding implications of NDEs. As Emily Kelly has written: "In the absence of any adequate explanatory framework for NDEs, it may be useful . . . to remain open to all interpretations, particularly the one that is compelling to nearly all persons who have experienced an NDE."[48]

* * *

The most intriguing evidence for the extra-subjective nature of NDEs is this. Many claim to have seen, while under anesthesia or otherwise unconscious, and from a point of view outside the body, things that they should not have been able to see. If even a single such claim is true, standard accounts of sense perceptions cannot, to understate the matter, be the whole picture.

Some cases are well-known and appear in the literature again and again. There is the story of the man who, after a massive heart attack, was cyanotic and comatose before surgery. Immediately preceding intubation, a nurse removed his dentures and put them on a crash cart. Regaining consciousness a week later, he said to the nurse, "You know where my dentures are. Yes, you were there when they brought me into the hospital, and you took the dentures out of my mouth and put them on that cart; it had all these bottles on it, and there was a sliding drawer underneath, and you put my teeth there."[49] There is also the story of Maria, who suffered a heart attack while in the hospital. She told her social worker that, during her NDE, she had seen a dark blue tennis shoe on a ledge on the third floor, near a window. The social worker subsequently found the shoe and reported that it could not be seen from inside the hospital.[50] And then there is the story of Pam Reynolds. In order to treat a large brain aneurysm, her doctors induced hypothermic cardiac arrest. They chilled her blood, stopped her heart, then drained the blood from her brain. During repair of the aneurysm, her EEG was flat. Nevertheless, upon awakening she reported a detailed NDE. It included describing the little saw used to cut open her skull and hearing things she should have been unable to hear.[51]

Doubters, always starting from the premise that the idea of a soul or something analogous is no longer credible, have, of course, dissected each of these cases. They are not without useful observations and decent arguments. Once in a while anesthesia does fail to prevent a patient from hearing and recalling things said during surgery. People are not always able to distinguish dream from reality, and minds can indeed construct false memories. The fear of death might help explain why subconscious selves might fashion scenarios that suggest life after death. And stories, based on partial, imperfect memories, can grow in the telling because of our will to believe and our desire to confirm our convictions. Such facts amount to an arsenal with which to shoot down NDEs, including those with purportedly veridical elements.

It strikes me as a bit odd, however, that so many who report NDEs offer details about operating rooms and hospitals. I have undergone surgery several times. I do not recall ever, after waking up, wondering or fantasizing about what might lie on the roof of the hospital, or what the surgical instruments used on me looked like, or who exactly was in the operating theater or what they were wearing. I was instead wholly focused on more pressing matters. Did everything go OK? Can you get me something for the pain? One understands why an anxious, unconscious mind might conjure visions of beloved grandparents in heaven or praying relatives down the hall; but why invent the sorts of existentially unimportant yet vivid details that often show up when NDErs tell their stories? Maybe the answer lies in their perceptual experiences, mysterious as those may be.

One is also impressed by the seeming accuracy in some reports. Pam Reynolds may not have described perfectly the saw used on her, but she was close enough ("like an electric toothbrush"). What explains this? If some imaginations, unlike mine, are disposed to concoct detailed pictures of operating rooms, why do so many reports of NDEs seemingly contain veridical details?[52] One possibility, of course, is that only hits gets reported. If a patient recounts a surgical scene that a doctor or nurse instantly brushes aside because it is wildly off the mark, the fact-drained tale ends there. Still, researchers have asked cardiac patients not reporting an NDE to guess what transpired during CPR, and their answers do not impress.[53] Further, a recent study concluded that, of 287 NDErs who purported observing events that could be objectively confirmed, 280 related nothing unrealistic. Beyond that, 65 reported investigating for themselves and confirming what they had seen.[54] Was every one of them naive, self-deceived, or dishonest?

It is not just that thousands have purported that, during their NDE, they saw things they should not have been able to see. In quite a few instances—one count reckons the number in the literature to be over 300[55]—third-party confirmation has been claimed.[56] This includes confirmation from medical professionals on the scene. Consider these firsthand testimonies:

- These are the words of an ICU doctor: "I operated on a woman under general anesthetic. And when she woke up, she described her operation as if she had been on the ceiling. Not only that, she also described the operation that took place in the next theater, the amputation of a leg. She saw the leg; she saw them put the leg in a yellow bag. She couldn't possibly have invented that and she described it as soon as she woke up. I checked afterwards and the operation had indeed taken place in the next theater. A leg had been amputated at the very same time that she was under anesthetic and thus totally disconnected from the world."[57]
- These are the words of a cardiothoracic surgeon: "He [the patient] talked about the bright light at the end of the tunnel, as I recall, and so on. But the thing that astounded me was that he described that operating room, floating around, and saying, 'I saw you and Dr. Cattaneo standing in the doorway with your arms folded, talking. I saw the . . . I didn't know

where the anesthesiologist was, but he came running back in. And I saw all of these Post-its sitting on this TV screen.' And what those were, were any call I got, the nurse would write down who called and the phone number and stick it on the monitor, and then the next Post-it would stick to that Post-it, and then I'd have a string of Post-its of phone calls I had to make. He described that. I mean, there is no way he could have described that before the operation, because I didn't have any calls, right? . . . He described the scene, things that there is no way he knew. I mean, he didn't wake up in the operating room and see all this stuff."[58]

- These are the words of another cardiologist: "He told me everything that I had said and done, such as checking the pulse, deciding to stop resuscitation, going out of the room, coming back later, looking across at him, going over and rechecking his pulse, and then restarting the resuscitation. He got all the details right, which was impossible because not only had he been in asystole and had no pulse throughout the arrest, but he wasn't even being resuscitated for about 15 minutes afterward. What he told me really freaked me out, and to this day I haven't told anyone because I just can't explain it. . . . I just can't explain it. I don't think about it anymore."[59]

- These are the words of an emergency medicine physician: "In theory, he [a patient who was successfully resuscitated] could have heard what we said aloud and recounted it later, but [he also] visually described the room and the 'dark-haired nurse' in detail and what she did even when she was not talking. This should have been impossible, as he never spontaneously opened his eyes and had no signs of the visual brain centers working. There were approximately 60 staff members or more in the emergency department. Additionally he described in detail what the specific woman did to him. I cannot imagine that random chance would've allowed him to pick her up from a previously known population and then describe in detail what she did."[60]

- These are the words of the neurosurgeon who worked on Pam Reynolds: "There was absolutely no question that Pam Reynolds was clinically dead. Her EEG was completely flat, and her evoked potential too was completely gone. I believe that Pam recalled things that were remarkably accurate. I do not understand from a physiological perspective how that could possibly have happened. I hope not to be arrogant enough to say it can't happen, but from a scientific perspective, there is no acceptable explanation to me. . . . As a neurosurgeon, I have encountered so many things that I didn't have an explanation for. You keep it in the back of your mind and if in your lifetime you come up with another explanation, then you can recall it and say, 'Aha, this is how it works.' In Pam's case, I'm far, far from that."[61]

· These are the words of an orthopedic surgeon: "Her observations of the minutest details of her [cardiac] arrest were things that no one would have known. My mind raced to find a logical scientific explanation for what she was telling me, but I could not. She had not been conscious, her eyes were closed, and she had no logical way of knowing what took place in the OR that day."[62]

· These are the words of a cardiac anesthesiologist: the patient "went on to describe the number of surgeons in the operating theater, where they were positioned, the actions of the nurses, and other events that made it clear he had been observing events from somewhere above us. I could hardly believe what he was saying. Over the course of my twenty-five-year career . . . there had been patients who claimed to see deceased friends during their cardiac arrest, or who saw lights and the end of tunnels, or who claimed to see people made of light, but I chalked that off to some kind of fantasy and referred them to the psychiatrist. . . . But what happened to this man was different. He had accurately described the operating room I was working in with great clarity. He not only showed signs of being alive when his heart and brain were inert but also of being awake."[63]

· These are the words of an inpatient medical director for a hospice center: "I continued my conversation with Ricardo, hoping there was something he would say that would prove his experience. 'Dr. Lerma, I need your help. . . . When I was out of my body and floating up above the trauma room I spotted a 1985 quarter lying on the right-hand corner of the 8-foot-high cardiac monitor. . . . Could you please check for me? It would mean so much.' I was curious and skeptical enough to oblige him, and went to the emergency room with a ladder. I climbed up, with the nurses standing by. They were also curious to know if a patient had really been able to see something while we were bringing him back to life. . . . To our total amazement, there it was, just as he had seen it, and even the year was right: 1985. . . . Still skeptical, I wondered if this man could have put the quarter there, so I checked some of the details, and found there was no way he could have known the quarter was there. It had been years since he had been able to climb a ladder. . . . I could find no connection with anyone who had worked on the newly built trauma rooms."[64]

- These are the words of a psychiatrist on call at an ER, recounting his response after a patient told him what he had been doing down the hall while she was unconscious: "The hair rose on the back of my neck and I felt goose bumps. . . . There was no way Holly could have known that I had spoken with Susan, let alone been familiar with the content of our conversation or the stain on my tie. And yet she did. Every time I tried to focus on what she'd said, I found my thoughts getting muddled. I couldn't deny that she knew the details of my conversation with her roommate. I'd heard it with my own ears; it definitely happened. But I couldn't figure out how she knew them. I told myself that it had to be a lucky guess or some kind of trick."[65]

- Here is one more testimony, this from a critical-care physician and ICU director: "Howard not only remembered the events of his cardiac arrest—what was said, what people were wearing, who was present—but he recounted it in such detail that it was clear he was a witness to his own event, even though he was completely unconscious at the time. I could have rationalized some of his memories away by accepting that perhaps, while unconscious, he was able to hear on some level. . . . But Howard was not only telling me what he *heard* but also what he had *seen* with incredible accuracy. . . . [He said,] 'I felt myself rising up through the ceiling and it was like I was going through the structure of the ceiling. . . . There were individual rooms all around the edge and on some of the beds were these people, except they were not people, exactly. They looked like mannequins and they had IVs hooked up to them but they didn't look real. In the center was an open area that looked like a collection of work stations with computers. . . .' That's when my jaw really dropped. . . . Right above the ICU is a nurse-training center where new hires spend a few days rotating through different scenarios. There are simulated hospital rooms around the perimeter with medical mannequins on some of the beds. In the center there is indeed a collection of workspaces with computers. I was amazed . . ."[66]

I acknowledge that these accounts are anecdotal. This does not, however, leave us free to discount them without compunction. There is often strength in numbers, and if the anecdotes come from on-the-scene experts, who admit to being flummoxed, does this not intimate a genuine anomaly?

Those who believe, because of their worldview, that the testimonies just quoted cannot imply what they seem to imply are like David Hume on miracles: the impossible is impossible, whatever the testimony to the contrary. Such people are immovable objects. What, however, of the rest of us, who are subject to persuasion? How many perplexed testimonials from attending medical professionals do we need before the skeptical dissections begin to feel strained? I am unsure, but maybe we are already there.

* * *

If, like me, one looks upon NDEs as metaphysical insurgents that are consistent with human beings being more than bounded batches of biochemical processes and if, beyond that, one is open-minded about the possibility that such experiences may intimate something about postmortem possibilities, what follows?

In trying to answer this question, I have found professional theologians and biblical scholars of next to no help. Most of them display not even a modicum of curiosity as they continue to write about death and eschatology with nary a word on NDEs.[67] The unstated implication is that such experiences are irrelevant for theology and of no significance for deciding whether there might be something beyond death or what it might look like.

Now this is, I grant, a defensible opinion, but not to defend it is a recipe for irrelevance in the wider world. Near-death experiences have captured the public's imagination. This is manifest from all the best-selling books and from the large number of TV shows, movies, documentaries, websites, and YouTube videos that, in one way or another, deal with the subject. My guess is that most in contemporary America, when they imagine what might lie beyond, now entertain first the standard scenario Moody popularized. That generalization includes many who sit in conservative church pews. To ignore NDEs is, then, to ignore the public. Eschewal of this subject does nothing to diminish the familiar prejudice that, nowadays, Christian theologians are pretty much irrelevant.

Indifference toward NDEs among theological professionals also makes no sense given that NDErs think of their experiences as religious and frequently use the word "God" when retelling their stories. In this connection I can appeal to Jeffrey Long's book *God and the Afterlife*.[68] This volume has its problems, among them its failure to contemplate the various conceptions of "God" embedded in the reports. Nonetheless, Long makes the empirical claim, for which he offers sturdy support, that NDEs are firmly correlated with "increased belief in God." More than that, NDEs are, in his judgment, linked with such belief more than with any other—to use his words—"specific life event."[69] It is dumbfounding that a theologian or pastor would not sit up and take notice at such a verdict. For many, NDEs function just like—or rather are—experiences of profound religious conversion, whose effects can be transformative and lifelong. How can this be of no interest to a theologian or pastor?

Even more disconcerting than those Christian thinkers who ignore NDEs are those who debunk them. John Haldane and Michael Marsh have attempted to undercut the phenomenon on scientific grounds, imagining this to be a victory for theology, because for them the doctrine of the resurrection invalidates the dualistic anthropology of NDEs.[70] They know not what they do.

If all NDEs turn out to be wholly endogenous, if they are, without remainder, brain-bred hallucinations, the consequences are more than dispiriting. We would be forced to conclude that a widespread, cross-cultural human experience, one that commonly moves people to use the word "God" and regularly prods them to become more loving and less selfish,[71] an experience that far more often than not feels wholly real and indeed self-authenticating, an experience that even children only two or three years old have reported, is, at bottom, illusory. And if the NDE is illusory, nothing but a vacuous cerebral dream, a meaningful but deceptive phantom, then religious experience and testimony, whether past or present, amount to little or nothing. The only qualified interpreters of all religious experience would inescapably be the reductionistic neuroscientists, who can explain to us why what we think happened did not really happen.

This would be, to my mind, the final victory of secularism, and I do not understand a theist who opines otherwise. Is the created world really this deceptive? Are the mind and its brain truly this untrustworthy? Are NDEs, despite the overwhelming firsthand testimony to the contrary, hallucinations through and through, ontologically akin to childhood dreams of monsters? In this matter I side not with Haldane and Marsh but rather sympathize with Jerry Walls, who has asked: "Why would God design us in such a way that many people would form strong convictions that they had encountered him, had experienced his love and the like, when in fact they had not really done so? Would the positive psychological benefits outweigh the apparent deception required to achieve this? I am inclined to think they would not, so I judge it unlikely that God would deceive us in this fashion."[72]

We should consider the possibility that the end may turn out to be like the beginning. There was a time when theologians, Bible in hand, were the sole arbiters of knowledge regarding the creation of the world, human origins, and archaic history. That has changed radically since the nineteenth century. When looking into the distant past, theologians have learned that they cannot ignore what cosmologists, geologists, anthropologists, and ancient historians have uncovered. To stick with the Bible alone would be irrational. What if, then, we are beginning to learn some truly new things about the process of death? And what if, at some point, the evidence that NDEs offer a glimpse into the earliest stages of or transition to a postmortem existence becomes compelling? In such a situation, the *sola scriptura* theologian who talks about death without taking into account new knowledge would be an obscurantist.

* * *

If we do not ignore or dismiss NDEs, we might contemplate any number of things, some quite far-reaching. They seem to suggest, against a number of influential theologians and biblical scholars, the existence of something like a traditional soul. Additionally, NDEs with confirmed observations speak against scientific materialism, which rules so much of today's academy (and has helped underwrite the soulless economic materialism that afflicts our world). Such NDEs should also help us to keep open minds about extraordinary narratives in general. If one species of out-of-the-ordinary experiences can contain veridical elements, perhaps the same is true of other species.

Although these are all very large and important matters, I here leave them aside. I rather wish to raise questions about three other matters. Each has pastoral implications. The first question is this. Why do some but not all who approach the brink of death report NDEs?

Four decades ago, as I noted in a previous chapter, a drunk driver sped through a red light and destroyed my car. The point of impact was the driver's door. Further details are irrelevant, except that I was unconscious for a time before an ambulance arrived on the scene, and throughout the evening awareness came and went.

I did not, despite nearly dying, have an NDE. I wish I had, so that I could supplement my secondhand knowledge with firsthand knowledge. The periods between wakefulness were, however, blanks. Or that at least is what I recall: absolutely nothing. The same appears to be true for most who have found themselves near death's door. Those who study such things estimate that 15–20 percent of those who were unconscious and near death can recollect some portion of an NDE.[73] This means 80–85 percent cannot. How many of the latter, if familiar with the contemporary lore of NDEs, feel disappointment (as did I), or wonder whether something is wrong with them?

In thinking through this issue, two possibilities present themselves. Both could be part of the truth. One option is that many, most, or all who fail to recall an NDE do so because they have nothing to remember. That is, when they were unconscious, they were in an abyss of oblivion. Maybe this is because they were, despite dire straits or compromised brains, further from death than those who report NDEs.

I am, however, more attracted to another possibility.

We all, the experts tell us, dream every night. Yet some are better at recalling their dreams than are others. A friend once told me that, with a single exception, he has never, over the course of a lifetime, remembered any of his dreams. By contrast, it is a rare morning when I fail to recollect a dream or some part of it. Although the explanation for such disparity is unknown to me, the fact is unsurprising. Everything human spans a spectrum. Some are very tall, some very short, and the rest fill up the spaces in between. Some learn to speak exceptionally early, some learn to speak exceptionally late, and the rest fill up the spaces in between. And some remember their dreams nearly always, others hardly ever, and the rest fill up the spaces in between.

Could it not be similar with memories of NDEs?[74] This is not to imply that the NDE is a dream. My point is instead this. To narrate an NDE is to remember it, and perhaps, just as the ability to recall dreams differs (for whatever reason) from person to person, so the ability to recall NDEs may differ (for whatever reason) from person to person or (for whatever reason) from situation to situation. Sam Parnia has suggested that, at least with regard to cardiac patients, those with recall have "suffered less damage [than others] to their brains and specifically to the memory circuits in the days and weeks after the cardiac arrest," whereas those without recall have had their memories "wiped away by the extensive postresuscitation inflammation and damage that occur in the brain after a cardiac arrest."[75]

Whatever the physiological explanation, it is plausible that many who have had NDEs remember them partially or not at all, that they are victims of some sort of amnesia. Reports rarely if ever include all the features listed at the beginning of this chapter. Accounts typically contain only some elements, often just two or three. Again, then, we have a spectrum. One way to account for it is to posit that people with a similar experience have dissimilar success recalling it.[76] This accords with the following comments from NDErs:

- "I have no doubt that there was more to my experience than I can remember."[77]
- "I cannot remember much about the return."[78]
- "I saw fragmented things of other people and events. But, those things were taken from me once I found myself in the room."[79]
- "That's all I can really remember."[80]
- "He (the god of death) asked me to extend my hand. I don't remember whether he gave me something or not."[81]
- "I remember small bits of it now, but barely anything."[82]
- "I heard a voice say, 'Go back!' . . . [After that] I don't remember anything . . . the blackness or nothing. I only remember waking up in intensive care two days later."[83]

These sentences imply or state that something happened that a subject cannot remember. In other words, they confess or betray limited recall.

If the memory of an NDE can, like other memories, be partial and imperfect, it can also lie wholly dormant. There are reports of people recounting an NDE upon awakening and then later forgetting it.[84] In addition, while up to 90 percent remember their NDE as soon as they stir from apparent insentience, others do not.[85] Of the latter, the time between event and memory varies considerably. It can be a month, more than a month but less than a year, more than a year but less than a decade, or more than a decade. The memory of an NDE—which sometimes appears not all at once but in stages—can, then, exist without being accessed, like the grooves in a record: the latter are only silent potential until a needle touches them to make music. If, further, some NDEs stay submerged for years, it stands to reason that others might never surface at all. Having an NDE and remembering it are, clearly, two different things. The memory switch can be in the off position.

Some data indicate that those who remember an NDE directly after an operation have better memories for events before and after surgery than those not reporting an NDE.[86] This matters because surgery or extreme trauma is often accompanied by a lack of recall for circumstances immediately preceding and following such trauma or surgery; and if those with no NDE to report tend not to recall other things, if the blank where the NDE would go belongs to a larger blank on either side of it, this is one more reason for supposing that a lack of memory is not proof that nothing happened.[87]

* * *

If some may be puzzled because they did not, when death was nigh, have an NDE, others may wish that they had never had one. This is because the good NDE has an unwelcome relative, the distressing NDE. Whereas most NDEs are positive, others—less than or much less than 20 percent, depending on the survey[88]—leave people most miserable. These harrowing experiences seem to be, for the most part, of three sorts.[89] One resembles the more common NDE, except that what enthralls and pleases most leaves others distraught: similar stimuli evoke dissimilar emotional responses. Some are, for instance, alarmed to feel unglued to the body, or anxious to be moving through darkness toward a bright light, or upset to undergo a life review.

The second sort of negative NDE is disorientation in a void. One woman reported: "I found myself hurtling toward the final torment: I was to be suspended in a total vacuum with nothing to see or do for eternity."[90] Another elaborated more fully: "As the hours went on with absolutely no sensation, there was no pain, but there was no hot, no cold, no light, no taste, no smell, no sensation whatsoever. . . . It became horrific, as time goes on when you have no feeling, no sensation, no sense of light. I started to panic and struggle and pray."[91]

The third—and by far least common—type of frightening NDE issues in narratives that sound like the traditional hells of the world's major religions. Here is an instance: "I heard cries, wails, moans, and the gnashing of teeth. I saw these beings that resembled humans, with the shape of a head and body. But they were ugly and grotesque. . . . They were frightening and sounded like they were tormented, in agony."[92]

What should we make of such dislocating experiences (which, unlike convivial NDEs, do not, for obvious reason, diminish the fear of death)? One might urge, as have a few, that they are consistent with and offer support for the traditional Christian idea of hell.[93] Examination of the reports, however, eviscerates that idea. No correlation obtains between religious faith of any variety and whether one has a positive or negative NDE. Indeed, we know of no clear connection with any specific character trait. Individuals of deservedly ill repute have reported blissful NDEs while seemingly good and decent citizens have narrated inverted or hellish NDEs. The straightforward dualism that turns heaven into the destination of all the faithful and hell into the locale for all the impious does not line up with the phenomenology of NDEs.

Such clear-cut dualism also cannot explain why many of the distressing experiences are episodes within larger, otherwise positive experiences. People can move from a place or state of misery to one of bliss or—far less frequently— from a place or state of bliss to one of misery. Here is one account:

> What I interpret as the moment of death was so traumatic that I am still, in my early fifties [decades later], unable to remember it without trauma. My mind simply will not allow itself to bring back what came immediately after this moment of death. I know it was darkness because I recall what I can only describe as a "porthole of vision" closing. When this porthole closed, the feeling I had was of being trapped in a dark well. Because this feeling was so horrible, my whole being tells me that the darkness was horrible, too. I know that when I went to the light, I had no memory or feelings of the trauma. . . . That light was . . . was a warm, inviting, loving intelligence. The desire to go forward to meet the source of the light was so compelling that I cannot recall it without being moved to tears, and being consumed by a terrible loss because I was not allowed to go there.[94]

These words recall those medieval sources in which a seer reports on both heaven and hell.[95]

Our first response to a negative NDE should be, in my view, sympathetic understanding. Those who recount such an episode should receive the informed response that they are not alone, that other good people have had the experience and been puzzled and traumatized by it, that it says nothing about one's moral or spiritual condition. While I would not dissuade anyone from construing a negative NDE as motivation for personal reformation—this is a common response, and repentance is never a bad idea—it seems prudent to regard the disturbing NDE as akin to other experiences of evil, such as those documented in chapter 3. Evil picks its targets indiscriminately. This includes disturbing NDEs. Such upsetting experiences belong to "the mystery of iniquity" (2 Thess. 2:7). Further inferences are unwarranted.

* * *

The third issue to which I wish to call attention is the most difficult of all. Despite the similarities between so many stories, including similarities that traverse times and cultures, the differences remain. What accounts for them? What explains all the variety?

Those who deny that NDEs ever intersect with a transcendent realm have it easy here. They can avow that the discrepancies reflect the lack of objective referents. Why do NDErs who claim to have met Jesus give different descriptions of him?[96] Because, the skeptics are confident, he was nothing but the figment of their religiously imprinted imaginations.

This is not the only possibility. Narratives of NDEs inevitably reflect the culturally derived ideas of experiencers.[97] Furthermore, we typically relate and revise (consciously and unconsciously) our stories—and reports of NDEs are stories—toward this or that end: consolation, encouragement, warning, entertainment, instruction. NDEs additionally encode the expectations and agendas of the interviewers and those who write them up. The verbal reports are, in brief, constructed from beginning to end, and they cannot be casually equated with the experiences behind them.

It is helpful here to recall how ordinary visual perception seems to work. Seeing an object is the outcome of a complex process in which we are not passive but active. In the words of one expert on cognitive neuroscience,

The brain is located inside a bony skull. All it receives are ambiguous and noisy sensory signals that are only indirectly related to objects in the world. Perception must therefore be a process of inference, in which indeterminate sensory signals are combined with prior expectations or "beliefs" about the way the world is, to form the brain's optimal hypotheses of the causes of these sensory signals—of coffee cups, computers and clouds. What we see is the brain's "best guess" of what's out there. . . . Perception is a controlled hallucination, in which the brain's hypotheses are continually reined in by sensory signals arriving from the world and the body.[98]

In other words, and as Kelly Bulkeley puts it: "C[ognitive] N[euroscience] finds an unexpected harmony with postmodern philosophy from Nietzsche onward—reality is not a given but is actively created by the human psyche."[99] If this is true of visual perception, may it not also be true of perception during NDEs, however managed?

We should further not forget that NDErs behold what they have not beheld before. Imagine three individuals from societies wholly ignorant of American football. If one were to put them in the stands to watch the Pittsburgh Steelers play the Baltimore Ravens for five minutes and then ask them what they had seen, the result would not be three identical narratives. The reports might in fact barely overlap. Without prior knowledge and experience of the game, and without words such as "quarterback," "sideline," "goalpost," and "football," our three observers would have difficulty relating their experiences. They might at best be able to draw some analogies with their own worlds: "It was like this," or "It was a bit like that."

Near-death experiencers are perhaps in a similar position to that of my hypothetical spectators. The reality they purport to enter is radically different because it is outside their usual space-time orientation. Person after person accordingly confesses that words fail.[100] These remarks are typical:

- "There really are no words. . . . I cannot describe it. You could not compare it to anything here. The terms I'm using to describe it are so far from the thing, but it's the best I can do."[101]
- "I regret that words can't do my experience justice. I must admit that human language is woefully inadequate for conveying the full extent,

the depth, and the other dimension I've seen. In fact, no pen can describe what I went through."[102]

· "You know, I've tried to sketch this, but it's too difficult. I know I've never seen anything like it."[103]

· "Our vocabulary is just not rich enough to describe the experience in a way that is understandable. Perhaps this is why Jesus often spoke in parables."[104]

· "It's impossible to describe. It truly can't be put into words. It's the hardest thing to describe to someone."[105]

· "Try to draw an odor using crayons. You can't even begin to try, no matter how many crayons you have in your box. That's what it's like describing NDEs with words."

· "The memories when coming back into my body flattened, simplified, and became symbols of what really happened. I believe this flattening happens simply because the human brain can't understand a world so much more complex and possibly so alien."

I am reminded of Paul, who reported hearing, when in the third heaven, "words that cannot be put into words" (*arrhēta rhēmata*; 2 Cor. 12:4). Language and concepts fitted for our world were not designed to map other worlds. Given this, even those who believe that NDEs are not wholly subjective cannot expect picture-perfect representations.

Let me try another analogy. Aristotle wrote that sometimes, when people dream, they think "it is lightening and thundering, when there are only faint echoes in their ears, and that they are enjoying honey when only a drop of phlegm is slipping down (their throats), and that they are walking through fire and are tremendously hot, when there is only a slight heating about certain parts (of the body); but the true state of affairs becomes obvious when they wake up."[106] These dreams are literally false. There is no thunder. There is no honey. There is no fire. Yet the dream machine is, in each case, responding to incoming stimuli. It is not imagining *ex nihilo*. The dreams do, moreover, correlate in a loose sense with those stimuli. There is sound, there is liquid in the throat, and some part of the body is hot.

Perhaps reports of NDEs are a bit like this. Perhaps, just as the imaginative mind of Aristotle's sleeper turns what it imperfectly perceives into fictitious dreams, so the resourceful NDEr translates exotic perceptions into conventional, inadequate speech. Gregory Shushan, attempting to account for the cross-cultural differences in NDE reports, has remarked: "There is no reason to believe that disembodied individuals would cease to process their experiences in their own idiosyncratic modes, including the use of personal and cultural memory, imagination, and visual metaphor."[107]

Consider these sentences, all from NDErs, and all about their "return":

- "I tried to climb over the fence but this man stopped me and said that I wasn't to come yet and he sent me back down the tunnel and I was in the hospital again."[108]
- "I saw a frame—it looked like a doorframe. . . . It felt that if I went beyond that frame, I could not come back again."[109]
- "Each time I tried to get on the highway the stars would block my way. I just stood there not knowing what to do. After a while the highway and stars disappeared. I woke up and found myself in a hospital bed."[110]
- "I could either enter the gate or return to the lifeless body, which I immediately sensed below me. I had the impression that entry through this gate meant definitive physical death."[111]
- "I could see a gray mist. . . . I felt certain that I was going through that mist. It was such a wonderful, joyous feeling; there are just no words in human language to describe it. Yet it wasn't my time to go through the mist."[112]
- "I've almost gotten across . . . a still stream of water . . . but they seem to push me back and tell me it's not my time."[113]
- "Someone told me that if I banked, as an airplane would bank, to the right and didn't stay right over that [barbed-wire] fence, I'd be gone. I wouldn't come back."
- "There was a young woman standing behind a traditional wooden five-barred gate. . . . She kept telling me that I had to go back, that it was too soon for me to be there and that there were things I had to do still in my life."[114]

These descriptions, while quite varied, are plausibly deciphered as different mythologizations of similar experiences.

What holds for one element in NDEs—the border, the barrier, the wall, the limit—likely holds for the whole. One NDEr observed: "I knew that the clothes [my] father wore were assumed because they were familiar to me, so that I might feel no strangeness in seeing him, and that, to some lesser extent, his appearance was assumed also."[115] Bruce Greyson is of the opinion that the "variability in reported features reflects not the experience itself but rather the experiencers' ability to process and express an event that is largely ineffable and must be 'inevitably cast in the images, concepts and symbols available to the individual.'"[116] Jonathan Edwards, speaking of religious experience in general, already understood that preconceptions shape "persons' notions of . . . their own experiences," so that the latter are "insensibly strained" by what is brought to them.[117]

* * *

It is regrettable that, almost half a century after Moody, many medical doctors and academics, including theologians, still know little about NDEs. Perhaps their disinterest is partly rooted in a sort of snobbery: if the public is keenly interested, then the matter cannot be serious. Yet whatever the source of their apathy, and whether or not one thinks that NDEs undercut some of the dictates of ordinary science, they have become the object of serious analysis. In the words of Christof Koch, one of the world's leading authorities on the brain and consciousness, investigation of NDEs is "a field of empirical study."[118] Anyone who doubts this should go to ScienceDirect.com and enter "Near-Death Experience." Thousands of entries—book chapters, research articles, literature reviews—will come up. The authors include neuroscientists, medical researchers, social scientists, and psychologists. To be unaware of what they have been and are up to is to be ignorant of something not only inherently fascinating but also, from multiple points of view, important and even, potentially, revolutionary.

* * *

Theologian Paul Fiddes has contended that to be dead is to cease to be. The Christian's only hope is resurrection, for "the witness of scripture, of experience, of feeling, of biology, and of the great tragedies is that there is no thread of survival, no lifeline through death."[119] Fiddes is right about mainstream biology. Otherwise his assertion is curious. The New Testament at points clearly assumes continuance after death,[120] and Christian theology is grounded not in the great tragedies but in the canonical story of Jesus, which ends not in miserable ruin but in return from the dead. Matthew's Gospel is not King Lear.

As for feeling and experience, these last two chapters have demonstrated that many feel sure, because of what they have witnessed firsthand, that death is not the end. Neath-death experiences are, for the vast majority of those who report them, not akin to dreams, nor do they feel like hallucinations. They are rather recalled as real, and they produce or reinforce the conviction that death does not terminate our stories or put them on hold. It is much the same with the many who see, hear, or feel the presence of a dead loved one: their experience is that death does not snuff out personal identity. In short, it is empirically false that all experience and feeling support Fiddes's generalization about death. Much speaks directly, firmly against it.

Death is not one thing, and theology should not seek to reduce it to one thing. It is rather, like life, many different things. Death can be painful or it can be pain free. It can be a martyrdom embraced or an execution fought. It can, when the suffering of old age has become horrific, bring relief to all concerned, just as it can, when a young life is senselessly lost, cause unrelieved misery. It can be entered into with faith and hope, or it can be resisted with doubt and anxiety. It can, furthermore, come without any of the ELEs introduced in the last two chapters. Yet it can equally come with one or more of them. So a theological imagination that ponders death while overlooking such experiences and their meaningful impact fails to do justice to the real world.

8

Rational Analysis

"We can understand only in the modes of understanding that we have, and these are both contingent and drastically limited. . . . Today we can pick up radio signals from distant galaxies, signals that were 'there' throughout the whole of human history. Goodness only knows what else is surrounding us without our having any notion of its existence."

—*Bryan Magee*[1]

"We are desperate to understand the world; we struggle from the moment of birth to understand the world—but it is beyond our capacity. We thus sign on to simplifications of the world that give us the illusion of understanding. Experts are not less inclined to sign on to these simplistic explanations than outsiders; they are more inclined to sign on to them."

—*Bill James*[2]

"The materialists' belief—that the entire universe, as it exists independently of the human mind, consists solely of physical entities—entails a wild leap of anthropocentric faith. They are avowing that reality, as it exists independently of human concepts, fits neatly within the human conceptual construct of 'physical,' as we define this term in the twenty-first century."

—*B. Alan Wallace*[3]

Skepticism about religious beliefs and experiences is, for many today, an integral part of what it means to be educated. In the words of Edward

Said, "the true intellectual is a secular being."[4] For those so minded, all religious experience, like every alleged miracle, can be (in principle) explained without appeal to extra-mundane realities. On their view, up-to-date analysis inevitably reveals that the out of the ordinary is always the ordinary in disguise.

This book is not for them. It rather addresses those who are, because of their worldview, open-minded about its topics, or at least half open-minded. Doubts, nevertheless, assail us all. The pronouncements of skeptics inexorably give the rest of us pause. How can we trust reports of private experiences? Have not the neuroscientists discovered why we sometimes perceive what is not there? Does not new knowledge demand, as a matter of course, that we disbelieve all extraordinary claims? I would like, in this chapter, briefly to address these questions. For all but devout ostriches, they are unavoidable in our current cultural moment.

* * *

I begin with the problem of testimony. It is natural to have second thoughts when someone avows, however sincerely, "I saw an angel," or "My dead husband just visited me," or "Last night I felt a horrible evil force." People hallucinate, and they deploy religious ideas to transform indefinite stimuli into definite, concrete events. Wittingly and unwittingly, moreover, they retrospectively embellish and reshape malleable memories in order to tell themselves and others better, more meaningful stories. Why, then, should we think them reliable?

In deference to the inauspicious facts, I have, throughout this book, recurrently confessed that I cannot vouch for the veracity of this or that particular story. This limitation, however, does not strand us in a dead end. While a single case, standing alone, may amount to little,[5] a claim that recurs again and again is different; and recurring claims are what this book is all about. My major inferences and suggestions do not depend upon the accuracy of any one report or reporter. Whether discussing NDEs, visions of angels, experiences of transcendent love, or enigmatic encounters with stifling evil, I have focused on patterns that emerge when one compares story with story.

My conviction is this. If enough people independently report the same sort of experience, that is reason to take note. Similar firsthand accounts suggest similar real events. The issue of what accounts for those events may remain in the air, yet if patterns exist, they constitute data.

My thoughts here are similar to those of William James, who wrote the following regarding his investigation of anomalous claims:

> I am . . . constantly baffled as to what to think of this or that particular story, for the sources of error in any one observation are seldom fully knowable. But weak sticks make strong bundles; and when the stories fall into consistent sorts that point each in a definite direction, one gets a sense of being in the presence of genuinely natural types of phenomena. . . . I think differently of the whole type, taken collectively, from the way in which I may think of the single instance.[6]

While these words make sense to me, one often runs across the warning that we must be wary of anecdotal evidence. Yet we do not ordinarily reject a claim because it is anecdotal. We usually reject a claim because it deviates from our general sense of what goes on in the world. It takes only a little evidence of any kind to persuade us of X if X fits snugly within our worldview. If, however, X does not so fit, if it exceeds the bounds of what we deem possible, maybe no amount of testimony will persuade us.[7] Already formed convictions constitute the eye of the beholder, and such convictions are exceedingly hard to budge. A worldview, once assimilated, is of such weight that it usually stays put.

Beyond that, even lab reports are, from one point of view, anecdotal testimony.[8] They become more only when others repeat an experiment. It is not wholly different with narratives of religious experience. When someone says, "This happened to me," we cannot determine the truth of the matter by retrieving for analysis the original experience. We can, however, check a story's plausibility by comparing it with other stories. And the more parallels, the greater the plausibility. This is because, to reiterate, if many report much the same thing, then perhaps they have experienced much the same thing. In such a case, it is the pattern that becomes the evidence and the object of inquiry.

* * *

While the imperfections of human testimony are not an insuperable obstacle to gathering data, dogmatic secularism poses the problem of how to interpret that data. Its baleful shadow falls over a book such as this, which not only calls attention to certain subjectively real phenomena but also declines to brand them as objectively unreal through and through. Frequently herein I have entertained the possibility that some experiences gesture beyond themselves, to realms or realities that transcend common scientific knowledge. I have even at times spoken of God.

Many in our time and place would regard my ontological stance as atavistic, as a remnant of a defunct age, when religious ideas were not passé. They think of themselves as living on the near side of the great divide that marks the transition from the enchanted world of the past to the disenchanted world of the present. They firmly believe that, outside of human fancy, there are no transcendent, non-physical objects, forces, or beings. They may even reckon it a badge of honor to defend this doctrinal conviction over against what they suppose to be unschooled superstition.

Science, according to many of these naysayers, has figured out, or is in the process of figuring out, the biological mechanisms that trigger and shape religious experiences: the latter are artifacts of brain function or dysfunction. Demoting the transcendent to the mundane, they decode religious perceptions by means of non-religious categories, as in this stunning sentence: "the God-concept is a form of involuntary mentation produced by electrical activity in the temporal lobe, increased theta activity in the cortex, secretion of endogenous opiates and release of the 'love' hormone oxytocin."[9]

Some, moreover, do not mourn what they take to be the victory of science over religion. They rather revel in it. I recall the hullabaloo that surrounded Michael Persinger's claims about the so-called God helmet. This device, when placed over the head, supposedly caused a subject to sense unseen presences and enjoy mystical experiences. Aside from the truth of this claim—there are problems[10]—I note only that many in the media were enthusiastic, as was the atheist Persinger. The supposed demonstration that electromagnetic currents could induce religious states was not just news but good news. Our sense of God, some journalists informed us, is merely the side effect of electricity unsettling our temporal lobes.

The excitement accompanying multiple reports about the God helmet also displayed itself when, a few years later, a team of neuroscientists announced that they had created, through electrical stimulation of a woman's left temporoparietal junction, the illusion of sensing another person.[11] Their work received global attention, and again some reporters eagerly informed us that felt presences reside solely within our skulls. The implication was clear. When people report sensing God or a dead loved one, it is a cognitive lapse: their brains have tricked them into detecting what is not there.

We should not be naive. What gets reported is a function of interest, and public pronouncements about what neuroscience has established when it comes to religion often have a sharp ideological edge.[12] Some partisans want to ensure that nothing invades the self-contained causal nexus they project upon everything. These truth enforcers are as driven to explain away the sorts of experiences that fill this volume as this writer is motivated to do the opposite.

The everything-is-in-the-brain thesis is not, one should note, a recent idea. It goes back to the old materialists, who triumphantly hailed post-Newtonian science as the slayer of God and souls.[13] Julien Offray de la Mettrie wrote in 1748: "Since all the faculties of the soul depend to such a degree on the proper organization of brain and of the whole body, [so] that apparently they are nothing but this organization itself, the soul is clearly an enlightened machine!"[14] A few years later, Baron von Holbach expressed himself similarly: "All the intellectual faculties—that is to say, all the modes of action attributed to the soul, may be reduced to the modifications, to the qualities, to the modes of existence, to the changes produced by the motion of the brain; which is visibly in man the seat of feeling, the principle of all actions."[15] While some things are new under the sun, brain-centered materialism is not.[16]

* * *

In observing all this, I do not depreciate science. It would be imbecilic to subtract one jot or tittle from its astonishing contributions to knowledge. My bookshelves proudly hold numerous volumes on the brain, on evolutionary biology, on quantum physics, and on any number of additional scientific subjects. This is because I regard what many scientists, including neuroscientists, have to teach us as not just intrinsically fascinating but inordinately important for understanding ourselves.

We should not, however, equate science with scientism, with the rigid dogma that modern science potentially answers all important questions.[17] We should equally distinguish neuroscience from neuroscientism, the latter being the colonizing ideology that strives to explain almost everything about us, including our religious beliefs and experiences, exclusively in terms of the stuff in the skull.[18]

Despite prominent proponents of this totalizing ontology, it is not self-evident that brain events determine rather than mediate mental events. These are the words of Christof Koch, who has spent a storied career attempting to ascertain the neural correlates of consciousness:

> I used to be a proponent of the idea of consciousness emerging out of complex nervous networks. . . . But over the years, my thinking has changed. Subjectivity is too radically different from anything physical for it to be an emergent property phenomenon. . . . The phenomenal hails from a different kingdom than the physical and is subject to different laws. I see no way for the divide between unconscious and conscious creatures to be bridged by more neurons. . . . I believe that consciousness is a fundamental, an elementary, property of living matter. It can't be derived from anything else; it is a simple substance, in Leibniz's words.[19]

According to David Presti, who teaches neurobiology at the University of California, Berkeley, "exactly how mind is related to body and brain physiology remains a deep mystery," and "we know neither the necessary nor sufficient conditions for mind and conscious awareness to manifest in matter, in life, in nervous systems."[20] More than this, Presti believes that neuroscientists need "an expanded hypothesis," one that recognizes that "the brain/body allows for information from a novel transpersonal or transcendental domain to enter one's experience, something beyond the already known sensory mechanisms."[21] He is not the only neuroscientist to defend such a thought.[22]

* * *

As for the rest of us, who are not experts, modesty becomes us. Nonetheless, anybody can fathom certain observations.

Just as contemporary scientists know more than their predecessors knew, so too will future scientists know more than those alive today. "Science," in Bruce Greyson's words, "by its very nature is always a work in progress. Each generation of scientists looks back on the models of previous generations with amusement at their naivete. Why then should we expect any of our current scientific views of how the brain works to stand up to the scrutiny of future generations?"[23]

Current knowledge is not all-inclusive, and there is no supertheory of everything. Since, furthermore, we cannot, given our point on the timeline, measure the scope of present-day ignorance against future discoveries, that ignorance is necessarily indefinite. There may well then be, to use Donald Rumsfeld's famed phrase, not just "known unknowns" but "unknown unknowns." If so, there can be no know-it-alls.

We have no cause to imagine, aside from the conceit that our moment in history is supreme, that contemporary scientists have finally ascertained the big picture and need but work out a few more details. One recalls those late nineteenth-century scientists who thought they were about to cross the finish line in the race to explicate everything and then learned, from relativity theory and quantum mechanics, that they were still in the starting blocks, and not even on the right track. Given that past scientific revolutions have been truly revolutionary, perhaps modesty becomes everyone.

More directly to the point, however: even if all conscious experiences, including all religious experiences, have neural correlates,[24] the issue of causation is not thereby settled. It is true that much popular neuroscience, in this age of materialism, instinctively jumps from correlation to cause.[25] Yet brain states do not, all by themselves, explain even everyday perceptions. Why is the reader of this paragraph having certain thoughts? A full explanation would need to take into account the words on this page as well as the intentions miraculously encoded in them, all facts beyond the brain; and one cannot determine whether there is something beyond the brain—printed words in this case—by looking inside the brain. Sam Parnia has observed:

> All human experiences, irrespective of whether they occur in response to a real event or an imagined event . . . are mediated by a series of different neurotransmitters and modulators (e.g., hormones and neuropeptides) in multiple brain regions. Thus, the discovery of the circuitry that modulates a specific human experience, such as love, does not prove or disprove the reality of the experience. When the circuits involved with a specific experience, such as love, are activated in response to a real event (e.g., when seeing a loved one) or an illusory or hallucinatory event . . . the same experience will likely arise, as the neuromodulators involved are the same.

Consequently, there are no specific neuromodulators that can distinguish between experiences arising in response to a real or unreal event.[26]

To be sure, and as Parnia notes, subjective perceptions can arise without external input, as when we hallucinate; and the reductionist who downgrades all religious experiences to cerebral circumstances alone will contend that, in this respect, such experiences are like hallucinations: no outer stimulus energizes them. But how does one reach this conclusion without presupposing it?[27]

Perhaps an analogy will help. On the assumption that free will is not "a benign user illusion" (Daniel Dennett) but instead a power we sometimes exercise,[28] the fact remains utterly mystifying. Certainly no neuroscientist has found the will. (Benjamin Libet, whose pioneering experiments birthed the modern neuroscience of volition, found himself theorizing, at the end of his career, that the will is a mental field not delimited by known physical law.[29]) And as with the will, so with God or transcendent forces possibly affecting the brain: no one has found them. Yet if immaterial or extraordinarily subtle powers exist, they are, by definition, immaterial or extraordinarily subtle and so, perhaps for that reason, beyond current scientific detection.

One may depict ordinary perception along these lines:

External sources
↓
Pre-conscious perception, selection, and analysis
↓
Conscious awareness and evaluation
↓
Recall and interpretation

My view is simply that some external sources do not belong to the consensual material world, and that the ordinary senses—sight, hearing, taste, smell, touch—are not the only portals to what lies beyond.

* * *

One objection to this proposal is that it is otiose. Neuroscientists report being able, through electrical stimulation, to cause individuals to feel euphoric, to sense presences, and to think that they are out of their bodies. Given this, may one not safely infer that religious experiences are wholly byproducts of cerebral activity, of neuronal firing or misfiring?

There are at least two problems here. The first is theoretical. To show that X causes Z is not to establish that X alone causes Z. Perhaps Y also causes Z. That one can make people sick by giving them a pill does not mean that other things do not make them sick. That unemployment can cause depression does not entail that other circumstances do not. And that an artificial electromagnetic field activates some part of the brain hardly requires that no other force or condition ever activates it. If, then, an electrode can arouse a sense of presence, why could some supra-empirical force—a real but invisible presence—not do the same? One could, if so disposed, even regard the electrical intrusion as a sort of artificial counterfeit of divine activity. Experience of virtual reality does not mean there is no reality.

The other problem is evidential. The hard-nosed physicalist has to deny that people ever know what is going to happen before it does (precognition), deny that they ever know what someone else is silently thinking (telepathy), and deny that they ever see or sense what is happening from afar (clairvoyance).[30] These rogue phenomena—and there are more[31]—are not at home within orthodox materialism. Yet they are, or so it appears to many of us, well-established verities.[32]

Those who agree will judge current materialism to be inadequate to the facts. Those who disagree must, in order to save their worldview, insist that the discordant facts are not facts. In other words, they can continue in their materialism and preserve "ontological safety"[33] only by discounting the solid evidence that belies their beliefs. But if what one concludes at the end inexorably follows from what one excludes at the beginning, then one is not arguing but simply taking sides. A remark of John Henry Newman comes to mind: "Anything will become plausible, if you read all that can be said in its favor, and exclude all that can be said against it."[34]

* * *

If, however, one doubts that minds are wholly reducible to brains, how do we explain the intimate correlations between the two? If our heads do not create consciousness *ex nihilo*, why do disease, alcohol, drugs, and old age so affect our mental capabilities, and how is it that transcranial magnetic stimulation alters subjective experience? Is there, given the facts, a credible alternative to physicalism?

I suspect that the nature of the mind may be beyond our comprehension, not just now but forever: beholding ourselves we will always be children in wandering mazes lost. Nonetheless we must try.[35]

In his Ingersoll lecture on the subject of immortality, William James defended, against the materialism of his day, with its denial of life after death, a proposal that remains credible.[36] He granted that "our soul's life" is "in literal strictness the function of a brain that perishes." He went on, however, to distinguish between two types of function.[37] The first he called "productive function," as when a waterfall generates power. The second he labeled "permissive" or "transmissive function," as when a prism sifts and limits the light passing through it, or when the keys of an organ "open successively the various pipes and let the wind in the air-chest escape in various ways. The voices of the various pipes are constituted by the columns of air trembling as they emerge. But the air is not engendered in the organ. The organ proper, as distinguished from its air-chest, is only an apparatus for letting portions of it loose upon the world in these peculiarly limited shapes."[38] In like manner, James urged, our brains serve a transmissive function: they are "colored lenses in the wall of nature, admitting light from the super-solar source, but at the same time tingeing and restricting it."[39]

Were James alive today, he would doubtless appeal to television (as have many of his like-minded successors). An old-fashioned set with antenna on top enabled one to watch *I Love Lucy*. This was not, however, because the transistors and cathode ray tube inside the box generated the show. The TV rather served to mediate the show, or as James would have put it, the set had a transmissive function. It was the instrument through which signals in the air—signals invisible and insensible to ordinary perception—became apparent to viewers. Without the TV, no show appeared. Had one been ignorant of radio waves, one could have inferred, invoking Occam's razor—do not multiply entities beyond necessity—that the TV itself somehow produced the plots, the pictures, the sounds. This would have explained why the screen went blank when one pulled the plug, and why adjusting this or that knob altered the picture or sound. Yet the inference would have been erroneous. The show existed independently of the mechanism that allowed viewing. Destroying one's TV set would not have destroyed *I Love Lucy*.

Another partial analogy for the Jamesian view is Bruce Lipton's comparison of body and self to a NASA Mars rover.[40] A rover has cameras that function as eyes. It has vibration detectors that serve as ears. It has chemical sensors that are effectively its taste buds. Through these mechanisms its onboard computer gathers information, which the rover then beams back to earth. A rover also has antennae. These receive instructions from NASA's faraway command center. Information, then, goes both directions, enabling scientists to learn about Mars and distant controllers to guide the rover. Yet the latter also has autonomous systems on board. These can, when needed, act on their own, as when gyroscopes prevent the machine from tipping over. Hypothetical Martians, if unaware of the unseen signals going back and forth through space, would behold nothing but a machine, one capable of swiftly responding to environmental change. They might well conclude that the rover was doing everything on its own.

In addition to allowing for immortality, James's idea of the brain as both receiving and constraining consciousness had, for him, two advantages over its materialistic competitor. One was that it is consistent with those "glows of feeling, glimpses of insight, and streams of knowledge and perception [that] float into our finite world."[41] James had in mind certain atypical states of mind in which people sense that things have opened up, or occasions when they perceive things beyond the familiar senses. "In cases of conversion, in providential leadings, sudden mental healings, etc., it seems to the subjects themselves . . . as if a power from without, quite different from the ordinary action of the senses or of the sense-led mind, came into their life, as if the latter suddenly opened into that greater life in which it has its source."[42]

James believed that the filter or transmission theory is further favored by certain "obscure and exceptional phenomena reported at all times throughout human history," among them premonitions, visions of loved ones dying at a distance, clairvoyant impressions, and "still more exceptional and incomprehensible things."[43] A few items in the present book—some reports from death beds, for instance—fall under the latter category. James, judging (in part from personal investigation) that not all stories featuring "exceptional and incomprehensible things" are spurious, observed that ordinary sight and hearing do not explain them. He found in them evidence of a wider reality.

Some, I may add, have come to the idea of the brain as a sort of filter not through philosophical reflection (as did James) but via firsthand experience. In trying to unfold the meaning of an intense mystical experience, one person said: "I felt as if a filter had been taken from my senses and I was seeing the concrete world as it really is and the purpose and meaning of it all."[44] These words are similar to those of a man who came close to drowning and had an NDE: "It's made me think that our understanding of the brain is actually backwards. The brain filters out everything and doesn't help our thinking but hinders it, slows it down, focuses it."[45]

* * *

The passing of time has added evidence consistent with James's theory.[46] While I cannot offer a survey of it in a book such as this, I note that recent neuroimaging has revealed that certain drugs—psilocybin, LSD, ayahuasca, DMT—may intensify states of consciousness precisely by depressing brain activity.[47] Moreover, other disruptions of ordinary brain function can lead to expanded awareness.[48] The neuroanatomist, Jill Bolte Taylor, reported that, during a massive stroke on the left side of her brain, a stroke that took away her ability to read, speak, walk, and remember, she felt that her body "functioned like a portal through which the energy" of who she was could "be beamed into a three-dimensional external space."

> In the absence of the normal functioning of my left orientation associa-
> tion area, my perception of my physical boundaries was no longer limited
> to where my skin met air. I felt like a genie liberated from its bottle. The
> energy of my spirit seemed to flow like a great whale gliding through a
> sea of silent euphoria. . . . This absence of physical boundary was one of
> glorious bliss. As my consciousness dwelled in a flow of sweet tranquility,
> it was obvious to me that I would never be able to squeeze the enormous-
> ness of my spirit back inside this tiny cellular matrix.[49]

The most dramatic examples of dysfunction associated with intensi-
fied consciousness are those NDEs in which the brain is, by every current measurement, out of order.[50] If, as James theorized, cerebration ordinarily constrains rather than produces consciousness, the fact is intelligible. If, however, consciousness is the brain's by-product, why are "complex, coher-ent, intense" experiences sometimes associated "precisely with reductions, or even elimination, of brain metabolism"?[51]

One might object to all this that there is no *modus operandi* for what James proposed. What is the machinery, the means by which consciousness not wholly determined by a brain affects that brain? No one has the answer. James, however, already saw the futility of this complaint. The idea of the brain as canalizing and filtering consciousness may be abstruse, but the idea of brain activity generating consciousness is no less abstruse.

Why, if minds derive wholly from brains, is there no "empirical evidence of any phenomenon with the properties of phenomenal experience—namely intentionality, quality, unity, and first person perspective"?[52] There appears to be no path from the third person to the first person,[53] and so no solution to what philosopher David Chalmers has called "the hard problem of consciousness."[54] In the words of another philosopher, Thomas Nagel, "conscious subjects and their mental lives are inescapable components of reality not describable by the physical sciences."[55]

Additional riddles assail us. We have no good explanation as to why some neural incidents and structures correlate with consciousness while others do not, nor why the firing of particular cortical neurons are associated with consciousness on some but not all occasions, nor why false beliefs can repair or aggravate physical ailments (placebos and nocebos).[56] We further cannot elucidate why, if mental events depend entirely on bodily states and are physically determined, we feel free to make decisions and do indeed make them. Indeed, if consciousness is never a causal agent, never an independent, directing force, then its evolutionary function seems null and so enigmatic. As some have urged, if mental events are ineffective epiphenomena, then their subtraction would seemingly leave human history unaffected, which means there would still be conversations about mental events and even, incredibly, debates about their nature.[57] A world of zombies would be, to onlookers, just like our world.[58]

The facts about the brain do not shove us in one direction only. "The truth," as neuroscientist David Eagleman has written, "is that we face a field of question marks, and this field stretches to the vanishing point," so "any neuroscientist who tells you we have the problem cornered with a reductionist approach doesn't understand the complexity of the problem." Eagleman confesses that, for all we know, "the brain is like a radio" that picks "up signals from elsewhere."[59]

* * *

I have, in this chapter, referred to telepathy, precognition, and clairvoyance. Some things in this book, however, may induce in readers even more incredulity than those phenomena. So the question becomes, How open-minded should we be? Put otherwise, How weird is our world?

Remarkable stories abound.[60] How then should we assess them? The answer will vary from individual to individual. This is because, as Gregory of Nyssa observed, "most judge the credibility of what they hear according to the measure of their own experience, and what is beyond the power of hearers they insult with the suspicion of falsehood as outside the truth."[61] This is close to common sense, which is why Nietzsche, whose worldview was radically different than Gregory's, said much the same thing: "For what one lacks access to from experience one will have no ear."[62]

If one has run into nothing much out of the ordinary, one may well believe that nothing much out of the ordinary occurs. By the same token, if one has witnessed something aberrant, something truly confounding, something that one's public school education did not prepare for and cannot capture, then one will know that consensus reality is not all reality. This is my situation. Perhaps, then, it is not out of line to revert, as in the first chapter, to a personal experience.

One August mid-morning, in 1980, at the age of twenty-four, I entered my parents' kitchen in order to bake a batch of blueberry muffins. I began by collecting and then mixing the wet ingredients in a large bowl. They included honey. In pouring into a measuring cup the quantity of honey the recipe called for, I spilled some onto the outside of its large glass container. So after combining the milk, the eggs, the butter, and the honey, I screwed the lid back on the honey jar, took it over to the faucet, washed it clean with hot water, and set it down right beside the sink.

The next task was to gather and stir together the dry ingredients. I took down from a nearby cupboard a second bowl and began to mix together raisin bran and baking soda, splintered pecans and wheat germ. After that, I moved to the pantry, on the wall opposite the sink. I opened the cupboard door, leaned over, and started to lift from the lowest shelf a large aluminum tin full of flour. An instant after I picked it up, the tin suddenly seemed to gain weight and slipped out of my hands and onto the floor.

Upon meeting the carpeted ground, the tin popped its lid and spilled some of its powdery contents. Annoyed at myself, I kneeled to clean up the mess. Then came the mystifying discovery.

Enough flour had run out to reveal something buried at the bottom of the tin, something breaking the surface of the flour. Puzzled, I dug through the white stuff with my fingers and then pulled out, of all things, a glass honey jar exactly like the one I had held in my hands and washed a moment ago, a jar completely caked with flour, as if it had been placed in the tin while wet. Puzzled, I turned my head to assure myself that the bottle I had just rinsed was standing where I had left it. It was not.

That moment brought bafflement, and I sat on the floor for the next two or three minutes. During that time I stared, alternately, at the caked honey jar, the flour tin on its side, and the countertop across the room. I was looking at what could not be.

I repeatedly reviewed what had just happened, retracing every movement I had made. The effort did not cancel confusion but reinforced it. The obvious fact was on the floor. The wet honey jar had been moved from the sink and deposited on the bottom of the flour tin. No explanation, however, came to me. The kitchen had become a theatre of the absurd.

Not long thereafter, on the same day, I called a close friend, an MIT-educated engineer. He is a thoroughgoing skeptic. I recounted my story and asked for a rational explanation. Setting aside the possibility that I was lying, all he could come up with was this. My conscious mind had gone offline, after which I blankly went through the bizarre, complex act of emptying the flour tin, placing at its bottom the still-wet honey jar, filling the tin again with flour, replacing the lid, putting the container back where it had been, and cleaning up any trace of the mess that I must have made—I would have needed a vacuum cleaner—after all of which I woke up and headed to the cabinet to retrieve the flour.

I did not and do not credit this narrative. I have no history of blacking out, nor do I suffer from ambulatory automatisms. I am not like Joseph Fürst, the German somnambulist who at night promenaded atop the roof ridge of his house while playing the tuba. My mother, moreover, had been sitting nearby during the whole episode, and when I, while staring at the floor, asked if she had seen anything out of the ordinary, she said, without pause, no.

Above all, the unevidenced proposal that my conscious mind shut down while some other part of me robotically buried a large wet jar in a canister of flour—a proposal forwarded solely in order to sustain a humdrum view of the world—fails to explain what was so vivid at the time, namely, the sudden heaviness of the flour canister. It seemed as though the container gained weight the second after I removed it from the shelf. That is in fact why I dropped it. The circumstance is consistent with the fantastic thought that the honey jar lodged itself beneath the flour while the canister was in my hands. That possibility passes understanding.

What, then, do I believe? I believe I observed the impossible. Beyond that, I remain utterly nonplussed. What agent or power was responsible? Within the hour it occurred to me, half-seriously, that perhaps I had been the victim of an impish jinn, an unseen practical joker. Some people believe in such ethereal rascals. They thereby seek to explain how their keys and socks disappear and then reappear. I do not, however, know so much about the way things are.

Later, I wondered whether some part of my subliminal self, knowing that my conscious mind would appreciate a dramatic refutation of physicalism, somehow worked the trick via a faculty beyond my customary command. I have also toyed with the deeply unsatisfying, absurd idea that there was no agent. I just chanced to witness an incomprehensible quirk, a statistical aberration, the realization of an infinitesimal possibility.

Another option comes from a Christian pastor. He assures me that God must have been the culprit. The Supreme Being was trying to convince a skeptical historian of early Christianity that something supernatural could have happened to Jesus's lifeless body. If I saw for myself that a piece of matter can disappear from one location and then reappear in another, should it not be easier for me to believe that Jesus literally rose from the dead?

I find no reason to endorse any of the preceding possibilities (although I acknowledge that the answer to the pastor's question is, yes). I equally do not see how dogmatically to exclude any of them. The agent, if any, and its purpose, if any, remain opaque to me.

This does not, however, render the event meaningless. For one thing, this outlandish experience, all by itself, tells me that there is more on earth than my science teachers imagined. The world must be far odder than we regularly take it to be.

Another lesson I come away with is that I cannot be closed-minded about the incredible stories that so many others often tell. To behold the impossible with one's own eyes inexorably raises the odds that others have beheld it, too. Of course, for a historian such as myself, this opens Pandora's box. But I did not open the box. I just happened by when the lid popped off. And I cannot put it back on without lying to myself.

* * *

Maybe, however, the chief moral my experience imparts has to do with human understanding. To make the point, I return to the kitchen cabinet. At the time of the self-transporting honey jar, the pantry held not only an aluminum tin of flour but a twenty-five pound bag of dog food.[63] Claw marks badly scarred the maple door. Their source was Ralph, who was more German Shepherd than anything else. Ralph knew that we kept his food in the kitchen cabinet, and also that, when one of us went to that cabinet with bowl in hand, he was about to eat. That is why he then barked with excitement. Ralph further reasoned that, when he was hungry, he could get our attention by pawing at the cabinet door, whence all the scratches. Regarding his food, then, Ralph could think well enough.

There was, however, a fixed limit to his understanding. Although he knew where we kept his food, he did not know that bags of dog food come from grocery stores. Nor did he know that grocery stores obtain those bags from trucks, nor that trucks retrieve them from manufacturing plants. He had no conception of any of these things, nor of the system of economic exchange that makes them possible. Such knowledge was too high for him.

These were things, moreover, that he could never understand. Had I spent every waking hour trying to instruct him about the long chain of events that puts dog food in the kitchen cabinet, it would have been in vain. For his mind was constricted. Beyond a knowledge of certain facts about the cabinet and his bowl there was only fog. His mind ran out.

It must be the same with us. We sometimes imagine that, because we understand much, we should be able to understand everything. Yet we are animals, and like all other animals our minds are finite, not infinite. There is much we do not know, and surely many things that we will never know and can never know.[64] Just as Ralph's mind soon enough came up against facts it could not fathom, so too is it with us. This is why my inability to account for or explain an event, including the episode of the honey jar, is not, for me, good or sufficient reason to deny that it happened.

The Bible teaches that human beings are just a little lower than the angels. My view is that we are just a little bit above the dogs. Bryan Magee, without my religious orientation, advocates the same idea:

> A dog is enclosed in its dogness, its doggitude, and cannot get outside that. The cleverest dog that ever existed can do and understand only what it is possible for a dog to do and understand. . . . Anyone who claimed of any natural creature apart from ourselves that it is capable, in principle, of understanding anything whatsoever would be talking obvious nonsense. . . . Whatever our origin, how could limitations imposed on us by our nature not be untranscendable? Yet if it is so, it almost certainly means that there are whole universes of unknowability for us, just as there are for dogs, dolphins, orangutans, and every other living creature. The sort of reasons why most of reality lies permanently outside the ken of a dog, a dolphin, or an orangutan apply by parity of reasoning to us.[65]

The Dunning-Kruger effect is the psychological disposition of those with low ability to imagine that they have great ability. It is the cognitive bias to think ourselves smarter than we are. It afflicts us all.

* * *

Carl Sagan, echoing others before him, famously said: "Extraordinary claims require extraordinary evidence."[66] But the word "extraordinary" is not a fixed measure. It is rather relative to one's other beliefs. What is extraordinary for one may not be so for another, or at least much less so. Our sense of what can or cannot happen inevitably reflects what has or has not happened to us personally. This in part explains why I hold some beliefs Carl Sagan did not. My experiences move me to ponder possibilities he likely never explored. They preclude me from identifying our Flatland with all there is. There must be more—extra dimensions, other realities, additional intelligences.[67]

I favor this option all the more because immediate family members have their own remarkable stories to tell, stories that, if they happened as recounted, reveal an untamed world. They include a teenager interacting with an apparition identified only later from a picture album; a boy recurrently dreaming about a girl who turns out to live across the street after he moves to a new city; a man hearing the voice of his dead father asking him to call a woman he does not know in order to wish her happy birthday, after which, upon doing so, he learns it is in fact her birthday; a high school student dreaming about entering her church's sanctuary by the side entrance on Sunday morning, seeing all the lights go out, and hearing a friend say, "We lost the electricity," after which, a few weeks later, she walks into her church by the side door on Sunday morning, observes that all the lights are off, and hears her friend say, "We lost the electricity because of the storm"; and a father receiving (more than half a century before cell phones) a call from his son, asking to be picked up at the train station at a specific time while the son was then on an hours-long train ride and could not have placed the call; yet when he steps off the train, expecting to surprise his family, he is immediately greeted by his brother, who has been sent to collect him.

I cannot explain away such experiences without distrusting those I trust most; and if only one of their stories happened as told and is not the upshot of coincidence, then everything is different. As it turns out, then, I have little choice in the matter. Were I to distrust not only my own eyes but the eyes of those nearest and dearest to me, I would have no good reason to believe anything.

My liberal take on what is possible is additionally confirmed by this thought. The number of individuals within my inner family circle comprises only the minutest portion of humanity throughout the ages. This surely means that the number of stories like theirs is incalculably massive. And again, if only one of them is true, everything is different.

My conviction is that, once one leaves the crowd of conformity and begins to think outside the social censorship that envelops us, it is obvious that there is, with regard to astounding firsthand claims, an embarrassment of riches.

I realize, of course, that the line of thought I have just sketched will not work for all. It remains true, to recall Gregory, that we judge what is credible by our own experience, and those who have never seen the incredible, and whose friends and family have never seen the incredible, will have a different view of things. This is an obdurate fact, and I know of no argument to make it go away.

I nonetheless note that those who disbelieve that anything truly peculiar happens should be bothered by the fact that those of us who report impossible affairs cannot, one and all, be condescendingly scorned as uncritical or uninformed, or as the hapless victims of arrested intellectual development. Many of us are well-educated, well-read, and capable not only of perceiving what is in front of us but of reflecting on it thoughtfully.

* * *

This chapter's title is "Rational Analysis." Some would protest that I have, with telepathy and the transported jar of honey, entered irrational territory. My retort is that the truly reasonable thing is to follow the evidence wherever it leads, which is what I have done; and further that there is nothing irrational about recognizing that our minds, constrained by our mammalian brains, are unable to grasp everything in this incredibly complex, sometimes dumbfounding, wonder-filled world. We should not shrink experience to fit our understanding but enlarge our understanding to take in experience.

9

Some Theological Issues

"Since the comming of Christ in the flesh, and establishing of his Church by the Apostles, all miracles, visions, prophecies, & appearances of Angels or good spirites are ceased. Which serued onely for the first sowing of faith, & planting of the Church. Where now the Church being established . . . the Lawe and Prophets are thought sufficient to serue us, or make us inexcusable."

—King James I[1]

"With just a few exceptions among the Radicals, [Reformation] Protestants denied the possibility of mystical ecstasies, visions, apparitions, revelations, levitations, bilocations, and all other supernatural phenomena associated with intimate encounters between the human and divine."

—Carlos Eire[2]

"One would think that religious communities would be particularly interested in the frequency and meaning of paranormal experiences that constructively change people's lives and enhance their understanding of their spirituality. It is the case, however, that the prescribed nature of most religious life squelches openness to the spirit and to the reality and importance of numinous experiences."

—J. Harold Ellens[3]

One afternoon, many years ago, I awakened from a nap on my couch. I stood up and idly looked through the living-room window. Across the street was an aged, unremarkable apartment complex. Before then I had paid it scant attention. That changed in a moment. Out of nowhere, unbidden, came the engulfing sense that I was the building and the building was me. I somehow apprehended that the red bricks and I were the same subject, were one. All distinction was an illusion.

This hypnotic conviction, which lasted maybe five seconds, was like a revelation, and while I was inside the experience it commanded assent. After it departed, leaving me on my own, I remember having this thought: Were I a Hindu, I would know exactly what to think. *Tat Tvam Asi.* Thou art that. Atman is Braham. All is one.

I was not, however, a Hindu. I was instead a Christian. So my response was: Well, that was interesting.

Soon enough I had an additional thought, and it has stayed with me. Maybe doctrines, or at least some doctrines, are not just doctrines. That is, maybe religious people do not simply sit around and make things up. I suspected that, whether or not Atman is in fact Braham, I had stumbled upon why someone came up with the notion—it was the distillation of a real experience—and further why others went along: the mystical feeling of the oneness of all things had overwhelmed them, too.[4] If so, then perhaps, I mused—and later came to believe—this is not the only religious idea to have firm grounding in experience. Maybe now and again, or more than now and again, people have formulated and held a religious conviction because something unexpected and profound had happened to them or others of their acquaintance.[5]

* * *

Let me illustrate with two possibilities from my Christian tradition.

The old Protestant hymn "Go, Happy Soul" opens with these words: "Go, happy soul: thy days are ended, thy pilgrimage on earth below; go, by angelic guard attended; to God's own Paradise now go."[6] The phrase "by angelic guard attended" is a bit cryptic. Matthew Henry, the famed biblical exegete, was more expansive: angels "are ministering spirits to the heirs of salvation, not only while they live, but when they die, and have a charge concerning them, to bear them up in their hands, not only in their journeys to and fro on earth, but in their great journey to their long home in heaven, to be both their guide and their guard through regions unknown and unsafe."[7]

That angels escort the righteous dead to the postmortem paradise is not an idea hidden away in little-known hymns and old commentaries. It be-

longs rather to wider Western culture. Even the uncatechized may know it
from having read or heard what Horatio says to the dying Hamlet:

> Now cracks a noble heart.
> —Good night, sweet prince,
> And flights of angels sing thee to thy rest![8]

The motif of angels coming for the saints at death did not, of course,
originate with Shakespeare. It appears often in medieval hagiography,
old liturgical sources, and the church fathers before that.[9] Where did it
come from?

One might hazard that it comes straight out of the New Testament. The
parable of the rich man and Lazarus opens with this: "There was a rich man
who was dressed in purple and fine linen and who feasted sumptuously every day. And at his gate lay a poor man named Lazarus, covered with sores,
who longed to satisfy his hunger with what fell from the rich man's table;
even the dogs would come and lick his sores. The poor man died and was
carried away by the angels to be with Abraham" (Luke 16:19-22). Perhaps the
last line captured the Christian imagination and accounts, all by itself, for
what we find in so many later sources.

This, however, leaves Luke's angels unexplained. Where did they come
from? The answer is: Jewish tradition. The Talmud affirms that "when a
righteous individual departs from the world, he is welcomed by three com-
panies of ministering angels."[10] According to another rabbinic text, the souls
of the righteous dead are borne to the Garden of Eden by angels.[11] Earlier
than these sources is the Life of Adam and Eve, a Jewish pseudepigraphon
from the first century. In this, one of the six-winged Seraphim carries
Adam's disembodied soul to heaven (37:3 Greek). Similarly, when the long-
suffering Job expires in the Testament of Job, another pseudepigraphon from
the turn of the era, those "who come for his soul" arrive in gleaming chariots
and are clearly angels (52:5-7). Then there is this generalization from the
Testament of Asher, yet one more book from around the time of Jesus: when
righteous souls pass, they will meet "the angel of peace" and enter eternal
life (6:5).

Our question now becomes, Why did so many Jews suppose that angels
appear as the righteous slip away? Perhaps, one might hazard, they bor-

rowed the idea from the Greeks. Plato speaks of guardian spirits escorting the dead to judgment (*Phaedo* 107D), and in multiple sources the god Hermes serves as a psychopomp. But then, one might ask, Why did the Greeks believe what they did?

My suggestion is this. Wherever and whenever the notion that otherworldly beings come for us at death was conceived, and whoever conceived it, it was not a free-floating fiction. We should rather entertain the possibility that real experiences begot the notion and, once it was born, fortified it.

I observed, in an earlier chapter, that an oft-reported feature of modern NDEs is encounter with an extraordinary, personified light. Here, as a reminder, are a few illustrations from the literature:

- "Then I saw . . . a bright angel. An angel of light. I felt encompassed by this force of love from this angel that was searching and probing my deepest thoughts."[12]
- "Reaching the light, I was met by other beings of light and very gently encouraged to move on towards a life review."[13]
- "I saw this large light, like a spotlight with a Being in it, as if this Being was the light."[14]
- "Two angelic beings emerged into the tunnel. They exuded a powerful vigor—a charisma and energy that made them seem magnetic."[15]
- "There was a big bright light, but it wasn't like one man but maybe it was two in light. It wasn't a blinding, bright light at all. It was just a white light which looked like two people, but other than that, I actually didn't see who it was . . . like two people that were coming toward me. Although I couldn't distinguish them as people. Just outlines of light."[16]

Generalizing from his interviews with over a thousand NDErs, Bruce Greyson has written: "three-fourths reported an encounter with a 'loving being of light.'"[17]

While there might be some good reason for imagining this phenomenon to be altogether and uniquely modern, I have yet to run across it. I am inclined to suppose that, if modern people, in vast numbers, have—for whatever reason—reported seeing, when unconscious and near death, a benevolent light, then at least a few in olden times did also.[18] I am encouraged to think this not only because today's reports come from all over the globe but because worldwide lore tells again and again of deities, otherworldly escorts, and non-human spirits, including beings of light, meeting humans beings when they die.[19]

Circling back now to our religious forebears, to early Jews and Christians, what would they have concluded if someone, after seemingly swooning into death, returned to the living and told of encountering a kindly light? Given that angels were associated with both light and dream states,[20] some no doubt would have thought of angels, just as do many today.

Encountering a figure of light during an NDE is not the only experiential candidate for the belief that angels come for the dying. As observed in chapter 6, those near death often (outside NDEs) have visions, and sometimes these visions include figures with whom they are unfamiliar, figures they may identify as angels, as in these firsthand testimonies:

- "Don't cry, mother, it is very beautiful, there are angels round me."[21]
- "Death has come to get me. The angel of death is here. Oh, the angels of heaven are here, too."[22]
- "Look! She's in white. I've never seen anything so white. She's an angel—a real angel."[23]
- "'Do you see them?' he gasped with amazement. 'No, sir, but tell me. What are you seeing?' I [a hospice nurse] whispered back into his ear. [He answered:] 'The room here is now full of angels.'"[24]

Reports that use the word "angel" are, obviously, influenced by Jewish and Christian tradition.[25] Adherents of other religious traditions employ other terms, such as "deva" or "devi," or "Amida" or "Amitābha."[26] For my argument, however, this matters little. The different names and even differing descriptions do not require that everything is, at bottom, nothing but culture and language.[27] Although the latter may *affect* everything, they do not *effect* everything.

Mediation is one thing, origin another. If someone meets "a being of light," another "an angel" or "a diva" while yet another sees "the sun" speaking to him,[28] this scarcely demands or even suggests that their experiences are fundamentally dissimilar. The same phenomenon can provoke diverse interpretations, and the arrow of causation is not exclusively one way, from culture to experience. It also runs the other way, from experience to culture. To contend otherwise is perhaps a bit "like saying that the red fruit growing on trees is a function of the imagination because it is called 'apple' by Americans and 'pomme' by the French."[29] That one person, when tempted to do what she believes to be wrong, thinks that the impulse is from the devil whereas another, in a similar situation, equates her evil inclination with her unconscious mind does not mean that the two are having unrelated experiences.

* * *

As with angels at death, so too with the vexed doctrine of hell. It is unlikely that the latter was contrived in utter isolation from experiences surrounding death. Nor, once formed, is it credible that the expectation was miraculously insulated from ongoing experiences. People no doubt have endorsed hell for any number of reasons—in order to put their enemies there, or to inhibit behavior deemed sinful, or to prevent evildoers from never paying for their crimes. Yet it is more than plausible that belief in a place of other-worldly misery owes something to firsthand testimonies.

While most NDEs are pleasant, others are not. As recounted in chapter 7, some people report that, when close to death, they entered a terrifying void or place of agony and torment. Elements sometimes include "frightening or threatening beings, hellish landscapes, threatened or actual torture, and communications containing taunts or malevolence."[30] Here are three modern illustrations:

- "I was falling down a very dark tunnel. Demons appeared around me, and even though I was spirit—my body had stayed at the hospital—they were going through the motions of ripping my flesh off. It was intensely painful."[31]
- "I was in a place like hell. It was like a valley and the earth had been scorched. There were demons like in a Bosch painting. There was vapor rising from the ground like steam. The sky was overcast with grayish clouds. I felt awful—depressed and miserable. Unbearable."[32]
- "I was terrified in the darkness that surrounded me but very aware of the horrible pain burning and searing my entire body, agonizing pain beyond description that would never leave. There were the tortured screams of others but I could see nothing but the darkness. There was no fire, just this dreadful burning pain over every part of me and I knew that this was hell."[33]

Despite these last two accounts, both of which use the word "hell," most narratives of frightful NDEs avoid that label. They restrict themselves to description.[34]

Before going further I emphasize what I have emphasized before, that many NDErs confess that words fail them, that plain prose cannot capture what happened to them. Furthermore, and to reiterate another point made earlier, their memories are inescapably filtered through their already-formed minds.[35] We should not, then, be unimaginative about their accounts. This includes accounts of negative NDEs. All we have to go on are inadequate words or, perhaps it would be better to say, inadequate metaphors.

With this in mind, is it not reasonable to infer that, despite their differences, the world's hells—the Greek Tartarus, the Jewish Gehenna, the Muslim Jahannam, the Taoist Diyu, the Zoroastrian Dušox, the Hindu and Buddhist Narakas—are partly rooted in frightening experiences? This would help explain why hell is a worldwide phenomenon: behind it lies a worldwide set of comparable experiences.[36] The idea of a place of misery was, to be sure, inevitably encoded variously at various times and elaborated differently in different places. This is why we always know whether we are reading a medieval Catholic narrative about hell or a *délok* story from Tibet.[37] This fact, however, is no reason to insist that the cross-cultural hells are, one and all, uninformed by real experiences.[38] Differences do not annul similarities.

It is just thinkable, I suppose, that the gruesome pictures in various religious traditions and the unhappy experiences of some unfortunates were lines that never intersected, so that their shared elements are mere coincidence. One could also, in theory, hypothesize that religious authorities around the world independently conjured, without empirical input, the prospect of postmortem unpleasantries, only after which some individuals began to report postmortem unpleasantries. On this account, belief everywhere preceded and summoned experience.

The historical record is too spotty to establish beyond doubt what happened. Yet if in our time and place negative NDEs are not self-evidently cultural artifacts, why hazard that it was different ages ago? In the modern world, horrid NDEs befall atheists as well as Christians, cynics anticipating oblivion as well as pious souls hoping to go to heaven. In other words, they can surprise. This does not obviously accord with reducing everything to expectation. It is more sensible to suppose that negative NDEs are no more reducible without remainder to language and culture than is déjà vu or the migraine, seeing ghosts or feeling that all is one. The same play can be choreographed in multiple ways, and some things belong to human experience. This is why communication between different societies is possible, and why there are certain human universals.[39] We are, after all, members of the same species.

None of this helps us to decide what might cause negative NDEs or what they might mean. But whatever one's thoughts on those issues, why balk at the idea that miserable experiences helped foster the conviction that death can land one in misery?[40]

* * *

Before moving on, I wish to note, as an aside, that certain experiences do not just inform religious doctrine. They likewise contribute to making people of a certain sort. Appreciating this fact helps us to understand our contemporary situation.

The phrase "spiritual but not religious" is everywhere these days.[41] Many among us believe in a higher power and engage in spiritual practices yet remain unaffiliated with a religious institution. Some practice yoga. Some meditate. Many pray. Most practice an eclectic mix of this and that.

I know churchgoers who dismiss such folk as "New Agers." But to dismiss is not to understand.

What happens when someone unattracted to or alienated from organized religion—perhaps for understandable reasons—is nonetheless overcome by transcendent bliss, or meets God in an NDE, or beholds an angel, or enters via mystical rapture some world beyond this one? There are many such people. That they are spiritual but not religious makes perfect sense. Indeed, what else could they be?

This circumstance is one reason secularization may have limits.[42] Even when churches, synagogues, and mosques fail to flourish, human beings continue to have religious experiences of one sort or another. As David Hufford explains,

> There are classes of experiences that give rise to spiritual beliefs among practically all who have them, regardless of their prior beliefs. The per-

ception and interpretation of such experiences are similar among persons with very different backgrounds and expectations. Those who have had such experiences form a minimum core of "believers," a substantial fraction of any population below which certain basic spiritual beliefs will not drop regardless of cultural and social pressure.[43]

In other words, and to quote Hufford again, "a fundamental reason that spiritual beliefs have been able to resist the enormous social pressures toward secularization is that they are, in part, rationally founded on experience (that is, empirically grounded)."[44] Religious sentiments and ideas are still with us because, among other reasons, religious experiences are still with us.

When Christian faith dominated the West, religious experiences were deciphered within churches, usually by their leaders. Those days of supremacy are over. Secularization, however, has not vanquished the experiences, which continue as ever. Nor has it eliminated spiritual appraisals of them. What it has done is contract the reach of Christian theology, so that many now interpret what happens to them without the aid of church teaching.

* * *

I see no good reason why what I have urged so far in this chapter—that experiences can be internal to religious beliefs, that some doctrines have been occasioned by unusual experiences—should disturb anyone's theological sentiments.

Others, however, might regard my line of inquiry, as well as the focus of this book as a whole, as recipes for theological trouble. Does not attention to religious experience subtract authority from the foundational sources of Christian faith, such as the Bible and the creeds? Does it not almost inevitably land one in a quagmire of subjectivity and competing doctrinal claims? Does it not embolden people to stitch together their private theological quilts? And might it not incite some to endeavor to induce their own extraordinary experiences when instead the one thing needful on the long, arduous, and sometimes dreary road toward God is to love and serve one's neighbors amid the everyday? There are no shortcuts to what matters most.

N. T. Wright has written that

"experience" is far too slippery for the concept to stand any chance of providing a stable basis sufficient to serve as an "authority," unless what is meant is that, as the book of Judges wryly puts it, everyone should simply do what is right in their own eyes. And that, of course, means that there is no authority at all. Indeed, the stress on "experience" has contributed materially to that form of pluralism, verging on anarchy, which we now see across the Western world.[45]

I could, in response to these sentences, urge that they have little to do with this volume, which is neither a dissertation on authority nor an exercise in constructive theology. I am not seeking, on the basis of religious experiences, to reconfigure Christian belief à la Swedenborg or to lay a new dogmatic foundation à la Schleiermacher. Nor do I herein aim to commend or attack any creedal conviction or to defend or criticize any particular version of the Christian faith. My aspirations are much more modest. I wish to increase awareness of certain experiences and their prevalence, venture some generalizations about them, and offer some tentative suggestions for others to ponder.

I could also sidestep Wright's concerns about authority by observing that something can matter greatly without mattering doctrinally, and further that to demote some things because they do not necessitate uniquely Christian ideas would be a sort of theological solipsism. Were this a book on aesthetics or the pyramids of Egypt, no one would complain about its threat to or irrelevance for dogma.

Yet I do not wish to let myself off so easily.

(1) I share Wright's dismay regarding the radical relativism that today holds sway over so much of our culture and its public institutions. The prevalence of profound discord about what is right and wrong—words many now decorate with quotation marks—has landed us in a bad place. In addition, I am not one to take leave of the Bible. I have spent my professional life engaging Scripture. This includes devoting years to writing commentaries on biblical books and decades introducing future pastors to biblical studies. I nonetheless have a different take on things, for I cannot, except in an abstract and inconsequential way, disentangle the interpretation of Scripture from ongoing human experience.

The Methodist quadrilateral—so named by Albert Outler—holds that, in addition to Scripture, the chief sources for understanding and living the Christian faith are tradition, reason, and experience.[46] I regard this not as a theological imperative, as did Outler, but rather a statement of the inevitable. The quadrilateral is descriptive, not prescriptive, because the four elements, including experience, are inextricable.

We all, whether or not we reflect on the fact, interpret the Bible through one or more interpretive traditions—Roman Catholicism, Russian Orthodoxy, Greek Orthodoxy, Anglicanism, Methodism, Pentecostalism, conservative Lutheranism, liberal Lutheranism, American fundamentalism, liberation theology, womanist theology, German historical criticism, and so on. When we read, we do so within a history that hands us a set of questions, prompts us to see this rather than that, and encourages us to think one thing and not another. We are never free of tradition.

We likewise, because Scripture does not interpret itself, are always thinking hard when engaged in exegesis. This is why, as even hasty perusal will confirm, all commentaries are, among other things, compendia of arguments. They are, that is, exercises in reasoning.[47] Those exercises, moreover, constantly work with sources outside Scripture—Hebrew and Greek dictionaries, archaeological discoveries, Ancient Near Eastern texts, the Philonic corpus, rabbinic writings, and so on. Scripture without reason is dead.

Finally, we never understand anything without drawing upon beliefs already formed, and as those beliefs are in great measure the products of our experience, we never understand anything independently of the latter. It follows that we invariably fathom Scripture through our experiences, including our religious experiences, whatever they may be. To dispute this, out of fear of eisegesis, would be to deny, among other things, that monastic or African-American readings of the Bible have anything new or distinctive to offer. But it is not so. When we read, we are the readers.

(2) I also cannot isolate the Bible from contemporary religious reports because Scripture itself is, to great extent, a string of metanormal experiences. It is through dreams and visions that God speaks to Abraham, Jacob, Joseph, Isaiah, Daniel, and Jesus's parents. Angels appear to or address the patriarchs, Moses, Balaam, Gideon, Samson's parents, Elijah, Zechariah the prophet, and a dozen more. Ezekiel, while in Babylon, clairvoyantly sees things happening far away in Jerusalem, and Jesus exercises the same

talent on several occasions.[48] Both the law-giver and the Messiah are trans-figured into light. Early Christians speak in tongues. Paul meets Jesus in a vision on the road to Damascus. Later he writes of a mystical rapture in which he was "caught up to the third heaven" and heard things unutterable. Miracles great and small, and of one sort or another, are, moreover, nearly ubiquitous in the narrative portions of Scripture, above all in the Gospels and Acts. So large swaths of the Bible are accounts of unusual experiences and their consequences. Is there not, then, a strange disjunction between any theological project that professes to take the Bible seriously yet fails to take today's unusual experiences seriously?

I am not a charismatic Christian. I have never spoken in tongues. Nor do I have much faith in run-of-the-mill faith healers. Yet I understand the puzzled Pentecostal. How is it that so many mainline Protestants can pay attention to the visions, voices, dreams, and mystical experiences of olden times yet be apathetic about the visions, voices, dreams, and mystical experiences that come to people today? Does it make sense to esteem the former while deeming the latter to be, for every practical and theological purpose, bogus? What justifies sorting into two distinct piles experiences in the Bible and similar experiences everywhere else? Evelyn Underhill wrote: "the New Testament is . . . largely the record of a personal experience of God, which has been repeated again and again."[49] Are these words wholly off the mark?

(3) Wright is correct to urge that "the stress on 'experience' has contributed materially to that form of pluralism, verging on anarchy, which we now see across the Western world." It is equally true, however, that post-Gutenberg interpretations of the Bible have made their own contribution to the pluralism and religious anarchy of the modern world. Protestants, lacking a Pope, were free to read into the Bible what was right in their own eyes. They soon enough, and largely because of different interpretations of Scripture, segregated themselves into warring camps: Lutheran, Anabaptist, Reformed, Arminian, Anglican, Unitarian, etc. And as in the beginning, so ever since. The advocates of *sola scriptura* have, through incessant cytokinesis, been the best argument against the perspicuity of Scripture.[50]

Why is there, in the USA alone, such a plethora of different Presbyterian groups—the PCUSA, the Cumberland Presbyterian Church, the Covenant Presbyterian Church, the Christian Presbyterian Church, the Presbyterian Church in America, the Reformed Presbyterian Church of North America, the Westminster Church in the United States, the Evangelical Assembly of Presbyterian Churches in America, the Bible Presbyterian Church, the Orthodox Presbyterian Church, the Covenant Order of Evangelical Presbyterians, the Evangelical Presbyterian Church, the Associate Reformed Presbyterian Church, the Free Presbyterian Church, and so on? The priesthood of all believers has occasioned the reading authority of all believers, and they have not seen the same thing on the sacred page.

The biblical canon is not the one place in the world where everything is clear. Anyone familiar with the commentary tradition knows the hard, disheartening truth. Interpreting Scripture is a difficult and complex task. Second Peter observes that Paul's letters contain things that are hard to understand (3:16). The same holds for the Bible in its entirety. Indeed, numerous questions without self-evident answers confront conscientious readers at every turn. The remark, made by the early French Calvinist Joseph Scaliger, that "religious discord depends on nothing except ignorance of grammar," is ludicrous.[51] The books of the Old and New Testaments speak with multiple and sometimes conflicting voices, and they regularly fail to clarify important matters. Although Arius and Athanasius read the same Bible, they came to different conclusions. So too Luther and John Eck. Confusion and disagreement attend everything in life that matters. Scripture is not the exception to the rule.

Because of this, the Bible is never an authority in and of itself. It becomes an authority only when people interpret it (in part because of their experiences) a particular way, contend that their interpretation (as opposed to other interpretations) is the right one, and then win (not by ratiocination alone) the concurrence of others.

(4) Inadequate regard for private religious and mystical experiences can lead to misinterpreting the Bible. Paul wrote in 2 Corinthians 12:1-5:

> It is necessary to boast; nothing is to be gained by it, but I will go on to visions and revelations of the Lord. I know a person in Christ who fourteen years ago was caught up to the third heaven—whether in the body or out of the body I do not know; God knows. And I know that such a person—whether in the body or out of the body I do not know; God knows—was caught up into Paradise and heard things that are not to be told, that no mortal is permitted to repeat. On behalf of such a one I will boast, but on my own behalf I will not boast, except of my weaknesses.

These lines refer, according to John Chrysostom, not only to a "great revelation"—one sanctioning Paul as a bona fide apostle—but prove that he had many "visions and revelations."[52] John Wesley thought that Paul's experience was "beyond all doubt" a "foretaste" of the eschatological paradise and so "served to strengthen him in all his after-trials," whenever he called "to mind the very joy that was prepared for him."[53] Others have characterized Paul's ascent to the third heaven as a "momentous event in his spiritual life," or inferred that it "must have had an untold influence on Paul," or reasoned that the "amazing" event was "a signal proof of Christ's approval and commendation," or supposed that it was "dramatic and substantial even by Paul's standards."[54]

Contrast these positive, animated evaluations with that of Jerome Murphy-O'Connor, the well-known specialist on the Corinthian correspondence:

> Paul deflates his opponents' claim to visions and revelations by speaking of his own experience in the third person (2 Cor. 12:2–4). The technique distances him from the episode, and thereby underlines its irrelevance for his ministry. It did not change him in any way, and did not provide him with any information he could use. The criticism of his opponents is all the more effective for being unstated. If their experience was the same as Paul's, it contributed nothing to their ministries. If it was something about which they could talk, it was less ineffable than his![55]

Murphy-O'Connor is not alone in seeing nothing of great import in 2 Corinthians 12:1–5. J. Christiaan Beker, another prominent Pauline expert, wrote that the apostle's gospel is in no way "based on visionary constructions or apocalyptic revelations, and he does not ground his apostolic authority on an exaltation to the heavenly regions."[56] Beker made this assertion despite 2 Corinthians 12:1–5, despite Galatians 1:12—according to which Paul received his gospel "through a revelation (*apocalypsis*) of Jesus Christ"—and despite the tradition that the apostle was first commissioned through a visionary encounter with the risen Jesus (Acts 9, 22, 26).

To similar effect, C. K. Barrett, when commenting on 2 Corinthians 12:2, insisted that Paul was "ordinarily anything but a visionary," and further that "the striking thing is not that Paul should have experienced such a rapture but that he should go back fourteen years to find an example, and then depreciate its significance."[57] My copy of Barrett's commentary has, in the margin beside these words, a note in red pencil, a note I made in 1978: "you can sure tell what Barrett thinks of visions!"

It is not my purpose here to offer exegesis of 2 Corinthians or to reflect at length on Paul's inner life. I simply record my judgment that Barrett, Beker, and Murphy-O'Connor do not, in the comments I have cited, help us to understand the apostle better. Their dicta are rather efforts to tame him, to distance Paul from experiences from which the commentators themselves are distanced. Yet Paul was a visionary, that is, one who sees visions.[58] I indeed incline to agree with W. Robertson Nicoll that there was in him "a mystic element . . . a perpetual side-door for him into the unseen, a power of detaching himself from all sensible surroundings."[59] However that may be, Paul was hoping, when writing 2 Corinthians 12:1-5, and despite the ironic pose, that the Corinthians would, in the words of Ambrosiaster, "understand how great and how wonderful the things said to him were," and grasp that he was "not inferior in any way to the other apostles, as some of them thought he was."[60]

Tepid or belittling appraisals of the experiences to which 2 Corinthians 12:1-5 adverts, appraisals that direct us not to the real Paul but away from him, are not aberrations. Modern commentators often pay curt or unsympathetic attention to biblical passages that directly or indirectly touch matters of religious experience.[61] The result does not enrich understanding but obstructs it.

* * *

Whether or not my response to theological anxiety about religious experience is on target, we need to be exceedingly cautious and self-aware when it comes to arguments about authority. Those who insist on Scripture's preeminence are most often Scripture's mediators; that is, they are preachers, commentators, or theologians, persons whose vocation is to interpret the Bible for others. This means that they are protecting the territory over which they rule. In other words, defenses of biblical authority often function to sponsor the authority of those making the argument. The corollary is that devaluing religious experiences regularly serves to diminish the status of others.

Edward Taylor (d. 1729), the well-known Puritan poet and preacher, wrote that "extraordinary discoveries of the minde of God, ordinarily are made to Persons of more than an ordinary, or Common concern. . . . Hence it is from Satan that any should assert that Extraordinary discoveries are with ordinary and common people."[62] This is a blanket rejection of the significance of the remarkable experiences of "ordinary and common people"— that is, experiences of the laity, of individuals not belonging to the hierarchy of which the esteemed Taylor was a member.

In comparable fashion, Increase Mather (d. 1723) opined that if "White Angels appear to Females only, who are the weaker Sex, and more easy to be imposed on, that renders the case yet the more suspicious," especially because, in "former dark ages," many women won renown because of "pretended Angelical Apparitions and Revelations." Mather was confident that, "if ever an Age for Angelical Apparitions shall come, no question but men, and not women only will be honoured with their Visage."[63] He had in mind, one presumes, female Catholic mystics, and since he was neither female nor Catholic, it was the experiences of Christians unlike himself that he was scorning as vacuous.

The same close-guarding of one's religious privilege appears in an affair from the life of Increase Mather's son, Cotton Mather (d. 1728). A Bostonian had a vision and heard a voice. She credited them to an angel. As she seemed to know some things she could not know through normal means, Mather went along. Yet only for a time. When the woman expressed a desire to be pastor instead of him, he quickly decided that her vision and voice were of the devil. After Mather managed to convince her of the same, she challenged her apparition: "I desire no more to hear from you; Mr. Mather saies you are a Divel, and I am afraid you are. If you are an Angel of the Lord, give mee a Proof of it."[64] The episode seems to have concluded there.

Given today's updated cultural assumptions, church leaders are less likely to be as brazen or transparent as were Taylor and the Mathers. Instead of open criticism based on gender or ecclesiastical station, they are more apt to render out-of-the-ordinary experiences inert either by ignoring them altogether or by politely listening and then, as soon as possible, changing the subject. The outcome, however, is the same—the functional irrelevance of someone's experience and maintenance of the status quo, over which the clergy and theologians preside.

* * *

Laying aside the issue of authority, there remains another theological reason for giving scant notice to experience. It is this. The world of religious experience seems to be a buzzing confusion, a chaos of conflicting claims. Diversity of reports and diversity of interpretation are everywhere. The subjective is the intractable. Should we not, then, lend our time and attention to matters that we can sensibly adjudicate?

The answer, for several reasons, is emphatically, no. (1) Observing that something is a mess will not make it go away; and imprudently giving a wide berth to religious experiences because they comprise a bewildering hodgepodge does nothing to reduce their incidence or—the more important point here—help those on whom such experiences, without invitation, have fallen.

Even if theologians and pastors pay no attention or prune experience to convenient proportions, people will continue to encounter the extraordinary and face the task of interpretation. To have nothing worthwhile to say about events that typically matter deeply and are often associated with God is to be inept and, at least in this particular, irrelevant. What good is an underinformed religious leader who is at a loss or dismissive in the face of mystical raptures, unexpected occurrences at deathbeds, visions of self-luminous figures, or encounters with dead loved ones?

Mystical and metanormal events neither a religion nor a life make. This is one reason the wise have, as a general rule, discouraged people from hankering after them. This, however, is not the same as calcified disinterest in spontaneous experiences that frequently shape lives and affect religious sentiments in profound ways.

(2) The variety of religious experiences and their competing interpretations do not set them apart from the rest of life. Theologians do not contend that, because rival religious claims are numerous, theology is impossible. Nor does the wide spectrum of political views on most subjects typically prevent citizens from going to the polls. Again, biblical interpreters do not abandon their line of work because there is an avalanche of contrary opinions about nearly everything.

The task, when facing a multiplicity of competing claims, is not to resign in despair but to work all the harder, to endeavor to find, if possible, the truth amid the discordant voices. We should sort the wheat from the chaff, not toss everything out to be burned.

(3) Religious experience is not the tangled, heterogeneous mess it once was. As I have observed throughout this book, a number of experiences have been categorized and investigated with profit. We can make informed generalizations about the Old Hag and NDEs, about visions of the dying and blissful ecstasies, about conversion experiences and disembodied voices. We also know what sorts of experiences tend to be common and what sorts tend to be uncommon, what is par for the course and what is idiosyncratic. It is, additionally, a bit easier today than in the past to judge when a report is or is not cause for concern about someone's mental well-being. "An angel appeared to me, declared that I am Jesus Christ, and I know for certain it's true" is not of the same order as "I was briefly paralyzed, felt overwhelmed by a malicious something, and don't know what to think." More often than not we can disentangle worrisome reports from what recurrently happens to the otherwise healthy-minded. It is one thing to be less than enthusiastic about an eccentric, self-aggrandizing, experientially based claim. It is quite another to discount an experience that is of a type not habitually associated with mental debility.

We have more maps for the territory than we used to have. Much, it is true, remains unclear and controverted, yet significant progress, taxonomic and otherwise, has been made, and the future will no doubt bring more of the same. So when pastors or theologians fail, for whatever reason, to attend seriously to religious experiences, they are walking away not from an unsortable pile of nonsense but from a growing body of knowledge.

(4) In attempting to account for variant—and sometimes vastly variant—interpretations of what may be similar experiences, we must not forget what previous pages have stressed: even everyday perception involves, to some degree, imagination and projection. We have no reason to think it is otherwise with discernment of supersensible realms or realities. Or rather we have every reason to think that it must be all the more true. I share William Alston's view: if there are "realms, modes, or dimensions of reality" that are "difficult for us to discern," then it is not surprising "that widespread agreement [about them] is extremely difficult or impossible to attain, even if *some* veridical cognition . . . is achieved."[65]

Personal histories, which belong to cultural histories, always shape our perceptive faculties. We never receive without giving. We never perceive without projecting. Light may enter us from outside, but we inescapably perceive the colors and shapes of our stained-glass selves.

* * *

In 1999, Sylvia Hart Wright, while working on a book about unusual incidents attending death, broached her subject with seven American clergy. They represented Protestant, Jewish, and Roman Catholic institutions. She disclosed what she was up to and asked whether they had stories to share. Two happily complied. Five, however, responded that they had nothing to say because they had never heard anything pertinent.[66] This seems peculiar given what we now know about the incidence of the types of events Wright was investigating. Perhaps these five clergy were newly minted and so of limited experience. If not, one wonders why they had nothing to relate.

Whatever the explanation for their empty stores, we know that some clergy are indifferent or even hostile when a parishioner recounts an extraordinary episode. A few years before Wright asked her questions, two British researchers, Meg Maxwell and Verena Tschudin, stated, on the basis of materials in the Religious Experience Research Unit, that some experiencers were not just misunderstood by clergy but rebuffed, as though they had done something wrong.[67]

More recently, Carla Wills-Brandon, author of a book on deathbed visions, has formed the impression that "most clergy perceive encounters with deceased relatives, angels, beings of light and celestial visions as nonsense."[68] She relates that, when trying to discuss her work with religious professionals in North America, she rarely evokes interest or empathy. "Instead, I am often confronted with some inaccurate, scientifically based explanation"[69]—as though clergy were trying to make the world safe for secularists. Wills-Brandon finds this maddening. She has decided that, instead of feeling discouraged or chastened, the best course is to chortle at smug ignorance.

Christian leaders have, unfortunately, often sought to suppress, marginalize, demonize, and erase otherworldly experiences. From a historical point of view, the reasons for this have been manifold. They include the Reformers' rejection of Roman Catholic beliefs and practices that allowed for contact with the dead; Protestant cessationism, which branded as bogus every Catholic miracle and healing; Enlightenment rationalism, which derided mystics and rejected all divine interference in the world; modern psychology's pathologizing of altered states of consciousness; mainline Protestant discomfort with Pentecostal and charismatic Christians (often derided as "enthusiasts"); and the liberal inclination to value social action over personal devotion.[70] The convergence of these skeptical currents is that the incredulity of some Christians is close to knee-jerk reflexive. They have become the bystanders at Pentecost who declared, "They are filled with new wine" (Acts 2:13).

Skepticism may also hold sway for more personal reasons. The sorts of experiences reviewed in these pages do not appear on demand. They are beyond beck and call. They transpire on their own schedule. This matters because we may be uncomfortable with or even fear what lies outside our control. Apprehension is likely to be all the greater when something fails to conform to everyday expectations or buttress one's doctrinal system. If there is a psychology of belief, there is also a psychology of disbelief. If there is a will to believe, there is also a will to disbelieve.[71]

We need, however, to overcome our historical and personal prejudices. Despite all the opinion to the contrary, a heap of firsthand testimony tells us that our world is not disenchanted, that intercourse with the transcendent has not gone away. The metanormal remains with us—amazing us, comforting us, assailing us, confusing us.

Philosopher Charles Taylor has distinguished between the modern bounded self and the premodern porous self. The latter was "vulnerable to a world of spirits and powers." The former is a "disengaged rational agent" who "no longer fears demons, spirits, magic forces."[72] Many of our contemporaries, however, do not have bounded selves. Even in this allegedly disenchanted age, multitudes, whether or not affiliated with a religious tradition, continue to report encountering invisible forces and transcendent realities, forces and realities that they deem to be real, not illusory. The modern conception of the enclosed, buffered human individual does not match their experience. The *sensus numinis* is not extinct. It is not even endangered.

* * *

I end this chapter on a personal note. Some theologians and pastors of my acquaintance are unconcerned with this book's subject matter. Their lack of interest puzzles me. Their apathy betrays a constricted, unimaginative mind. To fail to attend to experiences that inform many lives, experiences that in some cases suggest that reality may be larger and far more perplexing than widely presumed, is to lack curiosity. And being incurious is not a virtue.

10

The Pastoral Imperative

"Having had this great question of supernatural fact upon my hands now for a number of years . . . I have been surprised to find how many things were coming to my knowledge and acquaintance, that most persons take for granted are utterly incredible. . . . Indeed, they are become so familiar, after only a few years of attention thus directed, and without inquiring after them, that their unfamiliar and strange look is gone; they even appear to belong, more or less commonly, to the church and the general economy of the Spirit."

—Horace Bushnell[1]

"Subjectivity undoubtedly is a prerogative of the Christian faith, which affirms a personal God-human relationship and not just subscription to a collectively held package of dogma or nominal participation in a religious or social institution."

—Klaus Bockmuehl[2]

"All the mighty figures of our religious history possess in a certain degree this definite creative quality, a winning and yet awe-inspiring authority of their own; and, traced back, we find this always originates in a personal and first-hand experience of spiritual realities, a genuine contact with and surrender to a supernatural and more living world."

—Evelyn Underhill[3]

After a public lecture I gave a few years ago, a lecture that disclosed my open-mindedness about matters metanormal, a man of thirty years or so shyly approached me. He had waited until the audience was mostly dispersed so that we could be alone. He seemed nervous. After asking me not to think him crazy, he went on to unfold a long, complex tale full of unconnected details, a tale I had trouble following. The gist of it was that he had, a while ago, waded across a river and found himself near a large tree. Then, suddenly, he felt a violent thump, as something exited the tree and entered his body. It was, he said, the tree's spirit. I eventually asked him, after vainly trying to gain clarification on several matters, where the spirit was now. He told me that I was speaking with it. It had never left. He wished that it would. Could I help?

I do not recall how the encounter ended, although I recall much wanting it to end. This was beyond my competence. The man, whom I judged to be psychotic, needed help of a sort I could not supply. Had he been a friend, I would have tried to connect him with a mental health professional. As he was a stranger in a place I was only visiting, I was at a loss.

Some, when I raise with them the topics in this book, envisage straightway somebody like the poor soul who thought a dryad possessed him. They may then remark on how difficult it is to distinguish the salubrious experiences of the spiritually fit from the chimerical experiences of the religiously deluded. They may additionally ask me what I think about misguided or even catastrophic exorcisms. Or they may remind me of the saints and mystics who so much warned about misleading visions, false auditions, and subjective impressions.[4] Or they may brandish 2 Corinthians 11:14: "Even Satan disguises himself as an angel of light."

Legitimate concerns inform such remarks.[5] They become a problem, however, when they serve as excuses to ignore or marginalize religious experiences that interrupt the lives of stable, sensible folk. Although the number of troubling cases is not trivial, so that one needs some aptitude in spotting mental disorders, they represent neither the whole nor the majority. The unusual need not be the dysfunctional. The anomalous need not be the abnormal. That some experiences signal debility scarcely requires that all or most do. The maladies of the few would stand for the experiences of the many only if the former constituted a representative sample. They do not.[6]

Most who report the extraordinary are not victims of debilitating psychological disorders. Indeed, they tend to be, on average, a bit healthier than everyone else.[7] What characterizes them is not mental dysfunction but the circumstance that something remarkable has interrupted their lives, something that edifies, puzzles, or troubles them.

* * *

How then should we respond when the context is not mental disorder, when sober, well-adjusted individuals seek to confide in us and relate an unusual experience? I have a few suggestions.

The first is obvious. One should attend with real interest, without hurry, and without condescension. This means mustering more than vapid clichés, more than an adiaphorous, "And how does that make you feel?," or a spineless, "It doesn't matter what I believe, only what you believe." When individuals share extraordinary experiences they find either perplexing or full of meaning, they are trusting listeners to take them seriously. The last thing to do is to respond with thinly disguised indifference or, even worse, an easy explanation.

When we know that the world is a truly weird place, that human beings are more than complex, and that God works in unpredictable ways, we will own an open mind. The grooves in which our thoughts customarily run will not be imprisoning walls. We will be leery of simplistic, self-assured answers, and we will not affect curiosity because we will be genuinely curious. We will not be the unadventurous, uncharitable bore who feels it a duty to disbelieve every astonishing story, especially when it is heartwarming.

The second suggestion is to assure people, if they are anxious, that what has happened to them does not indicate pathology. Assurance will not be empty if one knows something of the more common religious and metanormal experiences and so can disclose that healthy-minded others have had the same experience. It is, one must keep in mind, not the experience, taken by itself, that should fix one's evaluation: the everyday state of mind of the person having the experience is no less consequential.[8]

Most are surprised and relieved to learn that they are not alone. I referred, in chapter 2, to the disorienting mystical rapture of Genevieve W. Foster. She reported that there was no one with whom she could share "the most important thing" that had ever happened to her. What helped her the most was Evelyn Underhill's book, *Mysticism*. This was, according to Foster, the chief help I got in understanding this tremendous experience. It was of crucial importance to me to know that what had come so suddenly into my life was not something totally new and unknown, but that such an event had a name and had been experienced and understood centuries ago. . . . I was extraordinarily fortunate in finding Evelyn Underhill's book when I did. The support of human understanding is so important in such an encounter, and that I lacked.[9]

To know oneself to be like others is to feel understood.[10]

My third point is a warning. A few moralize their experiences.[11] They may think in terms of reward and punishment. They may congratulate themselves for some inspiring event or blame themselves for some unhappy incident. It is, however, all but impossible to untangle cause and effect in the matters of this book. One may, then, wish to pose a question or two. As a respectful counter, one might, for instance, ask what someone makes of the blameless and upright Job, who feared God and turned away from evil, and yet lost everything; or of Paul who, even as he was "still breathing threats and murder against all the disciples of the Lord" (Acts 9:1), beheld the risen Jesus. Like the world at large, the metanormal does not reliably hew to moral rhyme or reason.

The safest generalization comes not from Job's three friends and their naive theology but from the social anthropologists who urge that two factors raise the odds of encountering invisible others. One is cognitive: belief that the self is not bounded but porous to outside, invisible sources.[12] The other is experiential: the ability to lose oneself in sensory experiences or internally generated imagery and scenes.[13] These factors are independent of moral considerations.

My final suggestion is this. Keeping the question of authority in abeyance, one should encourage people to be their own interpreters, to think for themselves about what an event might mean. This can be done through open-ended questions informed by what others with similar experiences have said and done. Such questions may be, according to the need of the experiencer, theoretical or practical. In the former case, one should be able to recommend relevant books, such as those listed at the end of this volume. In the latter case, one should be prepared to help people explore how an experience has changed the way they think, act, or feel.

* * *

Reviewers, to the dismay of authors, sometimes censure a book for what it fails to contain. I can imagine these pages suffering such a complaint. A critic might gripe that I have said little or nothing about any number of pertinent topics—speaking in tongues, conversion experiences, unexpected healings, providential coincidences, demonic possession, guiding voices, unitive mysticism, revelatory dreams, visions of Jesus, psilocybin-abetted states of mind, and mystical experiences of darkness and abandonment. Furthermore, and a bit like William James, I have one-sidedly focused on the individual rather than the communal, and on the dramatic rather than the unremarkable. I have also failed to discuss Christian pneumatology or to offer guidance as to how one might, when listening to an over-the-top story, come to suspect psychopathology as a contributing factor.

My preemptive defense is to plead a limited purpose. All the subjects just mentioned are important. They are also, each one of them, of interest to me. Were I to examine them all, however, this volume would pass the thousand-page threshold and suffer the disgrace of being self-published. It must, then, be an inadequate introduction to a vast subject, a deliberately truncated, elementary primer that covers but a handful of representative topics.

Perhaps I should also add, as the final word, that although I wish to stir interest and generate sympathy, I do not press any to hunger and thirst after the experiences I have written about. This is not a how-to book or a manual for would-be mystics. I am not a guru peddling or pushing peak experiences. My aim is not to promote the production of exotic encounters—as though I knew how to command angels, create synchronicity, or nudge an inscrutable Providence—but to enlarge understanding, as well as to counter ill-informed prejudices.

Notes

Preface

1. I venture no definition here but use "religious experience" only as convenient shorthand for the experiences discussed in this volume.

2. The serious student will find useful the collection of essays by editors Roger Trigg and Justin L. Barrett, *The Roots of Religion: Exploring the Cognitive Science of Religion* (Burlington, VT: Ashgate, 2014).

Chapter 1

1. Shakespeare, *A Midsummer Night's Dream*, Act 5, Scene 1.

Chapter 2

1. As quoted in Kevin Nelson, *The Spiritual Doorway in the Brain: A Neurologist's Search for the God Experience* (New York: Dutton, 2011), 109.

2. Philip Wiebe, *Intuitive Knowing as Spiritual Experience* (New York: Palgrave Macmillan, 2015), 111.

3. Susan L. DeHoff, *Psychosis or Mystical Experience? A New Paradigm Grounded in Psychology and Reformed Theology* (Cham, Switzerland: Palgrave Macmillan, 2018), 9.

4. For this and the following paragraphs see esp. Alister Hardy, *The Spiritual Nature of Man: A Study of Contemporary Religious Experience* (Oxford: Religious Experience Research Unit, 1979). The archive is now online and can be accessed for a small subscription fee; see https://www.uwtsd.ac.uk/library/alister-hardy

-religious-experience-research-centre/online-archive/. The Religious Experience Research Centre was formerly known as the Religious Experience Research Unit, so the relevant literature often refers to RERU, not RERC.

5. Jules Evans, *The Art of Losing Control: A Philosopher's Search for Ecstatic Experience* (Edinburgh: Canongate, 2018), 3. Hardy's method and results were partly anticipated by the (still interesting) work of Marghanita Laski, *Ecstasy: A Study of Some Secular and Religious Experiences* (Bloomington, IN: Indiana University Press, 1961).

6. J. M. Cohen and J.-F. Phipps, *The Common Experience* (Los Angeles: J. P. Tarcher, 1979), 142 (alluding to a famous line in Julian of Norwich, *Showings* 31).

7. Mark Fox, *The Fifth Love: Exploring Accounts of the Extraordinary* (n.p.: Spirit & Sage, 2014), 125.

8. A significant exception is the Christian philosopher Philip Wiebe; see his book *Intuitive Knowing as Spiritual Experience* (New York: Palgrave Macmillan, 2015).

9. See, e.g., David Hay, *Exploring Inner Space: Scientists and Religious Experience* (New York: Penguin, 1982), and Madeleine Castro, Roger Burrows, and Robin Wooffitt, "The Paranormal Is (Still) Normal: The Sociological Implications of a Survey of Paranormal Experiences in Great Britain," *Sociological Research Online* 19 (2014): 30–44, https://www.socresonline.org.uk/19/3/16.html.

10. James H. Leuba, *The Psychology of Religious Mysticism* (New York: Harcourt, Brace & Co., 1925).

11. A. Grimby, "Bereavement among Elderly People: Grief Reactions, Post-Bereavement Hallucinations and Quality of Life," *Acta Psychiatrica Scandinavica* 87 (1993): 72–80.

12. Dewi Rees, *Pointers to Eternity* (Talybont, Ceredigion, Wales: Y. Lolfa, 2010), 202.

13. Rees, *Pointers to Eternity*, 178.

14. This and the following quotation are taken from Michael Hirsch et al., "The Spectrum of Specters: Making Sense of Ghostly Encounters," *Paranthropology* 5 (2014): 7.

15. Edie Devers, *Goodbye Again: Experiences with Departed Loved Ones* (Kansas City: Andrews and McMeel, 1997), 112.

16. Elizabeth G. Krohn and Jeffrey J. Kripal, *Changed in a Flash: One Woman's Near-Death Experience and Why a Scholar Thinks It Empowers Us All* (Berkeley, CA: North Atlantic Books, 2018), 47.

17. Nancy Evans Bush, *Dancing Past the Dark: Distressing Near-Death Experiences* (Cleveland, TN: Parson's Porch Books, 2012), 23. Bush adds: "One participant, at the urging of her psychotherapist, eventually contacted one of the investigators. . . . and agreed to be interviewed *nine years after the study.*"

18. Nancy Clark, *Divine Moments: Ordinary People Having Spiritually Transformative Experiences* (Fairfield, IA: 1stWorld, 2012), 53.

19. David Hay, *Something There: The Biology of the Human Spirit* (Philadelphia: Templeton Foundation Press, 2006), 86–87.

20. Genevieve W. Foster, *The World Was Flooded with Light: A Mystical Experience Remembered*, with commentary by David J. Hufford (Pittsburgh: University of Pittsburgh Press, 1985), 36.

21. Foster, *Flooded with Light*, 43–45.

22. Foster, *Flooded with Light*, 178.

23. Barbara Ehrenreich, "A Rationalist's Mystical Moment," https://www.nytimes.com/2014/04/06/opinion/sunday/a-rationalists-mystical-moment.html; *Living with a Wild God: A Nonbeliever's Search for the Truth about Everything* (New York: Twelve, 2014), esp. 115–17.

24. This quotation and those following are from Ehrenreich, "A Rationalist's Mystical Moment."

25. This, however, may be changing. See Sam Harris, *Waking Up: A Guide to Spirituality without Religion* (New York: Simon & Schuster, 2015), and Alice Heron, "Godless Mystics: Atheists and Their Mystical Experiences: Towards a Grounded Theory" (PhD diss., University of Surrey, 2019).

26. See https://www.aapsglobal.com/taste/.

27. See, e.g., Andrew Greeley, *The Sociology of the Paranormal: A Reconnaissance* (Beverley Hills: Sage, 1975); Craig Murray, ed., *Mental Health and Anomalous Experience* (New York: Nova Science, 2012); David Hufford, "The Healing Power of Extraordinary Spiritual Experiences," *Journal of Near-Death Studies* 32 (2014): 137–56; and David Bryce Yaden et al., "The Varieties of Self-Transcendent Experience," *Review of General Psychology* 21 (2017): 143–60.

28. See, e.g., Andrew Newberg and Mark Robert Waldman, *Born to Believe: God, Science, and the Origin of Ordinary and Extraordinary Beliefs* (New York: Free Press, 2006); Ilkka Pyysiäinen, *Supernatural Agents: Why We Believe in Souls, Gods, and Buddhas* (Oxford: Oxford University Press, 2009); and Nelson, *Spiritual Doorway*.

29. See further Heiner Schwenke, *Transcendente Begegnungen: Phänomenologie und Metakritik*, Schwabe Mystica 1 (Basel: Schwabe, 2014), 192–230.

30. The words are those of David Hufford, as quoted by John W. Morehead, "From Sleep Paralysis to Spiritual Experience: An Interview with David Hufford," *Paranthropology* 4 (2013): 22.

31. Thomas Woolston, *A Sixth Discourse on the Miracles of Our Saviour*, 2nd ed. (London: Printed for the Author, 1729), 30. On Protestants and ghosts see Peter Marshall, *Invisible Worlds: Death, Religion and the Supernatural in England 1500–1700* (London: SPCK, 2017), 132–77.

32. Cf. Marshall, *Invisible Worlds*, 165–66. On the cross-cultural and cross-temporal prevalence of apparitions of the dead, see my book *The Resurrection of Jesus: Apologetics, Criticism, History* (London: T&T Clark, 2021), 216–22.

33. See "Many Americans Mix Multiple Faiths," Pew Research Center: Religion & Public Life, December 2, 2009, https://www.pewforum.org/2009/12/09/many-americans-mix-multiple-faiths/.

34. Brian Inglis, *The Hidden Power* (London: Jonathan Cape, 1986), 266–67.

35. These numbers are from the Pew Research Center: Religion and Public Life; see note 33.

36. David J. Hufford, *The Terror That Comes in the Night: An Experience-Centered Study of Supernatural Assault Traditions* (Philadelphia: University of Pennsylvania Press, 1982).

37. Morehead, "Sleep Paralysis," 21.

38. Hufford, *Terror*, 25.

39. Richard J. McNally, as quoted in Bruce Bower, "Night of the Crusher: The Waking Nightmare of Sleep Paralysis Propels People into a Spirit World," *Science News* 168 (2005): 29.

40. David J. Hufford, "Sleep Paralysis as Spiritual Experience," *Transcultural Psychiatry* 42 (2005): 19.

41. Hufford, "Sleep Paralysis as Spiritual Experience," 13. See further Hufford, "Beings without Bodies: An Experience-Centered Theory of the Belief in Spirits," in *Out of the Ordinary: Folklore and the Supernatural*, ed. Barbara Walker (Logan, UT: Utah State University Press, 1995), 11–45, and cf. below, pp. 42–46.

42. Hufford, "Sleep Paralysis as Spiritual Experience," 22.

43. As quoted in the television documentary "Your Worst Nightmare," https://www.youtube.com/watch?v=J_vDgu_o-s4&t=1037s (at 11:22). See further Hay, *Exploring Inner Space*, 199–207, on the topic of "the social control of religious experience."

44. See George Riddoch, "Phantom Limbs and Body Shape," *Brain* 64 (1941): 197.

Chapter 3

1. Howard Thurman, *The Creative Encounter: An Interpretation of Religion and the Social Witness* (Richmond, IN: Friends United Press, 1972), 33.

2. As quoted in Christopher C. H. Cook, *Christians Hearing Voices: Affirming Experience and Finding Meaning* (London: Jessica Kingsley, 2020), 79.

3. Leslie D. Weatherhead, *The Christian Agnostic* (London: Hodder & Stoughton, 1965), 39–40.

4. Henry Alline, *The Life and Journal of the Rev. Mr. Henry Alline* (Boston: Gilbert & Dean, 1806), 35–36.

5. Mark Fox, *The Fifth Love: Exploring Accounts of the Extraordinary* (n.p.: Spirit & Sage, 2014), 13.

6. David Hay, *Something There: The Biology of the Human Spirit* (Philadelphia: Templeton Foundation Press, 2006), 18–19.

7. Nancy Clark, *Divine Moments: Ordinary People Having Spiritually Transformative Experiences* (Fairfield, IA: 1stWorld, 2012), 141.

8. Clark, *Divine Moments*, 81.

9. Clark, *Divine Moments*, 93.

10. Meg Maxwell and Verena Tschudin, *Seeing the Invisible: Modern Religious and Other Transcendent Experiences* (London: Arkana, 1990), 56.

11. Paul Hawker, *Secret Affairs of the Soul: Ordinary People's Extraordinary Experiences of the Sacred* (Kelowna, British Columbia: Northstone, 2000), 37.

12. Phillip H. Wiebe, *Intuitive Knowing as Spiritual Experience* (New York: Palgrave Macmillan, 2015), 87.

13. Those interested may consult further Fox, *Fifth Love*; also Wiebe, *Intuitive Knowing*, 83–90.

14. See further Fox, *Fifth Love*, 76–83.

15. See further Fox, *Fifth Love*, 97–115.

16. C. S. Lewis, *The Four Loves* (San Diego: Harcourt, Brace & Co., 1991).

17. Lewis, *Four Loves*, 126.

18. See further below, pp. 179–80.

19. Fox, *Fifth Love*, 85.

20. Fox, *Fifth Love*, 13, 61, 77, 123.

21. Maxwell and Tschudin, *Seeing the Invisible*, 55.

22. Wiebe, *Intuitive Knowing*, 84.

23. Maxwell and Tschudin, *Seeing the Invisible*, 53.

24. Roshi Philip Kapleau, *The Three Pillars of Zen: Teaching, Practice, Enlightenment*, rev. ed. (New York: Anchor, 2000), 253.

25. Irina Tweedie, *Daughter of Fire: A Diary of a Spiritual Training with a Sufi Master* (Point Reyes, CA: The Golden Sufi Center, 2014), 338-39.

26. Robert W. Harner, "Dance of the Leaves," in *The World's Strangest Stories*, ed. Mary Margaret Fuller et al. (Highland Park, IL: Clark Publishing Co., 1983), 166-70.

27. Cf. the interpretation of visual perceptions during sleep paralysis in J. Allan Cheyne, "The Ominous Numinous: Sensed Presence and 'Other' Hallucinations," *Journal of Consciousness Studies* 8 (2001): 133-50.

28. Merete Demant Jakobsen, *Negative Spiritual Experiences: Encounters with Evil*, RERC Third Series Occasional Paper 1 (n.p.: Religious Experience Research Centre, 1999), 18.

29. Jakobsen, *Negative Spiritual Experiences*, 10.

30. Maxwell and Tschudin, *Seeing the Invisible*, 69.

31. Alister Hardy, *The Spiritual Nature of Man: A Study of Contemporary Religious Experience* (Oxford: Religious Experience Research Unit, 1979), 63.

32. Jakobsen, *Negative Spiritual Experiences*, 19.

33. See Hay, *Something There*, 11, 19.

34. As quoted in Cheyne, "Ominous Numinous," 14.

35. Jakobsen, *Negative Spiritual Experiences*, 10.

36. See Jakobsen, *Negative Spiritual Experiences*, pp. 13, 15, for additional narratives that refer to "the devil."

37. I have, however, been unable to make sense of the polling data, which ranges widely. It is not clear to me how many people in North America profess belief in the devil or Satan and what, when they do, they mean by it. Whatever the numbers, they must be lower for Europe and higher in much of the rest of the world.

38. The words are from Darwin's famous letter to Asa Gray, dated May 22, 1860. See "The Darwin Correspondence Project," https://www.darwinproject.ac.uk/letter/?docId=letters/DCP-LETT-2814.xml;query=darwin;brand=default. Darwin, however, went on to write: "I cannot anyhow be contented to view this wonderful universe & especially the nature of man, & to conclude that everything is the result of brute force. I am inclined to look at everything as resulting from designed laws, with the details, whether good or bad, left to the working out of what we may call chance. Not that this notion *at all* satisfies

me. I feel most deeply that the whole subject is too profound for the human intellect. A dog might as well speculate on the mind of Newton. — Let each man hope & believe what he can."

39. Jakobsen, *Negative Spiritual Experiences*, 8.

40. Jakobsen, *Negative Spiritual Experiences*, 5.

Chapter 4

1. C. F. D'Arcy, "Prayer (Christian, Theological)," in *Encyclopaedia of Religion and Ethics*, ed. James Hastings, vol. 10 (New York: Charles Scribner's Sons, 1919), 171.

2. William James, *The Varieties of Religious Experience: A Study in Human Nature* (New York: New American Library, 1958), 353.

3. Jean-Claudet Larchet, *The New Media Epidemic* (Jordanville, NY: Holy Trinity Publications, 2019), 131.

4. But my diminishing focus on petitionary prayer is in line with the finding that belief in the objective efficacy of petitionary prayer often declines with age; cf. L. B. Brown, "Egocentric Thought in Petitionary Prayer: A Cross-Cultural Study," *Journal of Social Psychology* 68 (1966): 197–210; Brown, "Some Attitudes Underlying Petitionary Prayer," in *From Cry to Word: Contributions towards a Psychology of Prayer*, ed. A. Godin (Brussels: Lumen Vitae Press, 1968), 65–82; Robert H. Thouless, *An Introduction to the Philosophy of Religion*, 3rd ed. (Cambridge: Cambridge University Press, 1971), 94; John R. Finney and H. Newton Malony Jr., "Empirical Studies of Christian Prayer: A Review of the Literature," *Journal of Psychology and Theology* 13 (1985): 104–15.

5. See, e.g., "American Prayer Practices: Survey of 1,137 Americans for Thomas Nelson and Max Lucado," LifeWay Research, 2014, http://lifewayre search.com/wp-content/uploads/2014/09/American-Prayer-Practices.pdf. On what people pray about see further below.

6. For an overview see Bernard Spilka and Kevin L. Ladd, *The Psychology of Prayer: A Scientific Approach* (New York: Guilford Press, 2013).

7. T. M. Luhrmann, *When God Talks Back: Understanding the American Evangelical Relationship with God* (New York: Alfred A. Knopf, 2012).

8. As an aside, and as a reminder of how things are always changing, a number of older folks have told me that they were taught to pray, "Now I lay me down to sleep, I pray the Lord my soul to keep. If I should die before I wake, I pray the

Lord my soul to take"—ending there or continuing on (in multiple versions). They associate this with a real fear of death and recall quarantines in the 1940s and worries about measles. There are, I note, updated versions of this prayer that avoid the thought of death, such as "Now I lay me down to sleep, I pray the Lord my soul to keep. Guard me Jesus through the night, and wake me with the morning light."

9. Cf. Luhrmann, *When God Talks Back*, 150: one woman said that "she didn't really have mental images. She had sensations or impressions when she prayed for people." Some, in my experience, perceive something that they cannot describe or put into words.

10. We typically use first names for those closest to us but often use less definite designations for those more distant, as in: "Ken and Val and their children."

11. The bilingual, I have learned, can pray in more than one tongue. A Chinese immigrant told me that, when praying for family, she uses Chinese, but when she prays for her American friends, she uses English. Some, of course, mingle intercessions with glossolalia.

12. For illustrations see Luhrmann, *When God Talks Back*, esp. 132–56.

13. Cf. Luhrmann, *When God Talks Back*, 54: "Most people whom I met at the Vineyard seemed to have a 'prayer journal.' They'd write down their prayers, either before or after they prayed them, sometimes praying through the act of writing." For a helpful introduction and analysis of modern "prayer journaling" see Courtney Bender, "How Does God Answer Back?," *Poetics* 36 (2008): 476–92.

14. My guess is that evening prayer is more common than morning prayer; one study found this to be true of adolescents: Jacques Janssen, Joep de Hart, and Christine den Draak, "A Content Analysis of the Praying Practices of Dutch Youth," *Journal for the Scientific Study of Religion* 29 (1990): 99–107.

15. Cf. the cover of Bruce Bickel and Stan Jantz, *Bruce & Stan's Pocket Guide to Prayer* (Eugene, OR: Harvest House, 2000): this depicts a man holding a telephone.

16. The Public Religion Research Institute obtains an even higher number—26 percent—in a 2014 poll of American "sports fans"; see Daniel Cox, Juhem Navarro-Rivera, and Robert P. Jones, "Half of American Fans See Supernatural Forces at Play in Sports," https://www.prri.org/research/jan-2014-sports-poll/.

17. For all this see "American Prayer Practices."

18. See the "Tearfund Prayer Survey," which is available on the Savanta: ComRes website, https://comresglobal.com/polls/tearfund-prayer-survey/.

19. See the Savanta: ComRes website: https://comresglobal.com/polls/premier-Christian-media-prayer-survey/.

20. John Calvin, *Institutes of the Christian Religion* 3.20.3.

21. Cf. the situation with the Han Chinese according to a survey in 2005: although only 4.5 percent called themselves Buddhists, 27.4 percent reported that they had prayed to Buddha or a Bodhisattva in the last year; see Xinzhong Yao and Paul Badham, *Religious Experience in Contemporary China* (Cardiff: University of Wales Press, 2007), 189.

22. See Michelle Boorstein, "Some Nonbelievers Still Find Solace in Prayer," *The Washington Post*, June 24, 2013, https://www.washingtonpost.com/local/non-believers-say-their-prayers-to-no-one/2013/06/24/b7c8cf50-d915-11e2-a9f2-42ee3912ae0e_story.html.

23. Frank C. Laubach, *Prayer: The Mightiest Force in the World* (London: Lutterworth Press, 1952), 22–24, 33–34, 49–50.

24. Maxie Dunnam, *The Workbook of Intercessory Prayer* (Nashville: The Upper Room, 1979), 116. John B. Cobb's *Praying for Jennifer* (Nashville: The Upper Room, 1985) is in large measure a theological exposition of this point of view.

25. John Hick, *The Fifth Dimension: An Exploration of the Spiritual Realm* (Oxford: Oneworld, 2004), 30.

26. For a philosophical defense of this view see W. Paul Franks, "Why a Believer Could Believe That God Answers Prayer," *Sophia* 48 (2009): 319–24. For a more popular presentation see Keith Ward, *Divine Action* (London: Collins, 1990), 154–69.

27. I have elsewhere discussed some of the rational problems with prayer and why I do not find them fatal for practice; see *The Luminous Dusk: Finding God in the Deep, Still Places* (Grand Rapids, MI: Eerdmans, 2006), 165–78. For the current state of the philosophical discussion see Scott A. Davison, *Petitionary Prayer: A Philosophical Investigation* (Oxford: Oxford University Press, 2017).

28. See https://news.gallup.com/poll/1690/religion.aspx. I note, however, that a recent UK poll (January, 2020) has a much higher number: 57 percent; see the previously cited "Premier Christian Media—Prayer Survey," https://comresglobal.com/polls/premier-Christian-media-prayer-survey/.

29. Sarah Bänziger, Jacques Janssen, and Peer Scheepers, "Praying in a Secularized Society: An Empirical Study of Praying Practices and Varieties," *International Journal for the Psychology of Religion* 18 (2008): 256–65.

30. As quoted in Harriet Sherwood, "Non-Believers Turn to Prayer in a Crisis, Poll Finds," *The Guardian*, January 13, 2018, https://www.theguardian.com/world/2018/jan/14/half-of-non-believers-pray-says-poll.

31. See, e.g., Janssen, de Hart, and den Draak, "Content Analysis," and Margaret M. Poloma and George H. Gallup Jr., *Varieties of Prayer: A Survey Report* (Philadelphia: Trinity Press Intl., 1991), 5, 46–48.

32. William R. Parker and Elaine St. Johns, in a well-known study, *Prayer Can Change Your Life* (Carmel, NY: Guideposts, 1957).

33. "Stress in America," https://www.apa.org/news/press/releases/2008/10/stress-in-america.pdf, p. 6.

34. Note, e.g., John Maltby, Christopher Alan Lewis, and Lizz Day, "Religious Orientation and Psychological Well-Being: The Role of Frequency of Personal Prayer," *British Journal of Health Psychology* 4 (1999): 363–78; Leslie J. Francis and Thomas E. Evans, "The Psychology of Christian Prayer: A Review of Empirical Research," in *Psychological Perspectives on Prayer: A Reader*, ed. Leslie J. Francis and Jeff Astley (Herefordshire: Gracewing, 2000), 8–12; Rajni Moskowitz et al., "Socioeconomic Differences in the Effects of Prayer on Physical Symptoms and Quality of Life," *Journal of Health Psychology* 12 (2007): 249–60; John Maltby, C. A. Lewis, and Liza Day, "Prayer and Subjective Well-Being: The Application of a Cognitive-Behavioural Framework," *Mental Health, Religion and Culture* 11 (2008): 119–29.

35. Brandon L. Whittington and Steven J. Scher, "Prayer and Subjective Well-Being: An Examination of Six Different Types of Prayer," *International Journal for the Psychology of Religion* 20 (2010): 59–68, find a positive sense of well-being associated with adoration, thanksgiving, and "prayers focused on opening oneself up to closeness with God." They do not find this association with supplication, which they deem to be "self-focused." But petitionary prayer is, for many, habitually combined with the other types of prayer. When this is the case, distinguishing effects is impossible. Furthermore, prayers of supplication need not be self-focused or egoistic. People pray for others as much or more than they pray for themselves.

36. These are very large generalizations that ignore issues of age, gender, ethnicity, religious affiliation, and so on.

37. Simon Dein and Roland Littlewood, "The Psychology of Prayer and the Development of the Prayer Experience Questionnaire," *Mental Health, Religion and Culture* 11 (2008): 43.

38. E.g., Melvin Pollner, "Divine Relations, Social Relations, and Well-Being," *Journal of Health and Social Behavior* 30 (1989): 92–104; Shane Sharp, "How Does Prayer Help Manage Emotions?," *Social Psychology Quarterly* 73 (2010): 417–37; Kevin L. Ladd and Daniel N. McIntosh, "Meaning, God, and Prayer: Physical and Metaphysical Aspects of Social Support," *Mental Health, Religion & Culture* 11 (2008): 23–38. Cf. Kevin Rounding, Albert Lee, and Jill A. Jacobson, "Religion Replenishes Self-Control," *Psychological Science* 23 (2012): 635–42, and see further T. M. Luhrmann, *How God Becomes Real: Kindling the Presence of Invisible Others* (Princeton: Princeton University Press, 2020), esp. 136–84. Luhrmann takes prayer to be a mechanism by which God is made more real.

39. Julianne Holt-Lunstad, Timothy B. Smith, and J. Bradley Layton, "Social Relationships and Mortality Risk: A Meta-analytic Review," *PLOS Medicine* 7, no. 7 (2010), https://doi.org/10.1371/journal.pmed.1000316.

40. So Ladd and McIntosh, "Meaning, God, and Prayer," 33.

41. Amy L. Ai et al., "Prayers, Spiritual Support, and Positive Attitudes in Coping with the September 11 National Crisis," *Journal of Personality* 73 (2005): 763–91; Dein and Littlewood, "Psychology of Prayer," 43–44; Claire Hollywell and Jan Walker, "Private Prayer as a Suitable Intervention for Hospitalised Patients: A Critical Review of the Literature," *Journal of Clinical Nursing* 18 (2008): 637–51; Nathaniel M. Lambert et al., "Can Prayer Increase Gratitude?," *Psychology of Religion and Spirituality* 1 (2009): 139–49; Michael E. McCullough and Brian L. B. Willoughby, "Religion, Self-Regulation, and Self-Control: Associations, Explanations, and Implications," *Psychological Bulletin* 135 (2009): 69–93; Spilka and Ladd, *Psychology of Prayer*, 88–103.

42. Peter Sedlmeier et al., "The Psychological Effects of Meditation: A Meta-Analysis," *Psychological Bulletin* 138 (2012): 1139–71.

43. Michaël Dambrun et al., "Measuring Happiness: From Fluctuating Happiness to Authentic-Durable Happiness," *Frontiers in Psychology* 3 (2012), https://doi.org/10.3389/fpsyg.2012.00016; Michael Dambrun, "Self-Centeredness and Selflessness: Happiness Correlates and Mediating Psychological Processes," *PeerJ* 5:e3306 (2017), https://peerj.com/articles/3306/.

44. So Herbert Benson, as quoted by Augostino Bono, "Repetitive Prayer Can Reset Your Stress Thermostat," Catholic Online, https://www.catholic.org/news/health/story.php?id=23172.

45. Spilka and Ladd, *Psychology of Prayer*, 172. This helps explain why prayer

can be of immediate benefit even to those without a religious tradition to interpret what they are doing; cf. this testimony from Hardy, *Spiritual Nature*, 120: "In times of distress I have often found my own pleas or prayers answered, sometimes by an inexplicable feeling of peace which seems to arise simply from the fact of praying—although I do not know who or what I am praying to."

46. See Poloma and Gallup, *Varieties of Prayer*, 49–51; Luhrmann, *When God Talks Back*, 152–53.

47. Cf. the testimony from a member of the Vineyard in Lurhmann, *When God Talks Back*, 107–8: "Every once in a while there's like times when I'm just, like when it's like wow, something is different in prayer. It doesn't feel like it was just part of the daily routine, I just feel it was something more like there's some sort of connection, I'm more really talking to God. It feels better."

48. See Luhrmann, *When God Talks Back*, 132–56, 189–226.

49. For examples of this see Dein and Littlewood, "Psychology of Prayer," 47, and Luhrmann, *When God Talks Back*, 227–66. On the phenomenon of hearing voices, which is quite common in the general population, see Timothy Beardsworth, *A Sense of Presence: The Phenomenology of Certain Kinds of Visionary and Ecstatic Experience, Based on a Thousand Contemporary First-Hand Accounts* (Oxford: The Religious Experience Research Unit, 1977), 89–107, and John Watkins, *Hearing Voices: A Common Human Experience* (Melbourne: Michelle Anderson, 2008). Most often it is not pathological. I still hear my mother call my childhood name ("Dee") a couple of times a year.

50. As quoted in Maxwell and Tschudin, *Seeing the Invisible*, 184.

51. Beardsworth, *Sense of Presence*, 67.

52. Meaningful experiences during prayer are associated with subjective well-being; see Maltby, Lewis, and Day, "Prayer and Subjective Well-Being."

53. According to one survey, only 10 percent of Americans who pray report never receiving an answer; see the 2008 "U.S. Religious Landscape Survey" conducted by the Pew Forum on Religion and Public Life, https://www.pewresearch.org/wp-content/uploads/sites/7/2013/05/report-religious-landscape-study-full.pdf, 187. I here pass over the claim that we have empirical, statistical grounds for regarding prayer as objectively effective; this appears doubtful to me; see Spilka and Ladd, *Psychology of Prayer*, 139–60.

54. David Hay, *Exploring Inner Space: Scientists and Religious Experience* (New York: Penguin, 1982), 135.

55. Winston S. Churchill, *My Early Life* (London: Thornton Butterworth, 1930), 129–30.

56. As quoted in Vimal Patel, "As Gas Prices Soared, He Filled Up with Prayer," *Los Angeles Times*, August 14, 2008, https://www.latimes.com/archives /la-xpm-2008-aug-14-na-pump14-story.html.

57. Alvin J. Vander Griend with Edith Bajema, *The Praying Church Sourcebook* (Grand Rapids, MI: Church Development Resources, 1997), 243. Contrast Bickel and Jantz, *Pocket Guide*, 26: "If it is important to you, it is important to God."

58. Origen, *On Prayer* 17.

59. Cf. the sentence often attributed (rightly or not I do not know) to William Temple: "When I pray, coincidences happen, and when I don't, they don't." It does seem that, "if God exists and things are as supposed by classical theism, God causally contributes to every occurrence." So William P. Alston, *Perceiving God: The Epistemology of Religious Experience* (Ithaca, NY: Cornell University Press, 1991), 64.

60. Judson Cornwall, *Ascending to Glory: The Secret of Personal Prayer* (Mansfield, PA: Fire Wind, 1999), 81–82.

61. For what follows see Ken Gaub, *God's Got Your Number* (n.p.: New Leaf Press, 1998), 11–15. There is a slightly different account of this story, based on an interview with Gaub, in Peter Shockey, *Reflections of Heaven: A Millennial Odyssey of Miracles, Angels, and Afterlife* (New York: Doubleday, 1999), 40–43. Despite the differences, the main points agree.

62. Coptic Christians, however, tell me that they receive this story as history; cf. "Miracle," Saint Samaan The Tanner Monastery, https://www .samaanchurch.com/en/miracle.

63. George B. Stewart, *The Lower Levels of Prayer* (London: SCM, 1939), 163. See further Arndt Büssing, Stephan Winter, and Klaus Baumann, "Perception of Religious Brothers and Sisters and Lay Persons that Prayers Go Unanswered Is a Matter of Perceived Distance from God," *Religions* 11, no. 4 (2020), https:// www.researchgate.net/publication/340567998_Perception_of_Religious_Broth ers_and_Sisters_and_Lay_Persons_That_Prayers_Go_Unanswered_Is_a_Matter_of _Perceived_Distance_from_God.

64. Cf. Poloma and Gallup, *Varieties of Prayer*, 14–15.

65. For the effects of screens on reading see esp. Nicholas Carr, *The Shallows:*

What the Internet Is Doing to Our Brains (New York: W. W. Norton & Co., 2011), and Naomi S. Baron, *Words Onscreen: The Fate of Reading in a Digital World* (Oxford: Oxford University Press, 2015).

66. Philip Yancey, "Reading Wars," *Philip Yancey* (blog), July 20, 2017, https://philipyancey.com/reading-wars.

67. Howard Thurman, *The Creative Encounter: An Interpretation of Religion and the Social Witness* (Richmond, IN: Friends United Press, 1972), 34.

68. Simon Maybin, "Busting the Attention Span Myth," *BBC News*, March 10, 2017, https://www.bbc.com/news/health-38896790#; Faris Yakob, "The Goldfish Myth," WARC, https://www.warc.com/newsandopinion/opinion/the-goldfish-myth/2806.

69. Timothy D. Wilson et al., "Just Think: The Challenges of the Disengaged Mind," *Science* 345 (2014): 75–77.

70. "American Values, Mental Health and Using Technology in the Age of Trump," Findings from the Baylor Religious Survey, Wave 5 (2017), https://www.baylor.edu/baylorreligionsurvey/doc.php/292546.pdf.

71. Hay, *Exploring Inner Space*, 203.

Chapter 5

1. David Kessler, *Visions, Trips, and Crowded Rooms: Who and What You See Before You Die* (Carlsbad, CA: Hay House, 2010), 89.

2. David J. Hufford, "Visionary Spiritual Experiences and Cognitive Aspects of Spiritual Transformation," *Metanexus*, September 2011, https://www.metanexus.net/visionary-spiritual-experiences-and-cognitive-aspects-spiritual-transformation/.

3. Allan Kellehear, *Visitors at the End of Life: Finding Meaning and Purpose in Near-Death Phenomena* (New York: Columbia University Press, 2020), 20.

4. For what follows see Mickey Rooney, *Life Is Too Short* (New York: Villard Books, 1991).

5. Joan Wester Anderson, *Where Angels Walk: True Stories of Heavenly Visitors* (Sea Cliff, NY: Barton & Brett, 1992), 107–10. This was a *New York Times* best seller, and it eventually sold more than a million copies. It has been translated into over ten languages.

6. E.g., Judg. 13:1–21; 1 Kings 19:4–8; Ps. 34:7; Matt. 28:3–5; Mark 1:13; John 20:12.

7. See the online *Daily Mail* for August 7, 2013: https://www.dailymail.co
.uk/news/article-2386627/The-riddle-angel-priest-Holy-man-appeared-pray
-trapped-girl-rescuers-traffic-accident-told-OK-vanished.html.

8. The following story appeared in the October 24, 1992, edition of the *Wichita Eagle.*

9. This story is told in Hope MacDonald, *When Angels Appear* (Grand Rapids,
MI: Zondervan, 1982), 79–80.

10. For the following see Anderson, *Where Angels Walk*, 88–89.

11. Michael Murphy and Rhea A. White, *In the Zone: Transcendent Experiences in Sport* (New York: Penguin, 1995), 40–44.

12. Murphy and White, *In the Zone*, 42.

13. See Juliane Koepcke, *When I Fell from the Sky* (New York: Titletown, 2011).

14. Anderson, *Where Angels Walk*, 92–95.

15. MacDonald, *When Angels Appear*, 11–12.

16. Karen Goldman, *Angel Encounters: True Stories of Divine Intervention*
(New York: Simon & Schuster, 1995).

17. See Doreen Virtue, *Saved by an Angel* (Carlsbad, CA: Hay House, 2011),
23–41, and further below, pp. 85–86, 106–12. On the being of light in NDEs,
which is so often dubbed an angel, see Raymond Moody, *Life after Life: The
Investigation of a Phenomenon: Survival of Bodily Death* (New York: Bantam,
1975), pp. 58–64, and below, pp. 173–77.

18. For samples of these see Doreen Virtue, *Angel Visions* (Carlsbad, CA: Hay
House, 2000), 41–63.

19. This category presumably explains the title of Glennyce S. Eckersley's
book: *An Angel at My Shoulder: True Stories of Angelic Experiences* (London:
Rider, 1996). Note, e.g., 127–28.

20. Within these are three subcategories: the slow fall, helping hands, and
emergency flight. In addition to the stories introduced above see E. Lonnie Melashenko and Timothy E. Crosby, *In the Presence of Angels: A Collection of Inspiring, True Angel Stories* (Carmel, NY: Guideposts, 1995), 126–42, and Peter
Shockey, *Reflections of Heaven: A Millennial Odyssey of Miracles, Angels, and Afterlife* (New York: Doubleday, 1999), 113–23. Both of these include a slow fall story.

21. For examples see Virtue, *Saved by an Angel*, 157–71.

22. Examples in Virtue, *Saved by an Angel*, 183–93; *Angel Visions*, 125–39.

23. Illustrations in Carmel Reilly, *Walking with Angels* (Leicester: Silverdale
Books, 2005), 79–121.

24. On this phenomenon see D. Scott Rogo, *NAD: A Study of Some Unusual "Other-World" Experiences* (New York: University Books, 1970). It is a common motif in the literature on NDEs. In the books on angels, hearing beautiful or ethereal music without an apparent source is typically ascribed to angelic singing.

25. An exception is Susan R. Garrett, *No Ordinary Angel: Celestial Spirits and Christian Claims about Jesus* (New Haven, CT: Yale University Press, 2008).

26. The words are from Melashenko and Crosby, *In the Presence of Angels*, 125. Even if one is uneasy with their answer—"even in Scripture, God sometimes intervenes in trivial matters yet is silent at critical moments"—at least they pose the question.

27. I have, I may add, spoken with the author of one of the books cited in these footnotes, and I can attest that his stories, although lightly touched up here and there for stylistic reasons, are, with but a few exceptions, firsthand.

28. Evelyn Bence, *All Night, All Night Angels Watching Over Me* (Carmel, NY: Guideposts, 1995).

29. Here I may also appeal to Craig S. Keener, *Miracles: The Credibility of the New Testament Accounts*, 2 vols. (Grand Rapids: Baker Academic, 2011).

30. Melashenko and Crosby, *In the Presence of Angels*, 20.

31. Melashenko and Crosby, *In the Presence of Angels*, 156.

32. Eckersley, *Angel at My Shoulder*, 93.

33. Melashenko and Crosby, *In the Presence of Angels*, 108.

34. Glennyce S. Eckersley, *Angels and Miracles: Extraordinary Stories that Cannot Easily be Explained* (London: Rider, 1997), 145.

35. I have used the 2009 paperback edition: Emma Heathcote-James, *Seeing Angels: True Contemporary Accounts of Hundreds of Angelic Experiences* (London: John Blake, 2009).

36. All three of these quotations appear in Heathcote-James, *Seeing Angels*, 235.

37. MacDonald, *When Angels Appear*, pp. 12 and 32 respectively. Cf. Anderson, *Where Angels Walk*, 14–15.

38. I should note that seeing luminous human-like figures can be viewed as part of a larger phenomenon, that being encounters with a range of remarkable lights. On this subject see Mark Fox, *Spiritual Encounters with Unusual Light Phenomena: Lightforms* (Cardiff: University of Wales Press, 2008), and Annekatrin Puhle, *Light Changes: Experiences in the Presence of Transforming Light* (Guildford, UK: White Crow Books, 2013).

39. Heathcote-James, *Seeing Angels*, 170.

40. Cherrie Sutherland, *In the Company of Angels: Welcoming Angels into Your Life* (Dublin: Gill Books, 2008), 45.

41. Mark Fox, *The Fifth Love: Exploring Accounts of the Extraordinary* (n.p.: Spirit & Sage, 2014), 106.

42. Anderson, *Where Angels Walk*, 204.

43. Diane E. Goldstein, "Scientific Rationalism and Supernatural Experience Narratives," in *Haunting Experiences: Ghosts in Contemporary Folklore*, ed. Diane E. Goldstein, Sylvia Ann Grider, and Jeannie Banks Thomas (Logan, UT: Utah State University Press, 2007), 66.

44. Mary Boyce, ed., *Textual Sources for the Study of Zoroastrianism* (Chicago: University of Chicago Press, 1984), 75. I have changed her "Zardusht" to "Zoroaster."

45. *Diary of Cotton Mather*, ed. Worthington Chauncey Ford, vol. 1 (Boston: Massachusetts Historical Society, 1912), 87.

46. Interaction with a single angel appears to be the rule in NDEs.

47. For a popular overview see Oliver Sacks, *Hallucinations* (New York: Alfred A. Knopf, 2012). More demanding is André Aleman and Frank Larøi, *Hallucinations: The Science of Idiosyncratic Perception* (Washington, DC: American Psychological Association, 2008).

48. Henry Bourne, *Antiquitates Vulgares: Or, the Antiquities of the Common People* (Newcastle upon Tyne: J. White, 1725), 77.

49. Wolfhart Pannenberg, *Systematic Theology*, vol. 2 (Grand Rapids, MI: Eerdmans, 1994), 354.

50. See V. S. Ramachandran, *Phantoms in the Brain: Probing the Mysteries of the Mind* (New York: Quill, 1999), 88, 105, 107.

51. Puhle, *Light Changes*, 106.

52. As quoted in Phillip H. Wiebe, *Intuitive Knowing as Spiritual Experience* (New York: Palgrave Macmillan, 2015), 47. Cf. Heathcote-James, *Seeing Angels*, 46–47.

53. Lotte Valentin, "A Former Atheist's View of Her Death Experience," in *We Touched Heaven*, ed. Claudia Watts Edge (n.p.: Kindle Direct/LilyBud, 2021), 99.

54. Sir William Barrett, *Deathbed Visions* (1926; repr., Guildford, UK: White Crow Books, 2011), 52–53.

55. The same circumstance attends other sorts of religious experiences: they do not always accord with a percipient's cultural paradigm or religious expectations or lack thereof; see Caroline Francis Davis, *The Evidential Force of Religious Experience* (Oxford: Clarendon, 1989), 155–65.

56. John Lerma, *Into the Light: Real Life Stories about Angelic Visits, Visions of the Afterlife, and Other Pre-Death Experiences* (Pompton Plains, NJ: New Page Books, 2007), 111. She continued: "If randomness formed empathy and it was so specific, it's still an incredible experience. Funny how there were never living people in any of my angelic visions. Only the dead came to me. How can that be random?"

57. Ramachandran, *Phantoms*, 112. See further the TED Talk of Anil Seth, "Your Brain Hallucinates Your Conscious Reality," filmed April 2017, https://www.ted.com/talks/anil_seth_your_brain_hallucinates_your_conscious_reality?language=en.

58. Phillip H. Wiebe, *Visions of Jesus: Direct Encounters from the New Testament to Today* (Oxford: Oxford University Press, 1997), 82–83.

59. See Louise C. Johns, "Hallucinations in the General Population," *Current Psychiatry Reports* 7 (2005): 162–67; Aleman and Larøi, *Hallucinations*, 61–84; and V. Bell, P. W. Halligan, K. Pugh, and D. Freeman, "Correlates of Perceptual Distortions in Clinical and Non-clinical Populations using the Cardiff Anomalous Perceptions Scale (CAPS): Associations with Anxiety and Depression and a Re-evaluation using a Representative Population Sample," *Psychiatry Research* 289 (2011): 451–57.

60. Richard P. Bentall, "Hallucinatory Experiences," in *The Varieties of Anomalous Experience: Examining the Scientific Evidence*, ed. Etzel Cardeña, Steven Jay Lynn, and Stanley Krippner (Washington, DC: American Psychological Association, 2000), 95.

61. Cf. Peter D. Slade and Richard P. Bentall, *Sensory Deception: A Scientific Analysis of Hallucination* (Baltimore: Johns Hopkins University Press, 1988), 57–81, and Ralph W. Hood, Peter C. Hill, and Bernard Spilka, *Psychology of Religion: An Empirical Approach*, 5th ed. (New York: Guilford Press, 2018), 314 ("a massive literature" indicates that "hallucinations are not simply characteristic of organic deficiencies").

62. See, e.g., Walter Franklin Prince, *Noted Witnesses for Psychic Occurrences* (New Hyde Park, NY: University Books, 1963), and Sally Rhine Feather and Michael Schmicker, *The Gift: ESP, the Extraordinary Experiences of Ordinary People* (New York: St. Martin's Press, 2005). Also relevant are the countless reports of individuals in dire straits, such as mountain climbers lost and exhausted in a blizzard who sense a presence that stirs them on. This presence can take a visual, human form and offer guidance. See John Geiger, *The Third Man Factor:*

Surviving the Impossible (New York: Weinstein Books, 2009). As explanation, Geiger posits "a mechanism of the brain, activated in those who cross the line of physical or psychological tolerance," 238.

63. Heathcote-James, *Seeing Angels*, 239.

64. Heathcote-James, *Seeing Angels*, 170.

65. Sophy Burnham, *Angel Letters* (New York: Ballantine, 1991), 106–7.

66. For this and what follows see Burnham, *Angel Letters*, 110–13.

67. David J. Hand, *The Improbability Principle: Why Coincidences, Miracles, and Rare Events Happen Every Day* (New York: Scientific American; Farrar, Straus and Giroux, 2014), 6.

68. MacDonald, *When Angels Appear*, 39.

69. On angel books as assaults against secularism see Robert Wuthnow, *After Heaven: Spirituality in America Since the 1950s* (Berkeley: University of California Press, 1998), 114–41.

70. Melashenko and Crosby, *In the Presence of Angels*, 33–34.

71. William R. Miller and Janet C'de Baca, *Quantum Change: When Epiphanies and Sudden Insights Transform Ordinary Lives* (New York: Guilford Press, 2001), 147.

72. MacDonald, *When Angels Appear*, 26.

73. See further Melashenko and Crosby, *In the Presence of Angels*, 8–15.

74. See, e.g., Melashenko and Crosby, *In the Presence of Angels*, 91.

75. Eckersley, *Angel at My Shoulder*, 131.

76. This and the following quotations are from Anderson, *Where Angels Walk*, 207.

77. The idea of imitating angels goes back to early Christian times; see Karl Suso Frank, *Aggelikos Bios: begriffsanalytische und begriffsgeschichtliche Untersuchung zum "engelgleichen Leben" im frühen Mönchtum* (Münster Westfalen: Aschendorff, 1964).

78. Melashenko and Crosby, *In the Presence of Angels*, 230–43. Note also the final chapter of MacDonald, *When Angels Appear*, 115–20: this is about what angels "with skin on" can do for others.

79. Melashenko and Crosby, *In the Presence of Angels*, 242–43.

80. Rodney Stark, *Why God? Explaining Religious Phenomena* (West Conshohocken, PA: Templeton Press, 2017), 78.

81. I should note, however, that there is continuity with the tradition here. Luther could attribute good fortune to angels, and Cotton Mather could credit

angels with unexpected healings; see Martin Luther, *Lectures on the Minor Prophets III: Zechariah*, ed. Hilton C. Oswald, Luther's Works, vol. 20 (St. Louis: Concordia, 1973), 170; Cotton Mather, *The Angel of Bethesda: An Essay upon the Common Maladies of Mankind*, ed. Gordon W. Jones (1724; repr., Barre, MA: American Antiquarian Society; Barre, 1972), 51–52.

Chapter 6

1. As quoted in David Kessler, *Visions, Trips, and Crowded Rooms: Who and What You See Before You Die* (Carlsbad, CA: Hay House, 2010), 95.

2. Kessler, *Visions, Trips, and Crowded Rooms*, 108.

3. Henry L. Davis, "As People Lay Dying, Vivid Dreams or Visions Bring Comfort to Nearly All, Buffalo Research Suggests," *Buffalo News*, October 20, 2015, https://buffalonews.com/news/local/as-people-lay-dying-vivid-dreams -or-visions-bring-comfort-to-nearly-all-buffalo-research/article_735156c7-d214 -5657-b48f-30b215f3cd9c.html.

4. The motif has also, however, long been a staple of stories of Christian deaths; note, e.g., Izaak Walton, *The Life of Mr. Rich. Hooker, The Author of Those Learned Books of the Laws of Ecclesiastical Polity* (London: J. G. for Rich. Marriott, 1665), 147: Hooker's "Guardian Angel seem'd to foretell him, that the day of his Dissolution drew near."

5. The term became popular via Maggie Callanan and Patricia Kelley, *Final Gifts: Understanding the Special Awareness, Needs, and Communications of the Dying* (New York: Bantam, 1993).

6. Lisa Smart, *Words at the Threshold: What We Say as We're Nearing Death* (Novato, CA: New World Library, 2017), 3.

7. Smart, *Words at the Threshold*, 66.

8. Patricia Pearson, *Opening Heaven's Door: Investigating Stories of Life, Death, and What Comes After* (New York: Atria Books, 2014), 24–25.

9. Smart, *Words at the Threshold*, 55.

10. Sue Brayne, Chris Farnham, and Peter Fenwick, "Deathbed Phenomena and Their Effect on a Palliative Care Team: A Pilot Study," *American Journal of Hospice & Palliative Medicine* 23 (2006): 20.

11. Nick Bunick, *Transitions of the Soul: True Stories from Ordinary People* (Charlottesville, VA: Hampton Roads, 2001), 94.

12. Smart, *Words at the Threshold*, 56.

13. On this see below, pp. 173–77.

14. A. Brierre de Boismont, *Hallucinations: Or, the Rational History of Apparitions, Visions, Dreams, Ecstasy, Magnetism, and Somnambulism* (Philadelphia: Lindsay and Blakiston, 1853), 243.

15. Henry Halford, *Essays and Orations, Read and Delivered at The Royal College of Physicians*, 2nd ed. (London: John Murray, 1833), 90.

16. Michael Nahm, "Terminal Lucidity in People with Mental Illness and Other Mental Disability: An Overview and Implications for Possible Explanatory Models," *Journal of Near-Death Studies* 28 (2009): 87–106.

17. William Munk, *Euthanasia: or, Medical Treatment in Aid of an Easy Death* (London: Longmans, Green, and Co., 1887), 35.

18. One wonders whether modern drugs have depressed its incidence.

19. Nahm, "Terminal Lucidity," 89. Nahm has since written a book with two chapters on this subject: *Wenn die Dunkelheit ein Ende findet: Terminale Geistesklarheit und andere ungewöhnliche Phänomene in Todesnähe* (Amerang: Crotona, 2012), 19–86.

20. Scott Haig, "The Brain: The Power of Hope," *Time*, January 29, 2007, http://content.time.com/time/magazine/article/0,9171,1580392-1,00.html.

21. This and the following account are from Michael Nahm et al., "Terminal Lucidity: A Review and a Case Collection," *Archives of Gerontology and Geriatrics* 55 (2012): 140.

22. Smart, *Words at the Threshold*, 139.

23. See Marilyn A. Mendoza, "Terminal Lucidity Revisited," *Psychology Today*, September 30, 2019, https://www.psychologytoday.com/us/blog/understanding-grief/201909/terminal-lucidity-revisited, reporting on the work of Alexander Batthyány.

24. George A. Mashour et al., "Paradoxical Lucidity: A Potential Paradigm Shift for the Neurobiology and Treatment of Severe Dementias," *Alzheimer's & Dementia* 15 (2019): 1108.

25. Nahm et al., "Terminal Lucidity," 141.

26. Sue Brayne, Hilary Lovelace, and Peter Fenwick, "End-of-Life Experiences and the Dying Process in a Gloucestershire Nursing Home as Reported by Nurses and Care Assistants," *American Journal of Hospice and Palliative Medicine* 25 (2008): 195–206.

27. Stephen Claxton-Oldfield and Alexie Dunnett, "Hospice Palliative Care Volunteers' Experiences with Unusual End-of-Life Phenomena," *Omega* 77 (2018): 3–14.

28. Chi-Yeon Lim et al., "Terminal Lucidity in the Teaching Hospital Setting," *Death Studies* 44 (2018): 285–91.

29. A. S. Sandy Macleod, "Lightening Up before Death," *Palliative & Supportive Care* 7 (2009): 513–15.

30. For a survey of the germane statistics see Boris A. Chirboga-Oleszczak, "Terminal Lucidity," *Current Problems in Psychiatry* 18 (2017): 34–46.

31. Basil A. Eldadah, Elena M. Fazio, and Kristina A. McLinden, "Lucidity in Dementia: A Perspective from the NIA," *Alzheimer's & Dementia* 15 (2019): 1104–6.

32. Although some have speculated about a connection with the burst of electrical activity that seems to accompany death; see Mashour, "Paradoxical Lucidity," 1108–10. Cf. Lakhmir S. Chawla et al., "Surges of Electroencephalogram Activity at the Time of Death: A Case Series," *Journal of Palliative Medicine* 12 (2012): 1095–1100.

33. E.g., Hans Martensen-Larsen, *An der Pforte des Todes eine Wanderung zwischen den Welten* (Berlin: Furche, 1931); *Ein Schimmer durch den Vorhang: Vom Einbruch jenseitiger Mächte und Gewalten in das irdische Leben* (Berlin: Furche, 1930).

34. See the interview of Batthyány by Zaron Burnett III for *Mel Magazine*, https://melmagazine.com/en-us/story/terminal-lucidity-the-researchers-attempting-to-prove-your-mind-lives-on-even-after-you-die. Batthyány also says here: "Very, very many of the people who have terminal lucidity use the time to say farewell. I've never encountered one case where a person made plans for the next weekend. They say thank you to the nurse, thank you to the relatives or they make gifts. Then very often, very soon after, slip into unconsciousness and die. They do know they're dying. They make it very clear. How they know, I have no idea."

35. Nahm, *Dunkelheit*, esp. 255–74.

36. For White's firsthand account see Penny Sartori, *The Wisdom of Near-Death Experiences: How Brushes with Death Teach Us to Live* (London: Watkins, 2014), 100–101.

37. Smart, *Words at the Threshold*, 108.

38. Una MacConville, "Mapping Religion and Spirituality in an Irish Palliative Care Setting," *Omega* 53 (2006): 149.

39. Karlis Osis and Erlendur Haraldsson, *At the Hour of Death*, 3rd ed. (Norwalk, CT: Hastings House, 1997), 4.

40. Sir William Barrett, *Deathbed Visions* (1926; repr., Guildford, UK: White Crow Books, 2011), 34.

41. Emily Williams Kelly, Bruce Greyson, and Edward F. Kelly, "Unusual Experiences Near Death and Related Phenomena," in *Irreducible Mind: Toward a Psychology for the 21st Century*, ed. Edward F. Kelly et al. (Lanham, MD: Rowman & Littlefield, 2007), 410.

42. *The Zohar Pritzker Edition*, vol. 3, Va-Yh·i 1:218a, translation and commentary by Daniel C. Matt (Stanford, CA: Stanford University Press, 2006), 315.

43. Frances Power Cobbe, *The Peak in Darien, with Some Other Inquiries Touching Concerns of the Soul and the Body* (London: Williams & Norgate, 1882), 287–88.

44. Cobbe, *Peak in Darien*, 289–91.

45. Callanan and Kelley, *Final Gifts*, 88.

46. Callanan and Kelley, *Final Gifts*, 89–90.

47. John Lerma, *Into the Light: Real Life Stories about Angelic Visits, Visions of the Afterlife, and Other Pre-Death Experiences* (Pompton Plains, NJ: New Page Books, 2007), 161.

48. Karlis Osis and Erlendur Haraldsson, "Deathbed Observations by Physicians and Nurses: A Cross-Cultural Survey," *Journal of the American Society for Psychical Research* 71 (1977): 237–59; *At the Hour of Death*. Their results were consistent with Osis's earlier 1959–60 pilot survey that involved analysis of 640 returned questionnaires: Karlis Osis, *Deathbed Observations by Physicians and Nurses* (New York: Parapsychology Foundation, 1961).

49. Lerma, *Into the Light*, 227–30.

50. Kelly, Greyson, and Kelly, "Unusual Experiences Near Death," 409.

51. Tatsuya Morita et al., "Nationwide Japanese Survey about Deathbed Visions: 'My Deceased Mother Took Me to Heaven,'" *Journal of Pain and Symptom Management* 52 (2016): 646–54.

52. R. Morooka, "Deathbed Visions in the Context of End-of-Life Care," *Japanese Journal of Palliative Medicine* 24 (2014): 108–11.

53. Allan Kellenhear et al., "Deathbed Visions from the Republic of Moldova: A Content Analysis of Family Observations," *Omega* 64 (2012): 303–17.

54. Sandhya P. Muthumana, "Deathbed Visions from India: A Study of Family Observations in Northern Kerala," *Omega* 62 (2009): 97–109.

55. For what follows see Christopher W. Kerr et al., "End-of-Life Dreams and Visions: A Longitudinal Study of Hospice Patients' Experiences," *Journal of*

Palliative Medicine 17 (2014): 296–303, and Cheryl L. Nosek et al., "End-of-Life Dreams and Visions: A Qualitative Perspective from Hospice Patients," *American Journal of Hospice & Palliative Medicine* 5 (2015): 269–74.

56. Kerr, "Longitudinal Study," 302.

57. See esp. Christopher Kerr with Carine Mardorossian, *Death Is But a Dream: Finding Hope and Meaning at Life's End* (New York: Avery, 2020).

58. Nosek, "Qualitative Perspective," 272.

59. Franklin Santana Santos and Peter Fenwick, "Death, End of Life Experiences, and Their Theoretical and Clinical Implications for the Mind-Brain Relationship," in *Exploring Frontiers of the Mind-Brain Relationship*, ed. A. Moreira-Almeida and F. S. Santos (New York: Springer, 2012), 177.

60. Smart, *Words at the Threshold*, 107.

61. Neil Baldwin, *Edison: Inventing the Century* (New York: Hyperion, 1995), 407.

62. James Hyslop, "Visions of the Dying," *Journal of the American Society for Psychical Research* 12 (1918): 596.

63. Callanan and Kelley, *Final Gifts*, 111.

64. Santos and Fenwick, "Death," 180.

65. Kessler, *Visions, Trips, and Crowded Rooms*, 110.

66. Lerma, *Into the Light*, 143.

67. Allan Kellehear, *Visitors at the End of Life: Finding Meaning and Purpose in Near-Death Phenomena* (New York: Columbia University Press, 2020), 99.

68. See esp. Peter Fenwick, Hilary Lovelace, and Sue Brayne, "Comfort for the Dying: Five Year Retrospective and One Year Prospective Studies of End of Life Experiences," *Archives of Gerontology* 30 (2009): 173–79.

69. Very helpful here from a pastoral point of view is Martha Jo Atkins, *Signposts of Dying: What You Need to Know* (2016). This self-published book is available through Amazon.com.

70. Callanan and Kelley, *Final Gifts*, 103.

71. Barrett, *Deathbed Visions*, 28–29.

72. Ian Wilson, *The After Death Experience: The Physics of the Non-Physical* (New York: William Morrow and Co., 1987), 107. Wilson adds: "Janet T. is a thoroughly sensible teacher and housewife whom I have known for several years, and whose veracity on this deeply personal story I trust totally. Nor is the incident a tale that has grown with the years, for both she and her father wrote down what" the grandmother said shortly after her death.

73. Callanan and Kelley, *Final Gifts*, 92.

74. Raymond Moody Jr., with Paul Perry, *Glimpses of Eternity: Sharing a Loved One's Passage from This Life to the Next* (New York: Guideposts, 2010), 16.

75. Cobbe, *Peak in Darien*, 287.

76. Bruce Greyson, "Seeing Dead People Not Known to Have Died: 'Peak in Darien' Experiences," *Anthropology and Humanism* 35 (2010): 162.

77. Morita, "Nationwide Japanese Survey," 647.

78. Santos and Fenwick, "Death," 177.

79. Deborah O'Connor, "Palliative Care Nurses' Experiences of Paranormal Phenomena and Their Influence on Nursing Practice," unpublished paper presented at the Making Sense of Dying and Death Inter-disciplinary Conference, Paris, November 21–23, 2003.

80. Fenwick, Lovelace, and Brayne, "Comfort for the Dying," 176.

81. Sartori, *Wisdom*, 95–96.

82. Ian Stevenson, "Six Modern Apparitional Experiences," *Journal of Scientific Exploration* 9 (1995): 360.

83. Moody and Perry, *Glimpses of Eternity*, 49–50.

84. Moody and Perry, *Glimpses of Eternity*, contains several such stories.

85. Benedict Ward, *The Desert Christian: Sayings of the Desert Fathers: The Alphabetical Tradition* (New York: Macmillan, 1975), 214–15.

86. Wilhelm Schamoni, *Wunder sind Tatsachen: Eine Dokumentation aus Heiligsprechungsakten*, 3rd ed. (Würzburg: Johann Wilhelm Naumann, 1976), 237, 241; Patricia Treece, *The Sanctified Body* (New York: Doubleday, 1989), 64–66.

87. Catherine Crowe, *The Night Side of Nature, or Ghosts and Ghost Seers* (New York: E. P. Dutton, 1904), 363.

88. A decade ago, Michael Nahm, "Reflections on the Context of Near-Death Experiences," *Journal of Scientific Exploration* 25 (2011): 468, wrote that he had collected 142 cases of this phenomenon. He did not, however, indicate how many are from historical sources and how many from recent times.

89. This and the next two accounts are from Raymond Moody and Paul Perry, *Glimpses of Eternity*, 82, 85.

90. Peter Fenwick, "Dying: A Spiritual Experience as Shown by Near-Death Experiences and Deathbed Visions," unpublished paper, p. 4, http://citeseerx.ist .psu.edu/viewdoc/download?doi=10.1.1.510.682&rep=rep1&type=pdf.

91. This and the next two accounts are from Santos and Fenwick, "Death," 182.

92. Sartori, *Wisdom*, 88–89.

93. Melvin Morse with Paul Perry, *Parting Visions: Uses and Meanings of Pre-Death, Psychic, and Spiritual Experiences* (New York: Villard Books, 1994), 143.

94. Peter Fenwick and Elizabeth Fenwick, *The Art of Dying: A Journey to Elsewhere* (London: Continuum, 2008), 158–59.

95. Santos and Fenwick, "Death," 182.

96. Claudia Soares Dos Santos et al., "End-of-life Experiences and Death-bed Phenomena as Reported by Brazilian Healthcare Professionals in Different Healthcare Settings," *Palliative and Supportive Care* 15 (2017): 425–33.

97. Moody and Perry, *Glimpses of Eternity*, 83.

98. Fenwick, Lovelace, and Brayne, "Comfort for the Dying," 176.

99. Elizabeth F. McAdams, "Reported Near-Death Observations in a Hospice in California," in *The Synergy of Religion and Psychical Research: Past, Present, and Future*, ed. Mary Carman Rose (Bloomfield, CT: Academy of Religion and Psychical Research, 1983), 57–64.

100. Henry Marsh, *The Evolution of Light from the Living Human Subject* (Dublin: William Curry, Jun, & Co., 1842).

101. For all of the above see Marsh, *Evolution of Light*, 47–59.

102. Cf. Santos and Fenwick, "Death," 183: "Biophotons would be radiated by the collapse of energetic structures disintegrating when the body undergoes anoxic change."

103. Masaki Kobayashi, Daisuke Kikuchi, and Hitoshi Okamura, "Imaging of Ultraweak Spontaneous Photon Emission from Human Body Displaying Diurnal Rhythm," *PLOS One* 4 (2009), https://journals.plos.org/plosone/article?id=10.1371/journal.pone.0006256.

104. William R. Corliss, *Biological Anomalies: Human 1* (Glen Arm, MD: The Sourcebook Project, 1992), 46–50.

105. Sue Brayne and Peter Fenwick, "End-of-Life Experiences: A Guide for Carers of the Dying" (2008), is a helpful introduction to ELEs and is available free online, https://newcosmicparadigm.org/wp-content/uploads/2019/05/ENDOFLIFEPROF.pdf. On arresting coincidences see Fenwick and Fenwick, *Art of Dying*, 129–49. On supernal music see D. Scott Rogo, *NAD: A Study of Some Unusual "Other-World" Experiences* (New York: University Books, 1970), 51–72, and Nahm, *Dunkelheit*, 213–32. On sensing the presence of the dead see Dale C. Allison Jr., *The Resurrection of Jesus: Apologetics, Criticism, History* (London: T&T Clark, 2021), 262–66.

106. Cf. Kellehear, *Visitors at the End of Life*, 94: "In the light of the historical and current facts about the prevalence of experiences near death, among those with widely diverse beliefs and those who do not believe, it is more likely that the experience of contact with the dead *preceded* the beliefs [about an afterlife]."

107. Lerman, *Into the Light*, 186–90.

108. Peter Fenwick, "Non Local Effects in the Process of Dying: Can Quantum Mechanics Help?," *NeuroQuantology* 8 (2010): 159–60.

109. M. Renz et al., "Spiritual Experiences of Transcendence in Patients with Advanced Cancer," *American Journal of Hospice & Palliative Care* 32 (2015): 181.

110. Kerry Egan, "My Faith: What People Talk to Me about before They Die," CNN Belief Blog, January 28, 2012, https://religion.blogs.cnn.com/2012/01/28/my-faith-what-people-talk-about-before-they-die/?hpt=hp_c1. I strongly recommend Egan's captivating and moving book about her experiences as a hospice chaplain: *On Living* (New York: Riverhead Books, 2016).

Chapter 7

1. Elizabeth G. Krohn and Jeffrey J. Kripal, *Changed in a Flash: One Woman's Near-Death Experience and Why a Scholar Thinks It Empowers Us All* (Berkeley, CA: North Atlantic Books, 2018), 114–15.

2. Steve Taylor, *Spiritual Science: Why Science Needs Spirituality to Make Sense of the World* (London: Watkins, 2018), 101.

3. Bruce Greyson, *After: A Doctor Explores What Near-Death Experiences Reveal about Life and Beyond* (New York: St. Martin's, 2021), 200.

4. George M. Gould and Walter L. Pyle, *Anomalies and Curiosities of Medicine: Being an Encyclopedic Collection of Rare and Extraordinary Cases, and of the Most Striking Instances of Abnormality in All Branches of Medicine and Surgery, Derived from an Exhaustive Research of Medical Literature from Its Origin to the Present Day* (New York: Syndenham, 1937).

5. As quoted by Christine Kenneally, "The Deepest Cut," *New Yorker*, June 26, 2006, https://www.newyorker.com/magazine/2006/07/03/the-deepest-cut.

6. John Lorber, "Is Your Brain Really Necessary?," in *Hydrocephalus im frühen Kindesalter: Fortschritte der Grundlagenforschung, Diagnostik und Therapie*, ed. D. Voth, P. Gutjahr, and P. Glees (Stuttgart: Enke, 1983), 2–14; Lionel Feuillet, Henry Dufour, and Jean Pelletier, "Brain of a White-Collar Worker," *The Lancet*

370 (2007): 262; Donald R. Forsdyke, "Wittgenstein's Certainty is Uncertain: Brain Scans of Cured Hydrocephalics Challenge Cherished Assumptions," *Biological Theory* 10 (2015): 336–42; Michael Nahm, David Rosseau, and Bruce Greyson, "Discrepancy between Cerebral Structure and Cognitive Functioning: A Review," *Journal of Nervous and Mental Disease* 12 (2017): 967–72.

7. Forsdyke, "Brain Scans."

8. Yet a distinguished philosopher has confessed to being unfamiliar with NDEs until recently; see the interview with John M. Fischer on the website Skeptiko, at https://skeptiko.com/john-fischer-another-philosopher-tries-to-debunk -ndes-431/ (at 47:32). For a helpful overview of the phenomenology and issues see Janice Miner Holden, Bruce Greyson, and Debbie James, eds., *The Handbook of Near-Death Experiences: Thirty Years of Investigation* (Santa Barbara, CA: Praeger Publishers, 2009). For a convenient collection of accounts see the Near-Death Experience Research Foundation website: https://www.nderf.org/.

9. For the phenomenology of the life review—it has well-defined characteristics—see Judith Katz, Noam Saadon-Grosman and Shahar Arzy, "The Life Review Experience: Qualitative and Quantitative Characteristics," *Consciousness and Cognition* 48 (2017): 76–86.

10. See Charlotte Martial et al., "Temporality of Features in Near-Death Experience Narratives," *Frontiers in Human Neuroscience* 11 (2017), https://www .frontiersin.org/articles/10.3389/fnhum.2017.00311/full.

11. Gregory Shushan, "Near-Death Experiences," in *The Routledge Companion to Death and Dying*, ed. Christopher M. Moreman (New York: Routledge, 2018), 320.

12. Raymond Moody, *Life after Life: The Investigation of a Phenomenon: Survival of Bodily Death* (New York: Bantam, 1975).

13. I take the phrase from P. M. H. Atwater, *The Big Book of Near-Death Experiences: The Ultimate Guide to What Happens When We Die* (Charlottesville, VA: Hampton Roads, 2007), 25. For the statistical evidence see Rense Lange, Bruce Greyson, and James Houran, "A Rasch Scaling Validation of a 'Core' Near-Death Experience," *British Journal of Psychology* 95 (2004): 161–77. Given what we now know, NDEs are not rare. At a minimum, hundreds of thousands of people now living have had NDEs. On the problem of determining incidence see below, n. 30.

14. This is all the more obvious if NDEs alter temporal lobe functioning; see Willoughby B. Britton and Richard R. Bootzin, "Near-Death Experiences and the Temporal Lobe," *Psychological Science* 15 (2004): 254–58.

15. See Melvin Morse, *Closer to the Light: Learning from the Near-Death Experiences of Children* (New York: Ivy Books, 1991); Cherie Sutherland, "Near-

Death Experiences of Children," in *Making Sense of Near-Death Experiences: A Handbook for Clinicians*, ed. P. Mahendra Perera, Karuppiah Jagadheesan, and Anthony Peake (London: Jessica Kingsley, 2012), 63–78; and Penny Sartori, *The Wisdom of Near-Death Experiences: How Brushes with Death Teach Us to Live* (London: Watkins, 2014), 53–69.

16. See further Ian Stevenson and Bruce Greyson, "Near-Death Experiences: Relevance to the Question of Survival after Death," *Journal of the American Medical Association* 242 (1979): 265–67.

17. Nancy Evans Bush, *Dancing Past the Dark: Distressing Near-Death Experiences* (Cleveland, TN: Parson's Porch Books, 2012), 117.

18. Greyson, *After*, 158.

19. Kenneth Ring, *Life at Death: A Scientific Investigation of the Near-Death Experience* (New York: Coward, McCann & Geoghegan, 1980), 169.

20. His strange, idiosyncratic report appeared in *The Sunday Telegraph*, August 28, 1988, and is available online at: http://www.philosopher.eu/others-writings/a-j-ayer-what-i-saw-when-i-was-dead/. For a collection of the NDEs of atheists see Kevin R. Williams, "An Analysis of the Near-Death Experiences of Atheists," at https://near-death.com/an-analysis-of-the-ndes-of-atheists/.

21. Quoted in Peter Foges, "An Atheist Meets the Masters of the Universe," http://web.csulb.edu/~plowentr/Ayer%20NDE%202.pdf.

22. John Wren-Lewis, "The Darkness of God: An Account of Lasting Mystical Consciousness Resulting from an NDE," *Anabiosis: The Journal of Near-Death Studies* 5 (1985): 53–66.

23. Geena K. Athappilly, Bruce Greyson, and Ian Stevenson, "Do Prevailing Societal Models Influence Reports of Near-Death Experiences? A Comparison of Accounts Reported Before and After 1975," *Journal of Nervous and Mental Diseases* 194 (2006): 218–22.

24. See Gregory Shushan, *Conceptions of the Afterlife in Early Civilizations: Universalism, Constructivism and Near-Death Experiences* (London: Continuum, 2009); Michael Nahm and Joachim Nicolay, "Essential Features of Eight Published Muslim Near-Death Experiences: An Addendum to Joel Ibrahim Kreps's 'The Search for Muslim Near-Death Experiences,'" *Journal of Near-Death Studies* 29 (2010): 255–63; and Ornella Corazza and K.A.L.A. Kuruppuarachchi, "Dealing with Diversity: Cross-Cultural Aspects of Near-Death Experiences," in Perera et al., *Making Sense of Near-Death Experiences*, 51–62.

25. Jeffrey Long with Paul Perry, *Evidence of the Afterlife: The Science of Near-Death Experiences* (New York: HarperOne, 2010), 150–71.

26. Gregory Shushan, *Near-Death Experience in Indigenous Religions* (New York: Oxford University Press, 2018). See also his work cited above, *Conceptions of the Afterlife in Early Civilizations.*

27. Gregory Shushan, "Cultural-Linguistic Constructivism and the Challenge of Near-Death and Out-of-Body Experiences," in *The Study of Religious Experience: Approaches and Methodologies,* ed. Bettina E. Schmidt (Sheffield: Equinox, 2016), 83.

28. I am not of the view, however, that language is required for either awareness or meaningful experience; see Jason N. Blum, "The Science of Consciousness and Mystical Experience: An Argument for Radical Empiricism," *Journal of the American Academy of Religion* 82 (2014): 150-73. Mystical experiences, moreover, can (at least in my judgment) have "unmediated, nonlinguistic, and nonconceptual" components; see Blum, *Zen and the Unspeakable God* (University Park, PA: Pennsylvania State University Press, 2015); the quoted words appear on p. 162.

29. See Carol Zaleski, *Otherworld Journeys: Accounts of Near-Death Experience in Medieval and Modern Times* (New York: Oxford University Press, 1987).

30. Pim van Lommel, *Consciousness Beyond Life: The Science of Near-Death Experiences* (New York: HarperOne, 2010), 9. See further Hubert Knoblauch et al., "Different Kinds of Near-Death Experience: A Report on a Survey of Near-Death Experiences in Germany," *Journal of Near-Death Studies* 20 (2001): 15-29, and Mahendra Perera et al., "Prevalence of Near-Death Experiences in Australia," *Journal of Near-Death Studies* 24 (2005): 109-16.

31. See esp. Zaleski, *Otherworld Journeys.* On negative NDEs see below, pp. 144-46.

32. So Bruce Greyson, "An Overview of Near-Death Experiences," in *The Science of Near-Death Experiences,* ed. John C. Hagan III (Columbia, MO: University of Missouri, 2017), 20.

33. Ring, *Life at Death,* 138-58; Russell Noyes Jr. et al., "Aftereffects of Pleasurable Western Adult Near-Death Experiences," in Holder et al., *Handbook,* 41-62; S. Khanna and Bruce Greyson, "Near-Death Experiences and Spiritual Well-Being," *Journal of Religion and Health* 53 (2014): 1605-15.

34. David Hay, *Why Spirituality Is Difficult for Westerners* (Exeter: Societas, 2007), 24.

35. Here I may appeal to Kelly et al., eds., *Irreducible Mind: Toward a Psychology for the 21st Century* (Lanham, MD: Rowman & Littlefield, 2007). See also further below, chapter 8.

36. The possibility that NDEs occur right before or after cardiac arrest as opposed to during it does not fit every case; see Mario Beauregard, Évelyne Landry St-Pierre, and Philippe Demers, "Conscious Mental Activity During a Deep Hypothermic Cardiocirculatory Arrest?," *Resuscitation* 83 (2012): e19, and Sam Parnia et al., "AWARE—AWAreness during REsuscitation—A Prospective Study," *Resuscitation* 85 (2014): 1799–1805.

37. Bruce Greyson, "Near-Death Experiences," in David Presti et al., *Mind Beyond Brain: Buddhism, Science, and the Paranormal* (New York: Columbia University Press, 2018), 31.

38. Alexander Batthyány, "Complex Visual Imagery and Cognition during Near-Death Experiences," *Journal of Near-Death Studies* 34 (2015): 67.

39. See, e.g., V. Krishnan, "Near-Death Experiences: Evidence for Suvival?," *Anabiosis* 5 (1985): 21–38; Olaf Blanke and Sebastian Dieguez, "Leaving Body and Life Behind: Out-of-Body and Near-Death Experiences," in *The Neurology of Consciousness: Cognitive Neuroscience and Neuropathology*, ed. Steven Laureys and Giulio Tononi (Amsterdam: Elsevier Science, 2009), 303–25; and Costanza Peinkhofer et al., "The Evolutionary Origin of Near-Death Experiences: A Systematic Investigation," *Brain Communications* 3 (2021): fcab132, https://doi.org/10.1093/braincomms/fcab132. The latter attempt to link NDEs with the fascinating, cross-species phenomenon of thanatosis, the feigning of death when attacked. They leave unexplained the internal phenomenology of NDEs, such as the life-review and encounters with loved ones.

40. Bruce Greyson, Emily Williams Kelly, and Edward F. Kelly, "Explanatory Models for Near-Death Experiences," in Holder et al., *Handbook*, 214–34; Edward F. Kelly, review of *Out-of-Body and Near-Death Experiences: Brain-State Phenomena or Glimpses of Immortality?*, by Michael N. Marsh, *Journal of Scientific Exploration* 24 (2010): 279–37; Enrico Facco and Christian Agrillo, "Near-Death Experiences between Science and Prejudice," *Frontiers in Human Neuroscience* 6 (2012), https://www.frontiersin.org/articles/10.3389/fnhum.2012.00209/full.

41. Jeffrey Long, "Near-Death Experiences: Evidence for Their Reality," in Hagan, *Science of Near-Death Experiences*, 76.

42. Johann Christoph Hampe, *To Die Is Gain: The Experience of One's Own Death* (London: Darton, Longman & Todd, 1975), 50.

43. Michael B. Sabom, *Recollections of Death: A Medical Investigation* (New York: Harper & Row, 1982), 16.

44. This quotation and the next are from Greyson, *After*, 96.

45. This quotation and that following are from Ring, *Life at Death*, 83.

46. Arianna Palmieri et al., "'Reality' of Near-Death Experience Memories: Evidence from a Psychodynamic and Electrophysiological Integrated Study," *Frontiers in Human Neuroscience* 8 (2014), https://www.frontiersin.org/articles /10.3389/fnhum.2014.00429/full; Lauren E. Moore and Bruce Greyson, "Characteristics of Memories for Neath-Death Experiences," *Consciousness and Cognition* 51 (2017): 116–24.

47. See V. S. Ramachandran, *Phantoms in the Brain: Probing the Mysteries of the Mind* (New York: Quill, 1999), 88, 105, 107.

48. Emily Williams Kelly, "Near-Death Experiences with Reports of Meeting Deceased People," *Death Studies* 25 (2001): 251.

49. van Lommel, *Consciousness Beyond Life*, 21.

50. Kimberly Clark Sharp, "The Other Shoe Drops: Commentary on 'Does Paranormal Perception Occur in NDEs?,'" *Journal of Near-Death Studies* 25 (2007): 245–50; Sharp, "The Shoe on the Ledge," in *Surviving Death: A Journalist Investigates Evidence for an Afterlife*, ed. Leslie Kean (New York: Crown Archetype, 2017), 83–91. For the eerily similar but independent story of another NDEr spotting a shoe on a hospital roof, see Kenneth Ring and Madelaine Lawrence, "Further Evidence for Veridical Perception During Near-Death Experiences," *Journal of Near-Death Studies* 11 (1993): 226–27.

51. Michael Sabom, *Light and Death: One Doctor's Fascinating Account of Near-Death Experiences* (Grand Rapids, MI: Zondervan, 1998), 37–51.

52. See Janice Miner Holden, "Veridical Perception in Near-Death Experiences," in Holder et al., *Handbook*, 193–97; Holden, "Apparently Non-Physical Veridical Perception in Near-Death Studies," in Hagan, *Science of Near-Death Experiences*, 87–88.

53. Sabom, *Recollections of Death*, 81–115; Sartori, *Wisdom of Near-Death Experiences*, 134.

54. Long, *Evidence of the Afterlife*, 74–75.

55. Gary R. Habermas, "Evidential Near-Death Experiences," in *The Blackwell Companion to Substance Dualism*, ed. Jonathan J. Loose, Angus J. L. Menuge, and J. P. Moreland (Hoboken, NJ: John Wiley and Sons, 2018), 227–46.

56. See esp. Titus Rivas, Anny Dirven, and Rudolf H. Smit, *The Self Does Not Die: Verified Paranormal Phenomena from Near-Death Experiences* (Durham, NC: IANDS Publications, 2016).

57. The words are those of Dr. Jean-Jacques Charbonier, an ICU doctor in Toulouse, France, as quoted in the French documentary, *Faux Départ*. I reproduce the English transcription in Rivas et al., *The Self Does Not Die*, 59.

58. So Dr. Lloyd W. Rudy; see "Famous Cardiac Surgeon's Stories of Near Death Experiences in Surgery," July 27, 2011, https://www.youtube.com/watch?v=JL10DuvQR08 (beginning at 7:01).

59. Dr. Richard Mansfield, quoted in Sam Parnia, *What Happens When We Die: A Groundbreaking Study into the Nature of Life and Death* (London: Hay House, 2006), 79.

60. As quoted in Rivas et al., *The Self Does Not Die*, 120. For the story see Williams-Murphy's firsthand account at http://www.oktodie.com/blog/i-died-and-you-brought-me-back-to-life-how-one-patients-near-death-experience-changed-my-life/.

61. Dr. Robert Spetzler, as quoted in Kean, *Surviving Death*, 108–9.

62. Dr. David Mochel, as quoted in Scott J. Kolbaba, *Physicians' Untold Stories: Miraculous Experiences Doctors Are Hesitant to Share with Their Patients, or Anyone!* (North Charleston, SC: CreateSpace, 2016), 33.

63. Rajiv Parti with Paul Perry, *Dying to Wake Up: A Doctor's Voyage into the Afterlife and the Wisdom He Brought Back* (New York: Atria Books, 2016), 4.

64. Lerma, *Into the Light*, 12.

65. Greyson, *After*, 6.

66. Laurin Bellg, *Near Death in the ICU: Stories from Patients Near Death and Why We Should Listen to Them* (Appleton, WI: Sloan Press, 2016), 39–40.

67. Examples include N. T. Wright, *Surprised by Hope: Rethinking Heaven, the Resurrection, and the Mission of the Church* (New York: HarperOne, 2008), and Gerhard Lohfink, *Is This All There Is? On Resurrection and Eternal Life* (Collegeville, MN: Liturgical Press, 2018). It is hard to believe that the most sensible and sensitive reflections on NDEs from a Christian theological point of view remain those of the pastor and well-known journalist Johann Christoph Hampe, in a book originally published in German in 1975: *Sterben ist doch ganz anders*; this appeared the same year in English as *To Die Is Gain*; see n. 42.

68. Jeffrey Long with Paul Perry, *God and the Afterlife: The Ground-Breaking New Evidence for God and Near-Death Experience* (New York: HarperOne, 2016).

69. Long, *God and the Afterlife*, 40–41.

70. John Haldane, "A Glimpse of Eternity? Near Death Experiences and the Hope of Future Life," *Modern Churchman* 30 (1988): 20–28; Michael N. Marsh,

Out-of-Body and Near-Death Experiences: Brain-State Phenomena or Glimpses of Immortality? (Oxford: Oxford University Press, 2010). I note, however, that Haldane leaves open the possibility that, in the dream-like NDE state, God sometimes vouchsafes "previews" of the world to come. "That world does not yet exist, and so these 'meetings' are not real ones but can only be images of how life will be following the resurrection of the dead."

71. See Bruce Greyson, "Near-Death Experiences and Spirituality," *Zygon* 41 (2006): 401-5; Noyes et al., "Aftereffects," 24-53.

72. Jerry L. Walls, *Heaven: The Logic of Eternal Joy* (Oxford: Oxford University Press, 2002), 147-48.

73. Nancy L. Zingrone and Carlos S. Alvarado, "Pleasurable Western Adult Near-Death Experiences: Features, Circumstances, and Incidence," in Holden et al., *Handbook*, 29-36.

74. There seems to be some evidence that NDErs are better than average at remembering dreams; see Bruce Greyson, "Near-Death Experiences," in *Consciousness Unbound: Liberating Mind from the Tyranny of Materialism*, ed. Edward F. Kelly and Paul Marshall (Lanham, MD: Rowman & Littlefield, 2021), 20.

75. Sam Parnia with Josh Young, *Erasing Death: The Science That Is Rewriting the Boundaries between Life and Death* (New York: HarperOne, 2013), 256.

76. It also seems likely that experiences are of shorter and longer duration; cf. the testimony in Sabom, *Recollections of Death*, 123: "What in the world would have happened if I had kept on going I don't know."

77. Huston Smith, "Intimations of Immortality: Three Case Studies," *Harvard Divinity Bulletin* 30 (2001-2002): 14.

78. Parnia and Young, *Erasing Death*, 131.

79. Marc Wittmann et al., "Subjective Time Distortion during Near-Death Experiences: An Analysis of Reports," *Zeitschrift für Anomalistik* 17 (2017): 316.

80. Ring, *Life at Death*, 70.

81. John Belanti, Mahendra Perera, and Karuppiah Jagadheesan, "Phenomenology of Near-Death Experiences: A Cross-cultural Perspective," *Transcultural Psychiatry* 45 (2008): 126.

82. Peinkhofer et al., "Evolutionary Origin," 6.

83. Sabom, *Recollections of Death*, 54.

84. Parti and Perry, *Dying to Wake Up*, 79.

85. In this paragraph and the next I rely upon data supplied by Bruce Greyson in a personal communication (June 6, 2020).

86. According to Pim van Lommel et al., "Near-Death Experiences in Survivors of Cardiac Arrest: A Prospective Study in the Netherlands," *The Lancet* 358 (2001): 2039–45, in their study, patients who had memory issues after prolonged resuscitation reported fewer NDEs. I note, however, that according to Greyson, "Near-Death Experiences," 43, many NDErs "report that although memories of the NDE itself are clear and vivid, memories of events just before and after these episodes are confused or absent."

87. I should perhaps add that common components of the NDE are not exclusive to it. People near death are not alone in relating that they have apparently left their bodies and viewed them from above, or encountered beings of light, or met dead relatives or friends, or journeyed to other realms, and so on. Indeed, people not at all near death's door have reported several of these phenomena as part of the same experience. In other words, the phrase "near-death experience" can mislead, because its components and their combination are not affiliated solely with life-threatening situations. See esp. Vanessa Charland-Verville et al., "Near-Death Experiences in Non-Life Threatening Events and Coma of Different Etiologies," *Frontiers in Human Neuroscience* 8 (2014), https://www.frontiersin.org/articles/10.3389/fnhum.2014.00203/full, and Robert G. Mays and Suzanne B. Mays, "Explaining Near-Death Experiences: Physical or Non-Physical Causation?," *Journal of Near Death Studies* 33 (2015): 125–49.

88. Nancy Evans Bush, "Distressing Western Near-Death Experiences: Find a Way through the Abyss," in Holden et al., *Handbook*, 63–96. Greyson, *After*, 143, reports that 8 percent of NDErs he has interviewed over the years have reported an unpleasant experience.

89. See Nancy Evans Bush and Bruce Greyson, "Distressing Near-Death Experiences: The Basics," in Hagan, *Science of Near-Death Experiences*, 93–95.

90. Bush, *Dancing Past the Dark*, 32.

91. Bush, *Dancing Past the Dark*, 31–32.

92. Bush, *Dancing Past the Dark*, 36. The best known hellish NDE is that of Howard Storm, *My Descent into Death and the Message of Love Which Brought Me Back* (East Sussex: Clairview Books, 2000).

93. Maurice Rawlings, *Beyond Death's Door* (Nashville: Thomas Nelson, 1978).

94. Atwater, *Big Book*, 321–22. For another example see Richard J. Bonenfant, "A Child's Encounter with the Devil: An Unusual Near-Death Experience with Both Blissful and Frightening Elements," *Journal of Near-Death Studies* 20 (2001): 87–100.

95. On these see Zaleski, *Otherworld Journeys*.

96. See Janice Miner Holden, "Apparently Non-Physical Veridical Perception in Near-Death Experiences," in Hagan, *Science of Near-Death Experience*, 80, for different descriptions of Jesus.

97. The most substantial work here is Jens Schlieter, *What Is It Like to Be Dead? Near-Death Experiences, Christianity, and the Occult* (Oxford: Oxford University Press, 2018).

98. Anil K. Seth, "The Real Problem," *Aeon*, November 2, 2016, https://aeon.co /essays/the-hard-problem-of-consciousness-is-a-distraction-from-the-real-one.

99. Kelly Bulkeley, "Religious Conversion and Cognitive Neuroscience," in *The Oxford Handbook of Religious Conversion*, ed. Lewis R. Rambo and Charles E. Farhadian (New York: Oxford University Press, 2014), 248–49.

100. Ring, *Life at Death*, 84–85. Sixty-one percent of NDErs in his study unequivocally responded yes to the question, "Is your experience difficult to put into words?"

101. Raymond A. Moody, *Reflections on Life after Life* (New York: Bantam, 1977), 14.

102. van Lommel, *Consciousness Beyond Life*, 18.

103. Ring, *Life at Death*, 65.

104. Marcy C. Neal, *To Heaven and Back: A Doctor's Extraordinary Account of Her Death, Heaven, Angels, and Life Again* (Colorado Springs, CO: WaterBrook, 2012), 73.

105. This and the next two quotations are from Greyson, *After*, 47–48.

106. Aristotle, *On Prophecy in Sleep* 1, 463a.

107. Shushan, *Near-Death Experiences*, 234–35.

108. Penny Sartori, "Through the Eyes of a Child: Near-Death Experiences in the Young," in Hagan, *Science of Near-Death Experiences*, 90.

109. Parnia, *What Happens When We Die?*, 84.

110. Belanti et al., "Phenomenology," 127.

111. van Lommel, *Consciousness Beyond Death*, 38–40.

112. Moody, *Life after Life*, 76.

113. For this testimony and the next see Sabom, *Recollections of Death*, 51.

114. Parnia, *What Happens When We Die?*, 65.

115. Ian Wilson, *The After Death Experience: The Physics of the Non-Physical* (New York: William Morrow and Co., 1987), 154.

116. Bruce Greyson, "Western Scientific Approaches to Near-Death Experi-

ences," *Humanities* 4 (2015): 777, quoting Glen Roberts and John Owen, "The Near-Death Experience," *British Journal of Psychiatry* 153 (1988): 611.

117. Jonathan Edwards, *Religious Affections*, ed. John E. Smith (New Haven, CT: Yale University Press, 1959), 162. See further Lawrence Epstein, "A Comparative View of Tibetan and Western Near-Dear Experiences," in *Reflections on Tibetan Culture: Essays in Memory of Turrell V. Wylie*, ed. Lawrence Epstein and Richard F. Sherburne (Lewiston, NY: E. Mellen, 1990), 315–28. Epstein underscores the extent to which modern Western NDEs reflect modern Western concerns.

118. Christof Koch, "What Near-Death Experiences Reveal about the Brain," *Scientific American* 322 (2020): 70–75.

119. Paul S. Fiddes, *The Promised End: Eschatology in Theology and Literature* (Malden, MA: Blackwell, 2000), 89.

120. John W. Cooper, *Body, Soul and Life Everlasting: Biblical Anthropology and the Monism-Dualism Debate* (Grand Rapids, MI: Eerdmans, 2000).

Chapter 8

1. Bryan Magee, *Ultimate Questions* (Princeton: Princeton University Press, 2016), 73, 78.

2. Bill James, *Popular Crime: Reflections on the Celebration of Violence* (New York: Scribner, 2012), 290.

3. B. Alan Wallace, *Meditations of a Buddhist Skeptic: A Manifesto for the Mind Sciences and Contemplative Practice* (New York: Columbia University Press, 2012), 234.

4. So Edward W. Said, *Representations of the Intellectual* (New York: Vintage, 1966), 120.

5. There are exceptions, such as thoroughly investigated, well-documented NDEs that seem to defy conventional explanation; see, e.g., above, pp. 133–34.

6. William James, "The Final Impressions of a Psychical Researcher," in *William James on Psychical Research*, ed. Gardner Murphy and Robert O. Ballou (New York: Viking, 1960), 320–21.

7. As dramatic illustration I recall the words of a Protestant journalist, James Parton, writing in 1868. In evaluating a then-famous, well-attested Catholic miracle that involved the rapid disappearance of an inoperable tumor, this unpersuadable declared: "No amount or quality of testimony could convince a

Protestant mind that Mrs. Mattingly's tumor was cured miraculously. . . . For my part, if the President and Vice President [of the US], if the whole cabinet, both houses of Congress, and the Judges of the Supreme Court, had all sworn that they saw this thing done, and I myself had seen it,—nay if the tumor had been on my own body, and had seemed to myself to be suddenly healed,—still, I should think it more probable that all those witnesses, including myself, were mistaken, than that such a miracle had been performed." See James Parton, "Our Roman Catholic Brethren," *Atlantic Monthly* 21 (April 1868): 451.

8. Cf. Heiner Schwenke, *Transcendente Begegnungen: Phänomenologie und Metakritik*, Schwabe Mystica 1 (Basel: Schwabe, 2014), 187–91.

9. Ioannis Tsoukalas, *Conceiving God: Perversions and Brainstorms; A Thesis on the Origins of Human Religiosity* (Newcastle upon Tyne: Cambridge Scholars, 2010), 90.

10. See Pher Granqvist et al., "Sensed Presence and Mystical Experiences are Predicted by Suggestibility, Not by the Application of Transcranial Weak Complex Magnetic Fields," *Neuroscience Letters* 379 (2005): 1–6, and Mario Beauregard and Denyse O'Leary, *The Spiritual Brain: A Neuroscientist's Case for the Existence of the Soul* (New York: HarperOne, 2007), 101–24.

11. Shahar Arzy et al., "Induction of an Illusory Shadow Person," *Nature* 443 (2006): 287.

12. Note, e.g., Craig Aaen-Stockdale, "Neuroscience for the Soul," *The Psychologist* 25 (2012): 523: "Sceptics claiming that God is generated by a God-module pulsating away in the temporal cortex are making important empirical errors, but that's nothing compared to postulating the existence of an omnipotent, omniscient creator. . . . God will turn out to be something as prosaic as the internalisation of our parents combined with various cultural and evolutionary baggage."

13. These materialists of course had predecessors, the most significant being the Roman philosopher Lucretius.

14. Julien Offray de la Mettrie, *Man a Machine*, ed. Gertrude Carman Bussy (1748; Chicago: Open Court, 1912), 128.

15. Paul Henri Thiry (Baron d'Holbach), *The System of Nature*, vol. 1 (1770; New York: Snova, 2019), 79.

16. See further Saulo de Freitas Aranjo, "Materialism's Eternal Return: Recurrent Patterns of Materialistic Explanations of Mental Phenomena," in *Exploring Frontiers of the Mind-Brain Relationship*, ed. Alexander Moreira-Almeida and Franklin Santana Santos (New York: Springer, 2011), 3–15.

17. Cf. B. Alan Wallace, *The Taboo of Subjectivity: Toward a New Science of*

Consciousness (Oxford: Oxford University Press, 2000), and Schwenke, *Transcendente Begegnungen*, 179–91.

18. I have found most helpful here Raymond Tallis, *Aping Mankind: Neuromania, Darwinitis and the Misrepresentation of Humanity* (Durham, UK: Acumen, 2011).

19. Christof Koch, *Consciousness: Confessions of a Romantic Reductionist* (Cambridge, MA: MIT Press, 2012), 119.

20. David E. Presti, *Foundational Concepts in Neuroscience: A Brain-Mind Odyssey* (New York: W. W. Norton & Co., 2016), 255, 261.

21. David E. Presti, "An Expanded Conception of Mind," in Presti et al., *Mind Beyond Brain: Buddhism, Science, and the Paranormal* (New York: Columbia University Press, 2018), 142.

22. See, e.g., Mario Beauregard, *Brain Wars: The Scientific Battle Over the Existence of Mind and the Proof That Will Change the Way We Live Our Lives* (New York: HarperOne, 2012); Marjorie Hines Woollacott, *Infinite Awareness: The Awakening of a Scientific Mind* (Lanham, MD: Rowman & Littlefield, 2015); Imants Baruš and Julia Mossbridge, *Transcendent Mind: Rethinking the Science of Consciousness* (Washington, DC: American Psychological Association, 2017); and Eben Alexander, "Near-Death Experiences and the Emerging Scientific View of Consciousness," in *The Science of Near-Death Experiences*, ed. John C. Hagan III (Columbia, MO: University of Missouri, 2017), 123–37.

23. Bruce Greyson, *After: A Doctor Explores What Near-Death Experiences Reveal about Life and Beyond* (New York: St. Martin's, 2021), 81.

24. For an overview of the evidence regarding religious experiences see Helané Wahbeh et al., "A Systematic Review of Transcendent States across Meditation and Contemplative Traditions," *Explore* 14 (2018): 19–35.

25. Helpful here (and accessible) are Leslie Brothers, *Mistaken Identity: The Mind-Brain Problem Reconsidered* (Albany, NY: SUNY, 2001), and (even though he takes for granted that we are "physically bounded") Robert A. Burton, *A Skeptic's Guide to the Mind: What Neuroscience Can and Cannot Tell Us about Ourselves* (New York: St. Martin's Press, 2013).

26. Sam Parnia, "Death and Consciousness—An Overview of the Mental and Cognitive Experience of Death," *Annals of the New York Academy of Sciences* 1330 (2014): 81. See further William P. Alston, *Perceiving God: The Epistemology of Religious Experience* (Ithaca, NY: Cornell University Press, 1991), 230–33, and cf. Andrew Newberg, Eugene D'Aquili, and Vince Rause, *Why God Won't Go Away: Brain Science and the Biology of Belief* (New York: Ballantine Books, 2001), 37:

"both spiritual experiences and experiences of a more ordinary material nature are made real to the mind in the very same way—through the processing powers of the brain and the cognitive functions of the mind."

27. See further Matthew Dickerson, *The Mind and the Machine: What It Means to Be Human and Why It Matters* (Grand Rapids, MI: Brazos, 2011), 3-41. He shows that some arguments for physicalism beg the question by presupposing its truth.

28. For those interested in this long-standing, thorny topic I recommend Jeffrey M. Schwartz and Sharon Begley, *The Mind and the Brain: Neuroplasticity and the Power of Mental Force* (New York: Harper Perennial, 2002), and Alfred R. Mele, *Free: Why Science Hasn't Disproved Free Will* (Oxford: Oxford University Press, 2015). The former write: "The felt experience of willful effort would have no survival value if it didn't actually do something. . . . Positing that the feeling is the mere empty reside of neuronal action is antibiological reasoning and an unnecessary concession to the once-unquestioned but now outdated tenet that all causation must reside in the material realm" (318).

29. Benjamin Libet, *Mind Time: The Temporal Factor in Consciousness, Perspectives in Cognitive Neuroscience* (Cambridge, MA: Harvard University Press, 2004).

30. Some Christians, I note, also feel a need to discredit these phenomena; see, e.g., Malcolm Jeeves, *Minds, Brains, Souls and Gods* (Downers Grove, IL: IVP Academic, 2013), 90-99.

31. E.g., NDEs with veridical elements; see chapter 7. For additional relevant phenomena see esp. Edward F. Kelly et al., eds., *Irreducible Mind: Toward a Psychology for the 21st Century* (Lanham, MD: Rowman & Littlefield, 2007).

32. In addition to Kelly et al., *Irreducible Mind*, see Baruš and Mossbridge, *Transcendent Mind*; Eric Wargo, *Time Loops: Precognition, Retrocausation, and the Unconscious* (San Antonio: Anomalist Books, 2018); and Etzel Cardeña, "The Experimental Evidence for Parapsychological Phenomena: A Review," *American Psychologist* 73, no. 5 (2018): 663-77. As an aside, I note that the standard *Diagnostic and Statistical Manual of Mental Disorders*, 5th ed. (Washington, DC: American Psychiatric Association, 2013), 655-56, deems "belief in clairvoyance, telepathy, or 'sixth sense'" to be signs of schizotypal personality disorder. This is ludicrous.

33. The phrase is from Robert A. Orsi, *History and Presence* (Cambridge, MA: The Belknap Press of Harvard University Press, 2016), 64.

34. John Henry Newman, *Lectures on the Present Position of Catholics in England Addressed to the Brothers of the Oratory in the Summer of 1851* (Notre Dame, IN: University of Notre Dame Press, 2000), 6.

35. In the following pages I float only one possibility. For a popular introduction to other non-materialist theories see the overview in Jeffrey J. Kripal, *The Flip: Epiphanies of Mind and the Future of Knowledge* (New York: Bellevue Literary Press, 2019), 89–132. For more detailed review see Edward F. Kelly, Adam Crabtree, and Paul Marshall, eds., *Beyond Physicalism: Toward Reconciliation of Science and Spirituality* (Lanham, MD: Rowman & Littlefield, 2015).

36. See above all Kelly, *Irreducible Mind*. For the history of the transmissive theory, which Henri Bergson and Aldous Huxley adopted, see Michael Grosso, "The 'Transmission' Model of Mind and Body," in Kelly et al., *Beyond Physicalism*, 79–113.

37. William James, *Human Immortality: Two Supposed Objections to the Doctrine* (Boston: Houghton, Mifflin and Company, 1898), 11–12.

38. James, *Human Immortality*, 14–15.

39. James, *Human Immortality*, 19.

40. Bruce H. Lipton, *The Biology of Belief* (Santa Rose, CA: Mountain of Love/Elite Books, 2005), 192–93.

41. James, *Human Immortality*, 16.

42. James, *Human Immortality*, 27.

43. James, *Human Immortality*, 24–25.

44. Meg Maxwell and Verena Tschudin, *Seeing the Invisible: Modern Religious and Other Transcendent Experiences* (London: Arkana, 1990), 174.

45. Greyson, *After*, 121.

46. See above all Kelly et al., *Irreducible Mind*.

47. For references and general commentary see Bernardo Kastrup and Edward F. Kelly, "Misreporting and Confirmation Bias in Psychedelic Research," *Scientific American*, September 3, 2018, https://blogs.scientificamerican.com/observations/misreporting-and-confirmation-bias-in-psychedelic-research/.

48. See further Bernardo Kastrup, "Self-Transcendence Correlates with Brain Function Impairment," *Journal of Cognition and Neuroethics* 4 (2017): 33–42.

49. Jill Bolte Taylor, *My Stroke of Insight: A Brain Scientist's Personal Journey* (New York: Viking, 2006), 45 and 67, respectively.

50. The most famous case is the NDE of Pam Reynolds; see above, p. 134.

51. Bernardo Kastrup, "A Paradigm-Breaking Hypothesis for Solving the Mind-Body Problem," *Paranthropology* 3 (2012): 10.

52. Riccardo Manzotti and Paolo Moderato, "Neuroscience: Dualism in Disguise," in *Contemporary Dualism: A Defense*, ed. Andrea Lavazza and Howard Robinson (London: Routledge, 2014), 90.

53. Two seminal contributions are Thomas Nagel, "What Is It Like to Be a Bat?," *Philosophical Review* 83 (1974): 435–50, and Frank Jackson, "What Mary Didn't Know," *Journal of Philosophy* 83 (1986): 291–95.

54. David J. Chalmers, *The Conscious Mind: In Search of a Fundamental Theory* (New York: Oxford University Press, 1996).

55. Thomas Nagel, *Mind and Cosmos: Why the Materialistic Neo-Darwinian Conception of Nature is Almost Certainly False* (Oxford: Oxford University Press, 2012), 41.

56. On placebos and nocebos see Kelly, *Irreducible Mind*, 139–48, and Steve Taylor, *Spiritual Science: Why Science Needs Spirituality to Make Sense of the World* (London: Watkins, 2018), 83–99.

57. The key work here is Chalmers, *Conscious Mind*.

58. For an introduction to the philosophical issues in this connection see Robert Kirk, "Zombies," *The Stanford Encyclopedia of Philosophy*, spring 2021 edition, https://plato.stanford.edu/entries/zombies/.

59. David Eagleman, *Incognito: The Secret Lives of the Brain* (New York: Vintage Books, 2012), 220, 223, and 222, respectively.

60. For helpful introductions to this topic that do not operate from a theological point of view see John Michell and Bob Rickard, *Unexplained Phenomena: A Rough Guide Special* (London: Rough Guides Ltd., 2000), and Jeff Kripal, *Authors of the Impossible: The Paranormal and the Sacred* (Chicago: University of Chicago Press, 2010). For a compilation of modern Christian miracles see Craig S. Keener, *Miracles: The Credibility of the New Testament Accounts*, 2 vols. (Grand Rapids: Baker Academic, 2011).

61. "The Life of Saint Macrina," in *Saint Gregory of Nyssa Ascetical Works*, Fathers of the Church 58 (Washington, DC: The Catholic University of America, 1967), 190.

62. Friedrich Nietzsche, *On the Genealogy of Morals and Ecce Homo* (New York: Vintage Books, 1969), 261.

63. The following paragraphs rewrite what I have said elsewhere: *The Luminous Dusk: Finding God in the Deep, Still Places* (Grand Rapids, MI: Eerdmans, 2006), 173–74.

64. Our eyes perceive less than 1 percent of the electromagnetic spectrum, and our ears cannot register acoustic waves below 20 hertz or above 20 kilohertz;

and if dark matter and dark energy truly exist and make up over 90 percent of the universe, none of our scientific instruments have yet to register them. In other words, most of reality is beyond human detection.

65. Magee, *Ultimate Questions*, 81–82.

66. Sagan made the phrase famous when he used it in episode 12 of his PBS TV show, *Cosmos: A Personal Journey*.

67. I heartily recommend Edwin A. Abbott's classic, *Flatland* (1884), which is now available in various reprints. Christopher G. White, *Other Worlds: Spirituality and the Search for Invisible Dimensions* (Cambridge, MA: Harvard University Press, 2018), traces the far-flung influence of Abbott's ideas.

Chapter 9

1. King James I, *Daemonologie in Forme of a Dialogie Diuided into Three Bookes* (n.p.: Robert Walde-graue, 1597), 66.

2. Carlos Eire, "Incombustible Weber: How the Protestant Reformation Really Disenchanted the World," in *Faithful Narratives: Historians, Religion, and the Challenge of Objectivity*, ed. Andrea Sterk and Nina Caputo (Ithaca, NY: Cornell University Press, 2014), 136.

3. J. Harold Ellens, "The Normalcy of the Paranormal: Numinous Experiences throughout the Life Span," in *Being Called: Scientific, Secular, and Sacred Perspectives*, ed. David Bryce Yaden, Theo D. McCall, and J. Harold Ellens (Santa Barbara, CA: Praeger, 2015), 148.

4. As it turns out, the experience of oneness is not rare. One UK survey found 5 percent recalling an experience in which "all things are one." So Paul Marshall, *The Shape of the Soul: What Mystical Experience Tells Us about Ourselves and Reality* (Lanham, MD: Rowman & Littlefield, 2019), 3. The classic work on this sort of experience is W. T. Stace, *Mysticism and Philosophy* (Philadelphia: J. B. Lippincott, 1960). He discerns two main experiences of unity, one through the ordinary senses, the other via looking inward.

5. In addition to what follows see esp. David J. Hufford, "Sleep Paralysis as Spiritual Experience," *Transcultural Psychiatry* 42 (2005): 11–45. Hufford defends what he calls "the experiential source" hypothesis, according to which some religious beliefs and folk beliefs have experiential grounding. For related arguments see also Gregory Shushan, "Rehabilitating the Neglected 'Similar': Confronting the Issue of Cross-Cultural Similarities in the Study of Religion,"

Paranthropology 4 (2013): 48–53, and "Extraordinary Experiences and Religious Beliefs: Deconstructing Some Contemporary Philosophical Axioms," *Method and Theory in the Study of Religion* 26 (2014): 384–416.

6. Erik Routley, ed., *Rejoice in the Lord: A Hymn Companion to the Scriptures* (Grand Rapids, MI: Eerdmans, 1985), 590.

7. Matthew Henry, *Commentary on the Whole Bible, Vol. V.–Matthew to John* (New York: Fleming H. Revell, n.d.), *ad* Luke 16:22.

8. Shakespeare, *Hamlet*, act 5, scene 2.

9. Jean Danielou, *The Angels and Their Mission according to the Fathers of the Church* (Westminster, MD: Newman, 1957), 95–105; Pamela Sheingorn, "'And Flights of Angels Sing Thee to Thy Rest': The Soul's Conveyance to the Afterlife in the Middle Ages," in *Art into Life: Collected Papers from the Kresge Art Museum Medieval Symposia*, ed. Carol Garrett Fisher and Kathleen L. Scott (East Lansing, MI: Michigan State University Press, 1995), 155–82; Peter Marshall, "Angels around the Deathbed: Variations on a Theme in the English Art of Dying," in *Angels in the Early Modern World*, ed. Peter Marshall and Alexandra Walsham (Cambridge: Cambridge University Press, 2006), 83–103.

10. Babylonian Talmud tractate *Ketubim* 104a. Cf. *Pesikta Rabbati* 2:3.

11. *Targum on Canticles* 4:12.

12. Maurice Rawlings, *Beyond Death's Door* (Nashville: Thomas Nelson, 1978), 87.

13. Sam Parnia with Josh Young, *Erasing Death: The Science That Is Rewriting the Boundaries between Life and Death* (New York: HarperOne, 2013), 130.

14. Bruce Greyson, *After: A Doctor Explores What Near-Death Experiences Reveal about Life and Beyond* (New York: St. Martin's, 2021), 175.

15. Rajiv Parti, *Dying to Wake Up: A Doctor's Voyage into the Afterlife and the Wisdom He Brought Back* (New York: Atria Books, 2016), 57.

16. Michael B. Sabom, *Recollections of Death: A Medical Investigation* (New York: Harper & Row, 1982), 44.

17. Greyson, *After*, 139.

18. For the cross-cultural and cross-temporal character of NDEs see p. 225 n. 24 above.

19. For some examples see Gregory Shushan, *Conceptions of the Afterlife in Early Civilizations: Universalism, Constructivism and Near-Death Experiences* (London: Continuum, 2009), 159; Shushan, "Near-Death Experiences," in *The Routledge Companion to Death and Dying*, ed. Christopher M. Moreman (New York: Routledge, 2018), 198–99.

20. For angels and light see Exod. 3:2; Dan. 10:6; 4Q403 frag. 1 col. 1 45, col. 2 35; 4Q405 frags. 14-15 col. 1 5; Testament of Job 3:1; 4:1; Joseph and Aseneth 14:1-3; Matt. 28:3; Acts 12:7; 2 Cor. 11:14; Rev. 10:1; 18:1; 2 Baruch 25:6. For angels in dreams see Gen. 28:12; 31:11; 4QAmramb; Liber Antiquitatum Biblicarum 9:10; 2 Enoch 1; Matt. 1:20; 2:13, 19. If one wishes to ask, in turn, why angels were associated with light and dreams, the likely answer again lies in experience.

21. Sir William Barrett, *Deathbed Visions* (1926; repr., Guildford, UK: White Crow Books, 2011), 39.

22. David Kessler, *Visions, Trips, and Crowded Rooms: Who and What You See Before You Die* (Carlsbad, CA: Hay House, 2010), 26.

23. Kessler, *Visions, Trips, and Crowded Rooms*, 105.

24. Becki Hawkins, "Do You See Them?," in *We Touched Heaven*, ed. Claudia Watts Edge (n.p.: Kindle Direct/LilyBud, 2021), 266.

25. Many, of course, also identify the being of light with God. One is reminded of Genesis, where "the Lord" and "the angel of the Lord" alternate in confusing fashion.

26. On Amida, a golden Buddha of infinite light who appears at the moment of death, see Carl B. Becker, "The Centrality of Near-Death Experiences in Chinese Pure Land Buddhism," *Anabiosis* 1 (1981): 154-70.

27. Helpful here are Anthony N. Perovich Jr., "Mysticism and the Philosophy of Science," *Journal of Religion* 65 (1985): 63-85; Sallie B. King, "Two Epistemological Models for the Interpretation of Mysticism," *Journal of the American Academy of Religion* 56 (1988): 257-79; David J. Hufford, "Sleep Paralysis as Spiritual Experience," *Transcultural Psychiatry* 42 (2005): 11-45; Shushan, "Rehabilitating the Neglected 'Similar'"; Shushan, "Extraordinary Experiences and Religious Beliefs"; Shushan, "Cultural-Linguistic Constructivism and the Challenge of Near-Death and Out-of-Body Experiences," in *The Study of Religious Experience: Approaches and Methodologies*, ed. Bettina E. Schmidt (Sheffield: Equinox, 2016), 71-87; Mark Fox, *Religion, Spirituality and the Near-Death Experience* (New York: Routledge, 2003), 98-141; and Michael Winkelman, "Ethnological and Neurophenomenological Approaches to Religious Experiences," in Schmidt, *Religious Experience*, 33-51.

28. Cf. Gregory Shushan, *Near-Death Experience in Indigenous Religions* (New York: Oxford University Press, 2018), 53: "During a prolonged illness c. 1890, a Shoshone man named Enga-gwacu (Red-shirt) Jim had a vision in which the sun told him he was going to die, but that he could come back to life if he wished."

29. Oliver Nichelson, "The Luminous Experience and the Scientific Method," *Journal of Near-Death Studies* 8 (1990): 204.

30. Jeffrey Long with Paul Perry, *God and the Afterlife: The Ground-Breaking New Evidence for God and Near-Death Experience* (New York: HarperOne, 2016), 164.

31. Long, *God and the Afterlife*, 166.

32. Michael Sabom, *Light and Death: One Doctor's Fascinating Account of Near-Death Experiences* (Grand Rapids, MI: Zondervan, 1998), 170.

33. Greyson, *After*, 145.

34. Greyson, *After*, 146.

35. The *Tibetan Book of the Dead* acknowledges this fact; see *The Tibetan Book of the Dead or The After-Death Experiences on the Bardo Plane, according to Lāma Kazi Dawa-Samdup's English Rendering*, ed. W. Y. Evans-Wentz, 2nd ed. (London: Oxford University Press, 1949), 31–35.

36. See further James McClenon, *Wondrous Events: Foundations of Religious Belief* (Philadelphia: University of Pennsylvania Press, 1994), 168–84.

37. For the Catholic stories see Carol Zaleski, *Otherworld Journeys: Accounts of Near-Death Experience in Medieval and Modern Times* (New York: Oxford University Press, 1987). On the *délok* literature see Byran J. Cuevas, *Netherworld: Buddhist Popular Narratives of Death and Afterlife in Tibet* (Oxford: Oxford University Press, 2008). On the parallels between modern NDEs and Tibetan stories see Christopher Carr, "Death and Near-Death: A Comparison of Tibetan and Euro-American Experiences," *Journal of Transpersonal Psychology* 25 (1993): 59–109, and Joe Dixon, "Death and Afterlife in Tibetan Buddhist Biography: The rnam thar of Karma dbang 'dzin" (MPhil diss., Oxford University, 2017), 45–65; https://www.academia.edu/34221435/Death_and_Afterlife_in_Tibetan _Buddhist_Biography_The_rnam_thar_of_Karma_dbang_dzin.

38. See further Shushan, *Conceptions of the Afterlife*, 37–50. He argues persuasively that the NDE is a cross-cultural experience that people have interpreted in culturally specific ways.

39. Donald E. Brown, *Human Universals* (Boston: McGraw Hill, 1991).

40. As with hell, so with heaven: real experiences have informed ideas about its nature; see Dale C. Allison Jr., *Night Comes: Death, Imagination, and the Last Things* (Grand Rapids, MI: Eerdmans, 2016), 124–47.

41. For analysis see Diana Butler Bass, *Christianity after Religion: The End of Church and the Birth of a New Spiritual Awakening* (New York: HarperOne, 2012).

42. See further above, pp. 33–34.

43. David J. Hufford, "Beings without Bodies: An Experience-Centered The-

ory of the Belief in Spirits," in *Out of the Ordinary: Folklore and the Supernatural*, ed. Barbara Walker (Logan, UT: Utah State University Press, 1995), 28.

44. Hufford, "Beings without Bodies," 19.

45. N. T. Wright, *Scripture and the Authority of God: How to Read the Bible Today* (New York: HarperOne, 2011), 102.

46. Albert Outler, "The Wesleyan Quardrilateral in Wesley," *Wesleyan Theological Journal* 20, no. 1 (1985): 7–18. Wright, I should be clear, has a place for both tradition and reason, although he regards them as subservient to Scripture. As for experience, which he regards as "the necessary subjective pole of all knowing" (*Scripture*, 104), Wright says it is "that over which and in the context of which the reading of scripture exercises its authority" (103, italics omitted).

47. Reason, I note, is not "rationalism." Here I agree with Wright, *Scripture*, 78–81, 86–87.

48. Note, e.g., Mark 7:24–30; 11:1–10; 12:41–44; John 1:35–51; 11:11–14.

49. Evelyn Underhill, "The Authority of Personal Religious Experience," *Theology* 10 (1925): 15.

50. Helpful here is James Simpson, *Permanent Revolution: The Reformation and the Illiberal Roots of Liberalism* (Cambridge, MA: Belknap Press of Harvard University Press, 2019), esp. 259–314.

51. As quoted in Michael C. Legaspi, *The Death of Scripture and the Rise of Biblical Studies* (Oxford: Oxford University Press, 2010), 22.

52. John Chrysostom, *Homilies on 2 Corinthians* 26:1.

53. John Wesley, *Explanatory Notes upon the New Testament* (London: Epworth, 1950), 673.

54. J. H. Bernard, "The Second Epistle to the Corinthians," in *The Expositor's Greek Testament*, ed. W. Robertson Nicoll, vol. 3 (New York: George H. Doran Co., n.d.), 110; Ralph P. Martin, *2 Corinthians*, WBC 40 (Waco, TX: Word Books, 1986), 406; M. E. Thrall, "Paul's Journey to Paradise. Some Exegetical Issues in 2 Cor 12.2–4," in *The Corinthian Correspondence*, ed. R. E. Bieringer, BETL 125 (Leuven: Leuven University Press/Peeters, 1996), 361; and E. P. Sanders, *Paul: The Apostle's Life, Letters, and Thought* (Minneapolis, MN: Fortress, 2015), 261, respectively.

55. Jerome Murphy-O'Connor, *Paul: A Critical Life* (Oxford: Clarendon, 1996), 320.

56. J. Christiaan Beker, *Paul the Apostle: The Triumph of God in Life and Thought* (Philadelphia: Fortress, 1980), 116.

57. C. K. Barrett, *A Commentary on the Second Epistle to the Corinthians* (New York: Harper & Row, 1973), 308, 310.

58. Bernhard Heininger, *Paulus als Visionär: Eine religionsgeschichtliche Studie*, Herders biblischen Studien (Freiburg: Herder, 1996). In addition to the vision on the Damascus road, Acts tells of Paul having visions in 16:9–10; 18:9–10; 22:17–21; 23:11; and 27:23–24.

59. Robertson Nicoll, *The Church's One Foundation: Christ and Recent Criticism* (New York: A. C. Armstrong and Son, 1901), 139.

60. Ambrosiaster, *Commentaries on Romans and 1–2 Corinthians*, trans. and ed. Gerald L. Bray, Ancient Christian Texts (Downers Grove, IL: IVP Academic, 2009), 258.

61. See esp. Luke Timothy Johnson, *Religious Experience in Earliest Christianity: A Missing Dimension in New Testament Studies* (Minneapolis: Fortress, 1998); also Colleen Shantz, *Paul in Ecstasy: The Neurobiology of the Apostle's Life and Thought* (Cambridge, UK: Cambridge University Press, 2009).

62. Edward Taylor, *Harmony of the Gospels*, ed. Thomas Marion Davis, Virginia L. Davis, and Betty L. Parks (Delmar, NY: Scholars' Facsimiles & Reprints, 1983), 1:67.

63. As quoted in Elizabeth Reis, "Immortal Messengers: Angels, Gender, and Power in Early America," in *Mortal Remains: Death in Early America*, ed. Nancy Isenberg and Andrew Burstein (Philadelphia: University of Pennsylvania Press, 2003), 168–69.

64. See Reis, "Immortal Messengers," 167.

65. William P. Alston, *Perceiving God: The Epistemology of Religious Experience* (Ithaca, NY: Cornell University Press, 1991), 267.

66. Sylvia Hart Wright, *When Spirits Come Calling: The Open-Minded Skeptic's Guide to After-Death Contacts* (Nevada City, CA: Blue Dolphin, 2002), 73.

67. Meg Maxwell and Verena Tschudin, *Seeing the Invisible: Modern Religious and Other Transcendent Experiences* (London: Arkana, 1990), 16, 19.

68. Carla Wills-Brandon, *One Last Hug Before I Go: The Meaning and Mystery of Deathbed Visions* (Deerfield Beach, FL: Health Communications, Inc., 2000), 244.

69. Wills-Brandon, *One Last Hug*, 244.

70. For discussion of these matters see D. P. Walker, "The Cessation of Miracles," in *Hermeticism and the Renaissance: Intellectual History and the Occult in Early Modern Europe*, ed. Ingrid Merkel and Allen G. Debus (London: The Folger Shakespeare Library; Washington, DC: Associated University Presses, 1988), 111–24; Klaus Bockmuehl, *Listening to the God Who Speaks: Reflections on God's Guidance from Scripture and the Lives of God's People* (Colorado Springs, CO:

Helmers & Howard, 1990), 121–37; Eire, "Incombustible Weber"; and Andreas Sommer, "Geisterglaube, Aufklärung und Wissenschaft—Historiographische Skizzen zu einem westlichen Fundamentaltabu," in *Jenseits des Vertrauten: Facetten transzendenter Erfahrungen*, ed. Heiner Schwenke (Freiburg im Breisgau: Karl Alber, 2018), 183–215.

71. Helpful here is Neal Grossman, "Who's Afraid of Life After Death?," *Journal of Near-Death Studies* 21 (2002): 5–24, https://digital.library.unt.edu/ark:/67531/metadc799144/m2/1/high_res_d/vol21-no1-5.pdf.

72. Charles Taylor, *A Secular Age* (Cambridge, MA: The Belknap Press of Harvard University Press, 2007), 135 and 27, respectively. Taylor's generalizations about pre-secular times seem too simple to me, but that is beside the point here.

Chapter 10

1. Horace Bushnell, *Nature and the Supernatural as Together Constituting the One System of God* (New York: Charles Scribner's Sons, 1910), 457–58.

2. Klaus Bockmuehl, *Listening to the God Who Speaks: Reflections on God's Guidance from Scripture and the Lives of God's People* (Colorado Springs, CO: Helmers & Howard, 1990), 135.

3. Evelyn Underhill, "The Authority of Personal Religious Experience," *Theology* 10 (1925): 14.

4. On this matter see Evelyn Underhill, *Mysticism: A Study in the Nature and Development of Man's Spiritual Consciousness* (New York: E. P. Dutton & Co., 1961), 266–97.

5. Were I to pursue these matters, I could do no better than Jonathan Edwards and William James, who both reverted to the idea in Matthew 7:20 when evaluating the value or validity of a religious experience: "You will know them by their fruits."

6. I should add, however, that it is injudicious to assume that those with mental issues do not have genuine religious experiences. Helpful here is John Swinton, *Finding Jesus in the Storm: The Spiritual Lives of Christians with Mental Health Challenges* (Grand Rapids, MI: Eerdmans, 2020).

7. See the literature cited above, in fn. 27 on p. 199.

8. In line with this, the beliefs and values an individual brings to an experience affect whether it becomes inimical or beneficial; see Mike Jackson and K. W. M. Fulford, "Spiritual Experiences and Psychopathology," *Philosophy, Psychiatry, & Psychology* 4 (1997): 41–65.

9. Genevieve W. Foster, *The World Was Flooded with Light: A Mystical Experience Remembered*, with commentary by David J. Hufford (Pittsburgh: University of Pittsburgh Press, 1985), 44, 47.

10. In one study—see Genie Palmer and William Braud, "Exceptional Human Experiences, Disclosure, and a More Inclusive View of Physical, Psychological, and Spiritual Well-Being," *Journal of Transpersonal Psychology* 34 (2002): 29–61— sharing exceptional experiences with sympathetic listeners "was positively and significantly associated with meaning and purpose in life, positive psychological attitudes and well-being, and reduced stress-related symptoms." For an account of an Anglican priest starting, at his church, a "Mystics Anonymous" group see J. Hugh Kempster, "'Be Thou My Vision': Mystical Experience and Religious Calling," in *Being Called: Scientific, Secular, and Sacred Perspectives*, ed. David Bryce Yaden, Theo D. McCall, and J. Harold Ellens (Santa Barbara, CA: Praeger, 2015), 262–63.

11. A recent survey in Turkey found that over a quarter thought that "a pure heart and high morality" were requirements for "religious experience," the latter defined so as to include answers to prayer and awareness of God's presence; see Cafer S. Yaran, "Muslim Religious Experience: Recent Researches in Turkey," *Journal for the Study of Religious Experience* 1 (2015): 49–60. While the respondents were Muslim, ones doubts that results would be much different for Christians.

12. The terms "porous" and "bounded" come from Charles Taylor, *A Secular Age* (Cambridge, MA: The Belknap Press of Harvard University Press, 2007); see above, p. 191.

13. See T. M. Luhrmann, *How God Becomes Real: Kindling the Presence of Invisible Others* (Princeton: Princeton University Press, 2020), and Luhrmann et al., "Sensing the Presence of Gods and Spirits across Cultures and Faiths," *Proceedings of the National Academy of Sciences* 118, no. 5 (2021), https://doi.org/10.1073 /pnas.2016649118. This fact seemingly explains why meditation of various sorts seems to correlate with increased reporting of out-of-the-ordinary experiences; see J. Kim Penberthy et al., "Meditators and Nonmeditators: A Descriptive Analysis over Time with a Focus on Unusual and Extraordinary Experiences," *Journal of Yoga and Physiotherapy* 8 (2020), https://med.virginia.edu/perceptual-studies /wp-content/uploads/sites/360/2020/02/Combined-Meditators-and-non-medi tators-with-appendix-2020-Penberthy-et-al.pdf.

Suggested Reading

Cook, Christopher C. H. *Hearing Voices, Demonic and Divine: Scientific and Theological Perspectives*. London: Routledge, 2019. An up-to-date, scientifically informed survey of the phenomenon of hearing voices. Cook covers the Bible, Christian history, and contemporary experience.

Fox, Mark. *The Fifth Love: Exploring Accounts of the Extraordinary*. n.p.: Spirit & Sage, 2014. A compilation and analysis of experiences of transcendent love.

———. *Religion, Spirituality and the Near-Death Experience*. London: Routledge, 2003. A first-rate exploration of the religious side of NDEs.

———. *Spiritual Encounters with Unusual Light Phenomena: Lightforms*. Cardiff: University of Wales Press, 2008. The title indicates the content.

Greyson, Bruce. *After: A Doctor Explores What Near-Death Experiences Reveal about Life and Beyond*. New York: St. Martin's, 2021. One of the leading authorities on NDEs reviews his life-long study of the phenomenon.

Hardy, Alister. *The Spiritual Nature of Man: A Study of Contemporary Religious Experience*. Oxford: Religious Experience Research Unit, 1979. An overview of Hardy's work and the findings of the Religious Experience Research Unit/Centre.

Heathcote-James, Emma. *Seeing Angels: True Contemporary Accounts of Hundreds of Angel Experiences*. London: John Blake, 2009. The best of the books about reported encounters with angels.

Hufford, David. *The Terror That Comes in the Night: An Experience-Centered Study of Supernatural Assault Traditions*. Philadelphia: University of Pennsylvania Press, 1982. The pioneering work on sleep paralysis and associated phenomenology.

James, William. *The Varieties of Religious Experience: A Study in Human Nature.* The undisputed classic in its field; still of immense value.

Kelly, Edward F. et al. *Irreducible Mind: Toward a Psychology for the 21st Century.* Lanham, MD: Rowman & Littlefield, 2007. A trove and discussion of data incompatible with reductive materialism.

Luhrmann, T. M. *When God Talks Back: Understanding the American Evangelical Relationship with God.* New York: Alfred A. Knopf, 2012. An exceptionally insightful analysis of evangelical religious experience.

Maxwell, Meg, and Verena Tschudin. *Seeing the Invisible: Modern Religious and Other Transcendent Experiences.* London: Arkana, 1990. A compilation, classification, and discussion of experiences submitted to the Religious Experience Research Unit/Centre.

Pearson, Patricia. *Opening Heaven's Door: Investigating Stories of Life, Death, and What Comes After.* New York: Atria Books, 2014. A survey of surprising phenomena surrounding death beds.

Rivas, Titus, Anny Dirven, and Rudolf H. Smit. *The Self Does Not Die: Verified Paranormal Phenomena from Near-Death Experiences.* Durham, NC: IANDS Publications, 2016. An investigation of NDEs with seemingly verified perceptions.

Index of Names

Index of Subjects